What people are saying about . . .

Dollars & Sense
HOW TO BE SMART ABOUT MONEY

"I am unaware of any other books like this. It is the only thing I have seen that asks students to really think about their spending habits and understand how the decisions they make now can impact their financial futures."

Angela Szakasits
ACADEMICALLY AND INTELLECTUALLY GIFTED COACH,
TOPSAIL MIDDLE SCHOOL, PENDER COUNTY SCHOOLS, BURGAW, NORTH CAROLINA

"I like the meta-cognition approach of Dollars & Sense *which integrates critical thinking, problem solving, writing, and reflection. This helps students think about their thinking! I see this book as a preemptive strategy to promote future well-being personally, financially, and emotionally. What a great way to send students off to college, prepared for the future."*

Linnea Van Eman, PhD
ZARROW INTERNATIONAL SCHOOL, TULSA PUBLIC SCHOOLS
PRESIDENT-ELECT, OKLAHOMA ASSOCIATION OF GIFTED, CREATIVE, AND TALENTED, TULSA, OKLAHOMA

"This was a tool that greatly opened my eyes to real areas of concern regarding my spending habits. The learning activities really had me thinking of my own relationship with money."

Natalie Cancel
STUDENT, COLLEGE OF CHARLESTON,
CHARLESTON, SOUTH CAROLINA

"I feel this book could make a generation of spenders that are aware of their finances and won't get themselves in trouble with debt at an early age like generations before them. I wish I would have had something like this taught to me when I was in high school."

Angela Gillies
SPECIAL EDUCATION TEACHER, SOUTH PLAQUEMINES HIGH SCHOOL,
PLAQUEMINES PARISH, PORT SULPHUR, LOUISIANA

"High school is a start to adult life and this book teaches good ways to stay out of debt and manage our financial issues, banking and money when we get there."

Lily Davis
STUDENT, ROCKY MOUNTAIN HIGH SCHOOL,
POUDRE SCHOOL DISTRICT, FORT COLLINS, COLORADO

"I'm glad you tie math skills into these topics. I often think children learning math in school don't understand how important this skill will be to them in the future, or how they will use math in everyday life.

Karen Pynes
TEACHER, LAKEVIEW MIDDLE SCHOOL,
LEWISVILLE INDEPENDENT SCHOOL DISTRICT, FLOWER MOUND, TEXAS

"I see this book as a beginning guide to financial planning and investing, and why teens should be financially literate. Also, the book will encourage kids to think about money before money becomes an issue."

Colten Elkin
STUDENT, NORTH CENTRAL HIGH SCHOOL,
METROPOLITAN SCHOOL DISTRICT OF WASHINGTON TOWNSHIP, INDIANAPOLIS, INDIANA

I am long familiar with the work and people of LifeBound and am pleased to see Dollars & Sense join the collection of student success books already available to schools and districts. The need for financial literacy skills for students and adults alike is enormous. This resource couldn't have come at a better time to give a new generation the financial tools they require to make wise financial decisions.

Ben Branhinsky
PRESIDENT, LEAP FINANCIAL, INC., DENVER, COLORADO

Dollars & Sense

HOW TO BE SMART ABOUT MONEY

Carol Carter

LifeBound
DENVER, COLORADO

President/Publisher: Carol J Carter—LifeBound, LLC
Managing Editor: Angelica Jestrovich
Developmental Editor: Martha Roden
Copy Editor: Don Cameron
Cover and Interior Design: John Wincek, Aerocraft Charter Art Service
Printing: Data Reproductions

LifeBound
1530 High St.
Denver, Colorado 80218
www.lifebound.com

ISBN 978-0-9820588-3-1
ISBN 0-98-205882-9

10 9 8 7 6 5 4 3 2 1

Contents

Preface

Our goal is to educate a new generation of financially literate youth who can enter their adult lives with the skills they need to plan for a successful, happy, and secure future. All the financial skills, tips, and insights you will read in *Dollars & Sense* are mapped directly to the National Standards for Financial Literacy, established by the Jump$tart coalition to improve the financial literacy of youth from kindergarten through college.

The basic categories for the standards are:

- Financial responsibility and decision-making
- Income and careers
- Planning and money management
- Credit and debt
- Risk management and insurance
- Saving and investing

Flip to **Appendix F: Mapping National Standards for Personal Financial Literacy** for a detailed visualization of the six categories and how each chapter in *Dollars & Sense* correlates to those standards.

Dollars & Sense approaches the important topic of financial literacy in a colorful, creative, and fun way. This book brings the national standards and topic of financial literacy to life by including a number of real-life scenarios dealing with real-life issues as well as the following chapter features:

- It's a Fact!
- Now You Try It
- Financial Figures: Learning from the Experience of Others
- Financial Foul-ups: Learning from the Mistakes of Others

You may not know it yet, but you're holding much more than a book. By going to www.lifebound.com, you will find even more resources to get you smart about money, including financial assessments, online quizzes and tests, multimedia activities, and more interactive exercises for you to do individually, with a team, and with your family.

We are always looking for ways to improve our student success resources. If you have any suggestions or ideas about how you and your school can use this book, please send us your thoughts. Here's how to contact us:

E-mail:	contact@lifebound.com
Our toll-free number:	1.877.737.8510
Snail Mail:	Carol Carter
	LifeBound
	1530 High Street
	Denver, CO 80218

Acknowledgments

Special thanks to the following people for reviewing the manuscript and offering feedback:

Carrie Adams
Jerry Lee Anderson, PhD
Thomas Balchak
Ariel Baska
Sunit Bhalla
Ben Branhinsky
Natalie Cancel
Emily Davis
Lily Davis
Michael DeSantiago
Susan Dunbar
Chaz Elkin
Colten Elkin
Michelle Ewart
Angela Gillies
MaryPat Hayden-Davis
Dante Malara

Barten Nealy
Carly Nolan
Cynthia Nordberg
Piper Perry
Kaitlin Phelan
Karen Pynes
Deborah Rothenberg
Laura Santillan
Demetrious Skalkotos
Michelle Stout
Greg Strong
Angela Szakasits
Michele Thibodeau
Dr. Linnea Van Eman
Julia Watson
Jonathan Wolfer
Jean R. Wuensch

Special thanks to the following financial figures for sharing their financial experiences and expertise:

Anya Kamentez
Mark Kantrowitz
Alina Laikola
Judy Lawrence
Regina Leeds

Richard Martinez
Bobby Meacham
Kimberly Palmer
Russell Wild
Robin Wise

To Oseola McCarty *who despite working a lifetime on a washerwoman's salary was able to save enough money to give opportunity to deserving students at the University of Southern Mississippi with her generous donation of $150,000.*

And in honor of the World War II generation *who made personal sacrifices to create wealth and prosperity for our nation. We hope your legacy will live on for generations to come.*

C H A P T E R

1

Critical Thinking and Financial Skills

"Money has never made man happy, nor will it, there is nothing in its nature to produce happiness. The more of it one has the more one wants."

BENJAMIN FRANKLIN

Questions you will answer. . . .

1. What is financial literacy?
2. Can you tell the difference between needs and wants?
3. Are you aware of your spending habits?
4. Do you have a plan for the future?
5. How do you "if-then" think?
6. How can you see the big picture?

Test your financial skills with the Dollars & Sense chapter assessment at www.lifebound.com.

1

Meet Clint

Clint is a sophomore in high school and he's had a job ever since he was old enough to work. Currently, he's working at Little Caesar's Pizza. His parents pay for most of his day-to-day expenses, such as shelter, food, clothes, and car insurance. However, they expect Clint to pay for incidentals, such as meals at fast food restaurants, music downloads, video games, gas, and car maintenance. Plus, they expect him to put away money for college.

When Clint first started making money, he spent it as soon as he got it. A week before payday, he was usually counting change on the floorboards of his car to get enough gas money to drive to work. One day, he asked his dad for some cash for gas. His dad responded with a question of his own. "Where are you spending your money?"

Clint had never really thought much about it, so he decided to write down all his expenditures for the past week. He came up with quite a list: dinner and a movie with his girlfriend, lunch with his friends, a three-month subscription to World of Warcraft, gas for work, and daily mocha lattes from Starbucks before school. His dad asked him which of those things he really "needed." Clint was stumped—he bought them, so didn't that mean he needed them?

That's when Clint's dad decided to sit down with Clint and talk about financial literacy . . . of course he didn't call it that, he called it "spending money wisely." Together, Clint and his dad discussed how much Clint made, how much he spent, and what he spent it on. Clint realized that he spent more than he made and didn't put any money away for college.

Next, Clint's parents asked Clint to help them with a family budget. That meant listing all the family's bills and prioritizing them between needs and wants. "Needs" were bills the family had to pay, for services they could not do without: the house mortgage, groceries, car insurance, and utilities. "Wants" were items the family would like to buy, but could do without if they had to: a new television and a family vacation.

When Clint saw that his parents had to make hard decisions be-tween paying for needs and wants, he decided to make his own budget and do the same. His parents helped him get started and at first the budget felt restrictive. But after a while, Clint started to feel in control of his finances—he was making informed decisions about what to buy and when. By the time he was a senior, Clint was paying for the things he needed, some of the things he wanted, and was able to put money away for college. He was financially literate!

get ready

Like Clint, all of us struggle with telling the difference between what we want and what we actually need. It doesn't help that we're inundated daily with ads urging us to buy, buy, buy, or bombarded with images of what we're supposed to look like, wear, or own so we fit in with the "cool" people. We have become a consumer nation without any thought to how we'll pay for it all. Is it any wonder that so many people are in debt?

However, you don't have to wind up overspending and in debt. In-stead, you can follow Clint's lead by becoming aware of your spending, acknowledging what funds you have, making wise decisions about what you must have and what you can do without, and taking responsibility for those decisions.

In this chapter, we're going to introduce you to some of the concepts that you'll study in detail in later chapters. We want you to get a taste of things to come. You'll have a chance to get acquainted with financial literacy, tell the difference between needs and wants, become aware of your spending habits, think about the future, and see the big picture when it comes to making decisions about money.

WHAT IS FINANCIAL LITERACY?

 As we mentioned earlier, financial literacy is being able to man-age money wisely for lifetime security. There are a lot of people in the world today who don't feel very secure about their finances, and we want to make sure you are not one of them.

When you're **financially literate**, you are aware of your personal finances—you

Financial Literacy, noun

Ability to use knowledge and skills to manage your financial resources effectively for lifetime financial security.

Being literate involves more than being able to read; it involves being able to manage your finances wisely.

know what you own, what money you have, and where it's going. It means making conscious decisions about what to buy now and what to buy later. It means not always worrying about how you are going to pay for things.

When you are financially literate, you become aware of your **personal finances** and the financial issues that can affect you.

Personal Finance, noun

Methods you can use to acquire and manage income and assets.

Assets and Liabilities

As you probably noticed in the definition of personal finance, the word **income** was mentioned. Most of you already know this means money that you earn. But what about the other word: assets? That's a word you may not use very often. An **asset** is financial-speak for "what you own," specifically, anything that can be sold and converted into money. The opposite of an asset is a **liability** or "what you owe" (bills and expenses).

Income, noun

Monetary payment received for goods or services, or from other sources, such as rents or investments.

4

As a teenager, your income might include money you earn from a part-time job, interest from a savings account, or money gifts from relatives. Your assets might include a car (like Clint), a computer or a musical instrument. And your liabilities might include the money you spend on clothing or gas, as well as music and coffee (like Clint).

Asset, noun

Money earned, along with items that can be converted to cash, including cash, securities, real estate, machinery, and other possessions.

As you get older, your income, assets, and liabilities will change. Hopefully your income will grow. Your assets may eventually include a home, furniture, jewelry, or maybe even a boat or some rare books. And your liabilities will probably include groceries, utilities, a mortgage, a car loan (or boat loan), and educational expenses for your own children.

Whether you're a teenager, a college student, or an adult with a career, liabilities are usually what you worry about. Unfortunately, with credit card companies making it so easy to get credit cards and buy things that you can't afford, you can easily end up with a liability that grows and grows: credit card debt.

Liability, noun

Money owed, expenses.

Every teenager has some financial assets, either earned or unearned. Unfortunately, liabilities are more easily collected.

It's enough to make you want to pull your hair out! But there's no need to go bald yet. As a teenager, you probably have less knowledge of personal finance than someone older. So it's OK not to know everything you need to know about finances. Your knowledge will grow as you gain more responsibility and experience. This book provides a foundation you can build upon, the older you get.

quickcheck

What is financial literacy?

What is income?

What are assets and liabilities?

National Standards for Financial Literacy

Everything you learn in this book maps directly to the National Standards for Financial Literacy. In case you skipped the Preface, these standards were established by the Jump-$tart coalition to improve the financial literacy of children from pre-kindergarten through college-age. The basic categories for the standards are:

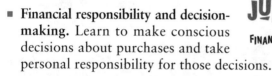

- **Financial responsibility and decision-making.** Learn to make conscious decisions about purchases and take personal responsibility for those decisions.

- **Income and careers.** Research different careers to learn what education is required, what job tasks are performed, and what income can be expected.

- **Planning and money management.** Manage your day-to-day expenses with a budget, and plan for the future.

- **Credit and debt.** Handle credit cards with care to prevent or reduce debt.

- **Risk management and insurance.** Identify the different types of insurance that help minimize risks.

- **Saving and investing.** Save money for emergencies and the future, and gain knowledge about different types of investments, such as stocks, bonds, and mutual funds.

Just think—unlike many adults today who had to figure out all this financial stuff on their own (making lots of mistakes along the way), you have a chance to learn some of the basic concepts by reading this book. And who knows? Maybe you'll make fewer financial mistakes in your life . . . at least that's our hope.

now you try it

ASSETS AND LIABILITIES

1. Think about the things you and your family own and list them. These are assets.

_____

_____

_____

_____

_____

2. Think about things that you and your family owe money on and list them. These are liabilities.

_____

_____

_____

_____

_____

CAN YOU TELL THE DIFFERENCE BETWEEN NEEDS AND WANTS?

A big part of financial literacy is learning to tell the difference between needs and wants, especially when they cost money. Remember Clint and his daily Starbucks coffees? Do you think that was a need or a want? Some of you with a caffeine habit may think it's a need, but it's not.

Needs

A **need** is something you must have to survive. Yes, sometimes it might feel like an iPod is an essential need. But really, we are talking about biological survival. So, for most of you, basic needs include:

We all have similar basic needs.

- Food and water
- Shelter (including heat and electric)
- Clothing
- Job (to pay for the other basic needs)

For many, those basic needs are met by your parents. And then there are additional needs that must be met to support those basic needs:

- Health (if you're sick, it's hard to work)
- Education (if you're uneducated, it's hard to get a job)
- Transportation (it's kind of hard to work if you can't get to your job)

Let's stop and consider Clint. Right now, his mom and dad are covering his basic needs by providing a home, paying the mortgage and utility bills, and buying all the groceries and supplies. More than likely, they are also supporting his health and education needs by paying for health and car insurance, and school costs. But Clint still has to pick up transportation costs by paying for his own gas.

Need, noun

A requirement, necessity, necessary duty, or obligation.

Wants

If all Clint did was attend to his basic needs, he wouldn't run out of money, since all he'd have to come up with is gas money. But now we move into the realm of wants. **Wants** are pretty unlimited, and they vary from person to person. However, we can artificially divide them into two categories:

- **Category A.** Wants related to things that would make it easier to meet a basic need.
- **Category B.** Wants related to things that would be nice to have, but are not directly related to any basic need.

Things that fall into **Category A** are directly related to your basic needs. For example, suppose you currently take the bus to a part-time job and have to make several transfers before you arrive. As a result, it takes you 45 minutes to get to work and 45 minutes to get home. Plus, in the winter, you have to wait at the bus stop, in the cold and dark, in a not so nice part of town. And sometimes the bus is late. As a result, your Category A want might be a car. With a car, it would take less time to get to work, you'd never miss the bus, and you wouldn't have to worry about waiting at the bus stop in the dark. Of course, you'd have to pay for insurance and gas, which might be more expensive than bus fare. So maybe your want is to find a person you could carpool with—then all you'd have to do is pay half of the gas costs.

> **Want,** noun
>
> *A wish, craving, demand, or desire.*

What about **Category B** wants? Wants in this category are rarely related to any basic need. Instead, these are personal desires for things that you could easily live without. These are often driven by advertising, peer pressure, or personal fantasy, as you will learn in the next section.

For example, suppose Clint drives an older vehicle that he "inherited" from his parents, and decides that what he really needs is a red Corvette. Hey, why not? Clint saw someone driving it on a reality TV show, and he looked really cool. Does Clint think about the fact that a Corvette costs about $75,000 new and has a monthly payment of $976 with four-year lease and $5,000 down?[1] And what about the sudden jump in his car insurance rate, not to mention the expensive new alarm system he's going to have to install in the car? Clint is definitely operating in the fantasy realm.

And that's what we want to help you with—telling the difference between fantasy and reality; discerning between reasonable needs and wants, and outrageous desires. A big part of being financially literate is becoming conscious of what's a need and what's a want. Keep reading this book and you will learn more about figuring out why you want something, whether your desire is reasonable or not, and whether you can actually afford it.

At this point, all you simply need to remember is that wants are not essential to our existence; needs are. Once you learn to differentiate between them, you may find yourself considering your purchases more carefully. Then, when you learn to prioritize those wants, you can figure out how to save the money you will need to afford them. You'll learn more about this process in **Chapter 3, Budgeting and Goal Setting for Success.**

The Source of Wants

Where do these "wants" come from? After all, we are not born with them. They come from a lot of sources, the most common of which include advertising, peer pressure, and family.

Advertising. Advertisers are very good at convincing you that you "need" a particular product. In fact, many advertisers are quite clever at making you think you have no choice—that you must buy the product, or else. However, if you do some research, you may discover that a) the advertiser's claims are untrue or b) there is another equally good product available, which is more affordable. Other times, you may discover that the product is really something you don't need at all. But you have to take time to do the research.

Unfortunately, after you impulsively buy something, it's easy to come up with all sorts

quickcheck

How is a want different from a need?

What is the difference between Category A and B wants?

of reasons why you can't do without it. In fact, you may even come up with new uses to support your imagined need. Why not? Isn't that what the advertisers tried to convince you of in the first place? That's why it's so important not to believe everything you see and hear, and instead to ask yourself: Do I really need this? Do I need it now? Can I afford it?

For example, our friend Clint saw an ad on TV about a new 55-inch flat screen, high-definition plasma television that would be perfect for playing hi-def video games. He told his dad, "We've got to get that!" But his dad reminded him that unless Clint could magically come up with $2,600, there would be no new television. Besides, Clint hardly played video games any more. Clint was so caught up in the ad that he forgot all about cost and whether or not the family even needed the television.

Peer Pressure. Whether you're young or old, what others think of you always seems to be an issue. Of course, the older you get, the more you realize that others' opinions of you really don't matter so much—what matters is what you think of yourself. But if you're not quite there yet, you can still listen to what others say without automatically assuming they know what they're talking about, or that their opinion is the only opinion. Like we mentioned earlier, do some research and ask yourself the same questions: Do I really need this? Do I need it now? Can I afford it?

Spending hard-earned money on clothing, electronics devices, and makeup won't change who you are.

Don't waste your money trying to fix yourself from the outside in just to fit in with everyone else. "Everyone else" isn't necessarily any better than you are. Instead, get to know yourself better and be true to who you are. You will probably find that other people will enjoy being around you when you are confident and like yourself—which has nothing to do with what you buy or don't buy.

Family. Families have their own views on money, careers, spending, and saving. As a child, you absorb these views without really thinking about them. Then, as you grow older, you start acting according to those views, without considering whether or not those are really your own.

For example, in Clint's family, his dad often says, "It's a tough world out there. You gotta get what you can before someone else does—and show them who's on top." Consequently, Clint is always worried that he's not going to have enough money. He's obsessed with making money and spending it to show others that he's not poor. Yet, most of the time, he feels unsure of himself and worries about money a lot. If only he could feel better about money and himself, but he doesn't know how. You'll learn more about this in **Chapter 2, Your Relationship with Money.**

quickcheck

Where do wants come from?

now you try it

NEEDS AND WANTS

■ List the basic needs in your life right now.

_____

_____

_____

■ List your wants and prioritize them.

_____

_____

_____

■ Where do most of your wants come from?

_____

FINANCIAL FIGURES

LEARNING FROM THE EXPERIENCE OF OTHERS

Richard Martinez, *president and CEO of Young Americans Bank, Denver, Colo.*

The banking world is not reserved for Donald Trumps and Warren Buffets. Denver-based Young Americans Bank opens the world of checking and savings to the 21 and younger crowd. It's the only bank on the planet with such a mission.

"Kids can understand what has to happen to conduct commerce at a very early age, at age 2 or the latest 3," says Richard Martinez, president and CEO of Young Americans. The key concepts his staff introduce are record keeping and goal setting. "It's hard to say, especially for young kids, that you have to save just for the heck of it. You've got to save for a goal, which gets you in the habit of saving. The younger the kids are, the shorter-term goals will be," Martinez says.

About 94 percent of the bank's 15,000 customers are from Colorado, but banking by mail is an option that out-of-staters can take advantage of. Checking customers can opt for online banking, too, but Martinez says young bankers are more like senior bankers in their preference for physical contact with the bills and coins. "The ability for it to be out in the virtual world is a little hard for some kids to grasp . . . even high schoolers and adults, too," Martinez says.

It's common for parents to wait in the parking lot as their kids head inside the Denver bank branch for some banking activity, eager to visit their favorite tellers, who instill confidence and teach valuable lessons. "The biggest benefit is a knowledgeable staff that is trained to educate you," Martinez says.

Young Americans offers a healthy dose of camps and curriculums to help kids and young adults become financially savvy, from the Young Entrepreneurs Marketplace to the Get aHead for Business program that gives high schoolers an entrepreneurial business experience and the chance to put their own business plan into action.

"There is some critical thinking," Martinez says of his young clients, "but it's financial planning, understanding risks and rewards and consequences. It's more life-based critical thinking."

13

ARE YOU AWARE OF YOUR SPENDING HABITS?

A lot of teenagers (and adults, for that matter) are rather unconscious of their own spending habits. They see something they want, they buy it, and never look back. Later, they never ask themselves these questions: Did I really need it? Could I afford it? Do I still have it?

The typical American spends $1.22 for every dollar he or she earns.[2]

If differentiating between needs and wants is the first step toward financial literacy, then becoming conscious of your own spending habits is the second. In **Chapter 3, Budgeting and Goal Setting for Success**, you will have a chance to keep a spending log, review it, and develop a budget. However, right now, all we want you to do is answer these questions on your own:

- How much money do you have?
- How much money do you make?
- What do you own?
- What do you spend?

Financial literacy often starts by simply becoming aware of your financial position through answering those questions—especially the last one!

Some people spend too little money; others spend far too much.

Depending on your relationship with money, you may be someone who refuses to spend money, or someone who overspends and buys compulsively. Neither behavior is a healthy relationship with money. In both cases, fear controls your behavior. In the first situation, you may be afraid to spend because you think you don't deserve it or won't have enough money to survive. In the second situation, you may be afraid not to spend because of what others will think of you or because you have a certain image you feel you have to maintain.

now you try it

SPENDING HABITS

1. Do you know how much money you spend each month?

   _____

2. Do you know how much money you make or receive from your parents?

   _____

3. Do you think you spend too much? Too little? Or just enough?

   _____

What we hope to teach you in this book is how to have a healthy relationship with money so that you can experience a future where you earn a decent income, can pay for what you need, have savings for emergencies, and still have money for fun activities.

In fact, let's look at things you might want to think about for the future.

DO YOU HAVE A PLAN FOR THE FUTURE?

One day (and for some of you, quite soon), you'll be on your own. You may be going to college or working. You may be renting an apartment by yourself or sharing with others. Or you may be buying a house. Whatever you will be doing, it's going to cost money.

Do you have any idea how much income you will need to live on your own? Do you know which careers will provide that income? Do you know how to budget your money so you can afford the things you need? And do you know how to wisely use a credit card so you don't end up in a sea of debt?

IT'S A FACT! *GUARANTEED*

The average American family is $54,000 in debt. This includes credit card, mortgage, home equity, and loans.[3]

By paying attention to what you learn in this book and actually performing the suggested activities, you improve your chances of not joining the ranks of Americans mentioned in **It's a Fact!**

What are you planning for? Everyone has different visions of their future, but here are some common things that people should think about:

- **Education.** As college looms on the horizon, you'll want to do some research into different colleges and their costs. You'll want to research scholarships and grants and other sources of financial help. **Chapter 9, Financial Planning in High School** and **Chapter 10, Financial Planning for College, Career, and Life** will look into the costs of education.

- **Emergencies.** No matter what your future plans, emergencies will always crop up. None of us have the power to plan and control everything. You'll want to have the funds to deal with these emergencies, no matter what they are. **Chapter 4, Components of Personal Money Management, Chapter 5, Balancing Credit and Debit,** and **Chapter 7, Avoiding Debt and Staying Out of Debt** will look into budgeting and saving for emergencies.

IT'S A FACT! *GUARANTEED*

Fifty percent of Americans working full time live paycheck to paycheck. They have no funds available for emergencies; only the money from their paychecks.

- **Home.** The American dream still seems to be to own or rent a nice home, condo, duplex, or apartment. What will that cost you and how will you afford it? **Chapter 10, Financial Planning for College, Career, and Life** will look into planning for the future.

- **Family.** Many of you probably plan to marry some day. Maybe you'll have kids; maybe not. But either way, you will have expenses associated with your family, like buying clothes, paying for health care, buying groceries, and paying for education. **Chapter 3, Budgeting and Goal Setting for Success** will look into budgeting for your life today so you're ready for tomorrow.

- **Career.** You are probably thinking about what you'll end up doing when you get out of school and how much money you will make. **Chapter 10, Financial Planning for College, Career, and Life** will look into careers and income.

- **Retirement.** It's unlikely that many of you are thinking about retirement—especially if you haven't even graduated from high school or started a career. However, retirement no longer means that you stop work and live off some big pension fund. Most companies today have no such funds and most workers end up working part time when they get older to add to whatever money they have managed to save, invest, or get from Social Security.

About 40 percent of people who work full time do not save money for retirement. Those who do save, tend to save very little.[4]

- **Charitable giving.** Now here's something that you might not have considered. With federal and state governments having fewer funds, many organizations and individuals depend on private donations. If you believe in helping animals, the environment, the disabled, or any group, you might want to consider donating money to worthy causes.

now you try it

PLANNING FOR THE FUTURE

When you think about the future:

1. What do you see yourself doing (school, work, home)?

   _____

   _____

2. How much money do you think you will make?

   _____

3. What kind of purchases might you want to make?

   _____

   _____

   _____

4. What kind of organizations do you think you might want to donate to?

   _____

   _____

   _____

How do you resist purchasing "wants"?

Jasper20: I think it's more empowering to say "no" than to say "yes" to advertisers.   3 minutes ago

FaeryWingz: Before I buy anything I ask myself if I can live without it. Most of the time, I can!
5 minutes ago

Bowie70: I think it's important people spoil themselves occasionally. BUT wait to buy your wants till after your bills are paid.   8 minutes ago

bfranklin: If you would be wealthy, think of saving as well as getting.   about 240 years ago

THE SOCIAL MEDIA FEED

FiNaNCiaL FouL-uPs

LEARNING FROM THE MISTAKES OF OTHERS

José's girlfriend, Jenn, decided she was tired of taking the bus every day and wanted new wheels of her own that would turn heads. The only problem was she had bad credit and her bank refused to give her a car loan. However, if she could get someone with good credit to sign, the car would be hers, the man at the car dealership explained.

She begged her mom and her grandparents but they refused to sign for it, saying they didn't want to have to suffer the consequences of her not making her payments. She didn't know what to do, so she went to the next closest person to her, José.

José didn't see a problem with signing for the loan; he even thought it was a little rude that her family didn't want to help her out. Jenn promised she would make the payments on time, and since he had known her, he had never had a reason to believe she would go against her word. Not only was this an opportunity to help out someone he loved, he thought, it was also a gesture that could help their relationship grow. He decided to sign on the dotted line.

A few months later, Jenn ditched the car—and not only that—she ditched José for some college-aged guy who had a lot more money than José or any of her friends. José got a notice from the bank that his car had been repossessed and that he had an outstanding payment of $18,000. He tried to explain the person who owed them money was his ex-girlfriend and that he had just done her a favor by signing for her. The collectors had heard it before.

Because his name was bound to the loan, there was nothing anyone could do to shift the burden of the payment to Jenn. José was responsible for the entire amount of the car, even though the state now owned the car and he had nothing.

Your spending decisions today will affect your ability to meet financial obligations in the future. If you are a **short-term** thinker, you tend to live moment to moment, rarely thinking beyond today. This means you may find yourself without the funds you need in the future. You may be unable to deal with an emergency, such as fixing your car, going to the health clinic, or getting a cavity filled at the dentist. You may be unable to afford a college education. Or you may be unable to afford a home.

If you are a true **long-term** thinker, you probably have no problem thinking about next week, next month, or next year. You are beginning to realize that your spending habits today affect your future. This means you are learning the power of "if-then" thinking. If you're unfamiliar with this term, read on.

HOW DO YOU PRACTICE IF-THEN THINKING?

Hopefully this brief introduction to financial literacy is sinking in, a few words at a time. That's why we've saved the best for last: "if-then" thinking.

What we're talking about is **hypothesizing**. You may have encountered the word, **hypothesis**, in a science class. If you remember, every scientific problem has a hypothesis associated with it. The hypothesis is a guess at how things are going to turn out, without actually experiencing the outcome.

In many cases, data suggests that without the ability to perform well-developed "if-then" thinking, many teenagers depend on their gut reactions, rather than evaluating the consequences of what they are doing. Hence, they are often more spontaneous and less inhibited.[5]

When you develop your if-then thinking skills, you become a force to be reckoned with. You gain the ability to look into the future and imagine the consequences of an action BEFORE you take it.

Hypothesize, verb

To form a hypothesis (a theory, a guess, or an assumption).

The ability to practice if-then thinking improves as the frontal lobes of your brain develop (usually by the age of 25). The younger you are, the easier it is to act impulsively, because the frontal lobes are not yet developed. However, impulsive acts can get you into trouble. So, even if your frontal lobe is not yet developed, you can exercise your if-then thinking by consciously trying to imagine what could happen if you followed a particular course of action.

If-then thinking helps you evaluate the results of something you are considering doing.

Neuro-scientists who study the behavior of the brain used to think human brain development was pretty complete by age 10. But today they know differently. In teenagers, a crucial part of the brain—the frontal lobes—are not fully connected. These lobes make up the part of the brain that says: "Is this a good idea? What is the consequence of this action?" Without fully developed and connected frontal lobes, it takes teenagers longer to consider the consequences of an action.[6]

If-then thinking, rather than impulsive behavior, is particularly important when looking at financial problems. For example, suppose Clint sees an ad for a new Android-powered, 4G smart phone, with a slideout keyboard, an ultra-fast processor, and a sleek, modern exterior. The ad says a new phone costs $150 for the two-year contract (Clint misses the fine print that says the cost is actually $250, but there's a $100 rebate). Clint decides it's the perfect phone for surfing the web, taking photos, sending text messages, downloading music, and calling people. He's got $150 saved up from his pizza job and decides he must have the phone. He goes to the mall and buys the phone without thinking about any of the other costs involved, like maintenance or monthly fees. This is an example of impulsive behavior.

But suppose Clint practices some if-then thinking and asks himself, "If I buy this, how much will it cost up front? What about the monthly costs?" Then suppose he asks himself, "Can I afford it? And if so, what will I have to give up to afford it?" Check out the **Real-World Math** example to see what Clint would discover.

REAL-WORLD MATH

Clint is considering buying a smart phone that supposedly costs $150. When he starts researching the phone, he learns there are other costs involved. Clint needs to figure out the actual cost before he can make a decision to buy it.

The phone actually costs $250 with a $36 one-time maintenance fee. Clint has to fill out paperwork to get the $100 rebate, which takes up to 8 weeks. So, Clint actually has to pay $286 plus tax, up front.

In addition, he has to pay for his calls, texts, photos, and videos. It's $0.45 per minute for outgoing or incoming calls, and $0.20 per text message, photo, or video he sends or receives. He estimates he makes or receives about 10 calls a day and sends or receives about 10 texts or photos a day. And that's 7 days a week.

CALLS:
10 × $0.45 × 7 days/week = $31.50 per week or $126 per month or $1,512 per year!

PLUS

TEXTS:
10 × $0.20 × 7 days/week = $14 per week or $56 per month or $672 per year!

EQUALS

GRAND TOTAL: $182/month or $2,184 per year![7]

There's no way Clint can come up with an extra $2,184 per year at his pizza job, so what's he going to have to give up to afford that phone? A lot! Clint decides it's just not worth it.

So, the next time an advertiser says, "This is what it costs," make sure to look further and consider any hidden costs. If the advertiser says, "This is an offer you can't refuse," trust me, you can refuse it. And if the advertiser says, "This is too good to be true," chances are that it is. Don't be a victim of compulsive buying.

✔ quickcheck

What is "if-then" thinking?

Why is "if-then" thinking harder for teenagers than for adults?

now you try it

IF-THEN THINKING

Consider a purchase scenario you may have
been considering and look at two possibilities:

- If I did X, what would happen?

_____

_____

- If I did Y, what would happen?

_____

_____

- Which possibility sounds best to you?

_____

HOW CAN YOU SEE THE BIG PICTURE?

At this point, you may be thinking, "Hey, I'm still young. Why should I worry about the future? Why not buy today and worry about paying later?"

The answer is simple. If you don't think about the consequences of your spending behavior today, you might very well end up like so many Americans tomorrow who:

- Have no money for emergencies.
- Have no money for retirement.
- Have huge credit card debt.
- Live paycheck to paycheck.
- Worry constantly about whether or not they will be able to pay their bills next month.

If this doesn't sound like the kind of future you want, it's important to look beyond the present. After all, you plan to live beyond high school. Right? And we bet you want to end up using your skills and talents to do something interesting, make some money, and have some good relationships with people.

Learning to see the big picture beyond high school helps you make wise decisions today. It helps you understand trade-offs. It helps you feel more in control of your own financial situation.

Well, we've covered the bases to get you warmed up for the rest of the book so you can begin your journey toward evaluating your options, making conscious choices, and taking responsibility for your financial decisions.

Now it's time for some review and activities. We know it's hard to remember everything you read without some review. We also know that the best way to learn is by doing. That's why we've created activities for you to do—to get those brain cells moving about and doing their thing!

LET'S REVIEW

 ere's your chance to think about what you've learned in this chapter. Reviewing stimulates your brain to remember important facts.

What Did You Learn?

- Financial literacy means being able to make wise decisions about money so that you have a safe financial future.
- Assets are things you own that have monetary value, and liabilities are expenses you have (including money you owe).
- Needs and wants are different. Needs are things you must have to survive. Wants are things you desire, but are not necessary for survival.
- Being able to consider the consequences of a purchase decision BEFORE you buy saves a lot of heartache later.
- Buying habits today affect your ability to fund your future needs tomorrow, such as education, emergencies, home, family, career, retirement, charitable giving.
- Frontal lobe development in teenagers affects their ability to do "if-then" thinking.

New Terms

- Financial Literacy
- Personal Finance
- Income
- Asset

- Liability
- Wants
- Needs

- If-then Thinking
- Long-term Thinking
- Short-term Thinking

END-OF-CHAPTER ACTIVITIES

Here's your chance to put your pen to paper, as well as discuss what you've learned with others. Doing activities and talking about them are great ways to make sure you really do understand the concepts you've read about.

Remember the Basics

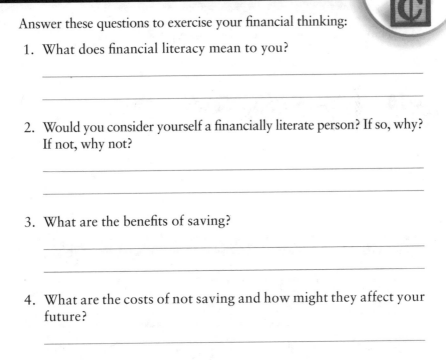

Answer these questions to exercise your financial thinking:

1. What does financial literacy mean to you?

   _____

   _____

2. Would you consider yourself a financially literate person? If so, why? If not, why not?

   _____

   _____

3. What are the benefits of saving?

   _____

   _____

4. What are the costs of not saving and how might they affect your future?

   _____

   _____

   _____

Work With a Team

Share your needs and wants results with others. In particular consider these questions:

1. Are some peoples' wants other peoples' needs, and vice versa? Why do you think that is so?

_____

_____

_____

2. Do you have similar needs to other people?

_____

_____

3. Do you have similar wants to other people?

_____

4. What is the biggest source of the group's wants?

_____

Put Your Math into Practice

This is your chance to analyze you and your family's assets and liabilities.

1. Sit down together with your parents or guardians and write down all sources of monthly income in the table below:

SOURCE	AMOUNT
What is the total of all the combined income?	

2. Gather all the monthly bills. List all the costs that you or your parents or guardians have to pay:

BILL	AMOUNT
What is the total of all the combined bills?	
How much income is left over after the bills are "paid"?	

Together, make a list of potential emergencies you might have to pay for. Do you think that the income left over is adequate to handle any of these emergencies?

For more activities, assessments, and examples, visit www.lifebound.com.

DID YOU KNOW?

- In 2011, there were over 300 million websites. The number continues to grow with 150,00 new URLs being added every day.[8]

- A study by the MacArthur Foundation found the time youth spend online is essential for developing the social and technical skills they need to succeed in the digital age.[9]

- There are more activities, online assessments, and financial learning materials available on the "Dollars & Sense" page at www.lifebound.com.

Your Relationship with Money

Studying your relationship with money inevitably leads to the questions, "Who am I," "What do I want," and "What do I want to do with my life?"

HELEN KIM, MONEY RELATIONSHIP MENTOR

Questions you will answer. . . .

1. What is your relationship with money?
2. Why do you spend money?
3. How do family, culture, and advertising affect your relationship with money?
4. How can you build a healthy relationship with money?

Test your financial skills with the Dollars & Sense chapter assessment at www.lifebound.com.

Meet Shoshana and Denzel

Shoshana feels stressed when she watches her mother spend money. Shoshana lives with her mom and her grandmother; her dad walked out when she was little. Her mom has never gotten over being angry with Shoshana's dad for leaving, and resents having so little money. The family has always lived paycheck to paycheck because when her mom gets paid, she buys whatever catches her eye whether it's needed or not. She always says, "We deserve it." But then a few days before the next paycheck, her mom is out of money.

Shoshana is always worried about being broke and feels her mom doesn't think about where the money is going.

Denzel hates the way his parents don't spend money. His family is very frugal with spending. They carefully budget everything, shopping at garage sales and thrift stores. They buy only items that are on sale, and usually buy only store brands at the grocery store. Denzel's parents take the money Denzel makes from his job and put it away in savings for his college fund.

Denzel still wants to save for college, but he also wants to spend some of his money on things that are fun, such as going out to dinner with his friends or picking up a new video game.

Whether they know it or not, both Shoshana and Denzel have been impacted by how their parents deal with money. Shoshana and Denzel need to decide what kind of relationship they want to have with money in the years to come.

get ready

Like Shoshana and Denzel, your relationship with money is influenced by how your family uses and misuses money. People need to understand and develop their own relationships with money. As unique individuals, we all have different spending styles and different spending priorities.

In this chapter, we will help you understand how you relate to money, and how your spending habits are influenced by your family, culture, and advertising. You will also get a chance to ask questions of your parents, your grandparents, your aunts and uncles, as well as your friends to find out what they really think about money. Many people are reluctant to talk about their relationship with money, but the best way to gather information is to talk to them as honestly as possible.

WHAT'S YOUR RELATIONSHIP WITH MONEY?

Think about how your family talks about and uses money. Do you believe their spending and saving habits help make them financially independent people? Do they take **responsibility** for their spending or saving choices? Are they happy in their **relationship** with money?

Think about how your friends talk about and use money. Do you believe their spending and saving habits help make them financially independent people? Do they take responsibility for their spending or saving choices? Are they happy in their relationship with money?

Now it's time to discover your own relationship with money. Read this list of statements, and respond **True** or **False** to each. Then answer the "why" or "how" question as honestly as you can. The more complete your answers, the better you will understand your relationship with money.

Responsibility, noun

Duty or obligation to satisfactorily perform or complete a task that you have been assigned, which has a consequent penalty for failure.

Relationship, noun

A connection, association, or involvement. An emotional or other connection between people, groups, countries.

MONEY & YOU
YOU & MONEY

1. I like paying bills. Why?

_____

_____

_____

2. I spend more money when I make more money. Why?

_____

_____

_____

3. I use money to celebrate good things and reward myself. Why?

_____

_____

_____

4. I make myself sick over how to use my money. Why?

_____

_____

_____

5. I envy people who have more money than I do. Why?

_____

_____

_____

6. I pity people who have less money than I do. Why?

_____

_____

_____

7. I am confused when I have to make money decisions. Why?

_____

_____

_____

8. I buy things on impulse. Why?

_____

_____

_____

9. I think I could spend my money more wisely. How?

_____

_____

_____

10. I spend money to make myself feel better. Why?

_____

_____

_____

11. I take responsibility for my spending choices. How?

_____

_____

_____

12. I wish I could save more money. Why?

_____

_____

_____

13. I think all my money problems could be solved by winning the lottery or inheriting a large sum of money. Why?

_____

_____

_____

Imagine you've received two job offers. The first, from Pete's Diner, pays $6.50 an hour. The second, from Burger Express, pays $8.50 an hour. Pete's Diner gives you a free meal worth $6 at each shift. It's down the street and you can walk to and from work. Burger Express charges $6 for a meal at work (which you plan to eat with each shift), and you have to take the bus to and from work, which will cost you $3 each day.

If you work 4 hours a shift, and have 3 shifts a week, which is the better job to take?

PETE'S DINER:
4 hours X 3 shifts = 12 hours a week
12 hours X $6.50 = $78 a week

BURGER EXPRESS:
4 hours X 3 shifts = 12 hours a week
12 hours X $8.50 = $102 a week

Subtracting for the meals:
$102 − ($6 X 3 shifts) = $84 a week

Subtracting for the bus fare:
$84 − ($3 X 3 shifts) = $75 a week

The job at Pete's Diner will give you $3 more a week once you factor in your other costs. Plus, since it's in walking distance it will probably save you time.

Some of the whys and hows were probably easy to answer, while others were not. If you did not know how to answer all the whys, you're not alone. Many people are confused about how they feel about money and what motivates them to make the financial decisions they do. However, you should now be aware of the emotions you experience when you think about money, and you should have a sense of the emotions you have surrounding money.

WHY DO YOU SPEND?

When it comes to spending money on things, the Federal Trade Commission classifies **necessary expenses** as housing, food, health care, insurance, and education. Every other thing is **optional**—everything.

People who have a healthy relationship with money know the difference between necessary and optional expenses. It's the same as knowing the difference between needs and wants (you learned about that in Chapter 1). People who have unhealthy relationships have difficulty knowing what's necessary and what's optional. They also have extreme emotional reactions to spending money. Just look at Denzel's parents and Shoshana's mother.

Denzel's parents are afraid they won't have enough money. They save every penny "just in case." When Denzel asks, "When *would* you spend money?" his parents can never come up with an answer. They can't imagine a situation when they would willingly spend money. They feel guilty spending their money.

"If you look at it, it seems the emotion most commonly associated with money is fear: of not having enough of it, or losing it once you do. The former might represent people who have large amounts of debt and therefore feel in a sense enslaved to money. The latter might include those who forget that money's purpose is to be used and not simply amassed. Finding a balance between these two teeter-tottering fears is a hard task, a never-ending process, because life is always changing."   **SUZE ORMAN**, FROM HER BOOK *WOMEN AND MONEY*

Shoshana's mother is so deeply in debt that she no longer cares about saving or investing money. "We can either spend it on ourselves, or pay bills with it." She is addicted to the pleasure "high" that shopping gives her.

Denzel's parents and Shoshana's mother are at the opposite extremes of many possible relationships with money: guilt vs. pleasure. Like many other things in life, it is best to have a balance between these two extremes. Think about your own spending patterns. Does spending cause you guilt or pleasure? Or do you only buy things that are necessity?

Guilt. There are several reasons why spending money can cause you to feel guilty. Some teens watch their families struggle to make money and don't want to make the family's burden greater. Some teens watch their parents fight about money and don't want to cause more arguments. Some teens believe that if they spend money, they won't feel as secure as if they hold on to it.

Pleasure. There are several reasons why spending money can cause you to feel pleasure. Some teens are excited to buy the latest fashion or gadget because they think it will help them fit in or improve their status so others will like them. Some teens feel closer to their friends when they shop together. Some teens feel like they deserve the reward of buying something they want rather than saving that money.

now you try it

NECESSITIES VS. OPTIONS; GUILT VS. PLEASURE?

1. Think about the things that you believe to be necessities in your life and list them.
   - Why do you need them?

   _____

   _____

   _____

   _____

   - Do you typically have enough money to buy them? How does that make you feel?

   _____

   _____

2. Think about all the things you buy that aren't necessities and list them.
   - Why do you want them?

   _____

   _____

   _____

   - Do you typically have enough money to buy them? How does that make you feel?

   _____

   _____

3. How do you feel when you spend money on yourself?

   _____

   _____

4. How do you feel when you spend money on others?

   _____

   _____

HOW DO FAMILY, CULTURE, AND ADVERTISING INFLUENCE YOUR VIEWS ABOUT MONEY?

It's one thing to come to grips with how money makes you feel. It's another to understand why you feel that way. Your family definitely influences how you view money, but so do other forces, like culture and advertising.

Influence of Family: Growing up Privileged or Poor

An excess or lack of money in a family has a tremendous influence on how you spend and save money. When your family works hard, but doesn't have enough for the basics—like food or rent—it can be very stressful. Money may become something you worry about all the time. You may resent others because they have more than you do. You may feel there is never enough to go around.

"Your first encounters with money are often watching your parents use money. A surprising number of people have shared their memory of parents who would buy items, then hide them from their spouse, telling their children not to divulge what then became 'their little secret.' Roping children into the parent's shame and inability to be truthful with money showed a clear lack of boundaries. It also implied that money carries secrets, never mind the confusion and effect it had on the (then) child's perception of money."[1]

HELEN KIM, MONEY RELATIONSHIP MENTOR

If you come from a family that has lots of money, you may begin to take money for granted. You may believe you are entitled to things without ever having to work for them. You may compare yourself to others based on how much money they have. Or you may be afraid of losing what you have and spend all your time trying to get more.

Whichever way you feel toward money, it's important to remember that money, or the lack of it, does not define who you are. You are who you are, regardless of how little or how much money you or your family has. Your self-respect does not come from money or things, it comes from deep inside of you—that part of you that says, "I am a valuable person. I have worth. I have skills. I can make a difference." Each of us is important and unique, regardless of our economic station in life.

Let's look at some of the similarities and differences in spending and saving habits between teens who grow up in wealthy families and those who grow up in poor families.

Spending similarities. Rich and poor alike spend money on the necessities of life: housing, food, health care, insurance, and education. However, the wealthy tend to purchase necessities that are expensive or exclusive. Those with little money purchase what they can afford, and often have little or no money for health care or private education.

Spending differences. The wealthy have more disposable income (what's left over after you pay for the necessities), which means they can buy more optional things, like designer clothes, computers, cell

phones, video games, televisions, college educations, cars, boats, and houses. Some wealthy people believe that owning more things gives them a higher status, so they buy more and live beyond their means just to keep up appearances. The poor have less disposable income, which causes some to make fewer purchases and others to live beyond their means so as not to appear poor. Often, to avoid debt, they must spend their money on items of less quality due to lower cost. However, those items often wear out sooner and have to be replaced, which costs more money.

Saving similarities. Both the wealthy and the poor save money, whether it is for a rainy day, a family vacation, a new car, a college education, or retirement. However, the amount of savings may differ greatly. Some wealthy families spend so much on daily expenses, that they actually have little savings; others have large savings. Some poor families religiously put aside money for the future, even though they earn very little.

Saving differences. Because the wealthy have more disposable income, they are able to put aside more money in savings, although many choose to overspend every dollar they earn, rather than save. They are also more likely to make investments because they have the money to do so. The poor often have difficulty building up their savings because they have to spend what they earn on day-to-day necessities and have little or nothing left over for savings or investments. However, poor families often believe strongly in saving because they know what it's like to be without. As a result, they learn the power of putting aside just a small amount of money each week into savings

To summarize, children of wealthy families are more likely to take money for granted, and assume it will always be there, believing they deserve it, whether they earned it or not. Some fear that they don't have enough money (compared to others) or that what they have will be taken away, so they spend most of their energy trying to earn as much money as they can and buy as much as they can.

Children of poor families rarely take money for granted and instead view it as something that is always in limited supply, negatively affecting their family's existence and preventing them from having a happy life. So, when they do have some money, they may spend it to reward themselves.

Defining yourself by the amount of money you have is a profoundly unhealthy attitude. Why? Because if that money is ever taken away, along with the things it buys, your identity will be taken away. Take the story of Josh and Haley. The brother and sister grew up in a very rich neighborhood. Their father was a CEO of a large software company and had a lot of money because of stock options, bonuses, and all the perks that went along with being the chief executive officer. Josh and Haley always got everything they wanted. Whatever it was, they would just charge it on the family credit card. They had absolutely no idea how much anything cost because they never had to worry about it.

During their senior year of high school, their father told them that the company was going out of business. Its earnings were dismal, the stock shares were worthless, and their father was accused of insider trading. This didn't only mean the family was losing their money; it also meant a possible jail term.

Josh and Haley didn't realize how this was going to affect them until their dad went to jail, their house got foreclosed on, their cars were repossessed, and they had to move to a small apartment with their mom. They couldn't use their credit cards anymore and all their former "friends" abandoned them, telling them they didn't want to associate with poor people whose dad was in jail. Even the college they wanted to go to was no longer an option because it was too expensive and they didn't have any financial aid lined up because they never believed they would need it.

For the first time in their lives they started thinking about who they really were, without all the "stuff" they used to own. Suddenly they had to live in the "real world" like everyone else, which meant researching a cheaper college that was on the bus route, applying for a student loan, and getting jobs that paid as much in one month as they would have previously spent in one day. They had no choice but to learn to live on less and stick to a budget.

now you try it

LEARNING PROJECT: INTERVIEW YOUR PARENTS

Ask your parents the following questions about their relationship with money.

1. Do you like paying bills? Why or why not?

_____

_____

2. Do you spend more money when you make more money? Why?

_____

_____

3. Do you use money to celebrate good things and reward yourself? Why?

_____

_____

4. Do you make yourself sick over how to use money? Why or why not?

_____

_____

5. Do you envy people with more money? If so, why?

_____

_____

6. Do you pity people with less money? Why?

_____

_____

7. Are you confused when you have to make money decisions? If so, why?

_____

_____

8. Do you buy things on impulse? Why or why not?

_____

_____

9. Do you think you could spend your money more wisely? How?

_____

_____

10. Do you spend money to make yourself feel better? Why?

_____

_____

11. Do you take responsibility for your spending choices?

_____

_____

12. Do you wish you could save more money?

_____

_____

13. Do you think all your money problems would be solved by winning the lottery or inheriting a large sum of money? Why?

_____

_____

Compare your answers from the Money Quiz to your parent's answers.

1. How are they the same?

_____

_____

2. How are they different?

_____

_____

Influences of family: frivolous or frugal spending

You just learned that your relationship with money can be greatly influenced by the amount of money your family has. However, it can also be influenced by your family's spending style, which doesn't reflect how much or how little money they have. Some families spend money **frivolously** and others spend it **frugally**.

Frivolous spending. This is inappropriate, silly, or wasteful spending. This type of spending typically occurs on impulse, because you are sad or bored. It also happens when you decide to buy something just because "everyone else has one."

"Frivolous purchases are aided by a difficulty with delayed gratification, not knowing how much is enough, or not knowing what is normal for other people."[2]

ARLENE MILLER, LICENSED SOCIAL WORKER

Frugal spending. This is a way of spending that involves managing your money and spending wisely. It means living without waste and being thrifty. It does not necessarily mean being stingy.

Think back to the questions that you asked your parents in the previous "Learning Project" activity. Given your parents answers to those questions, do you think your parents are frivolous or frugal spenders?

You've looked at the way your family influences your relationship with money. But are they your only influence? Of course not. Just as your wants and needs are affected by advertising and peer pressure (see Chapter 1), your relationship with money is also influenced by your culture.

quick*check*

How does your family influence your financial decisions?

What is frivolous spending?

What is frugal spending?

"Like saving or paying off debt, being frugal is a pattern of behavior that promotes patience. But being too frugal is forgetting that money is meant to be used, not hoarded."

SUZE ORMAN, FROM HER BOOK *WOMEN AND MONEY*

FINANCIAL FIGURES

LEARNING FROM THE EXPERIENCE OF OTHERS

Regina Leeds, *author, Los Angeles, Calif.*

Regina Leeds, the "Zen Organizer," offers teenagers a word of encouragement in the face of challenging financial realities. "Teenagers especially have an ability that, sadly, most adults lose over time," says Leeds, author of *One Year to an Organized Financial Life*. "That is the ability to have dreams. I don't think anybody should ever lose that quality. However there has to be a connection between the dream and how you make it a reality. That process is almost always going to require generous amounts of both time and money."

A former professional actress, including three years on the soap *The Young & the Restless*, Leeds says today's teens have opportunities to learn about finance that earlier generations did not. "It is no longer something you are supposed to absorb through osmosis," she says. "My dad was fabulous with money management but he didn't have a clue how to articulate or teach what he was doing. I had to learn through trial and error . . . I wish I had had a book to read or a financially savvy adult I could have gone to. I thought money was magical. When I needed it, my generous father would make it appear. I didn't get the cause-and-effect relationship between hard work and financial reward until much later."

Leeds' book *One Year to an Organized Life* was a *New York Times* bestseller, and *One Year to an Organized Financial Life* follows that successful blueprint. In her chapter "Children and Money," Leeds outlines a timetable for lessons parents can teach to their kids:

AGE	LESSON
under 11	Teach patience
11-12	Explain your values
12-13	Demonstrate charity
13-14	Show them the future
14-15	Forget about fate
15-16	Provide incentive
16-17	Demonize bad debt

Maybe the most important advice Leeds offers: Put fear aside, learn the basics, and when needed, seek out the financial experts. "Numbers are your friends because they don't lie nor do they have any emotion," Leeds says.

Influence of Culture: Consumer Nation

The United States, as well as most of Europe, Australia, and New Zealand, and parts of Asia, are called **consumer nations** because the citizens of those parts of the world purchase goods and consume materials in excess beyond their basic needs.

Americans have been brought up in a culture that celebrates excess; having the newest and the best clothes, phones, cars, and houses are all important indicators of status and success. As a result, people often buy more and more things to keep up their image. They believe that having more means they are more **successful** and have a higher **status**.

Consumerism, noun

Belief that ever-increasing consumption of goods and services forms the basis of a sound economy.

Status, noun

Position or rank in relation to others or relative rank in a hierarchy of prestige; especially high prestige.

Success, noun

Favorable or desired outcome; or the attainment of wealth, favor, or eminence.

"Perhaps the most shocking fact revealed by Annie Leonard's The Story of Stuff *extensive research is that our 'throwaway society' was carefully orchestrated by the government of the United States in order to revitalize the economy after World War II. At the time, retailing analyst Victor Lebow proposed an ambitious plan:*

'Our enormously productive economy demands that we make consumption our way of life; that we convert the buying and the use of goods into rituals; that we seek our spiritual satisfaction, our ego satisfaction, in consumption. We need things consumed, burned up, replaced and discarded at an ever-accelerating rate.'

And that's how the consumerism ball started rolling. Everyone in the U.S. is inundated with over 3,000 ads a day, telling them to buy more stuff. Companies design products to become obsolete as quickly as possible. Shelves are constantly loaded with disposable products for our convenience. The result?

Our entire lives are being narrowed down to working, shopping, and then working again to pay off for the stuff we just bought. And with such an endless treadmill, it's no surprise that polls show that our national happiness is actually declining."[3]

Influence of Advertisers: Your Age Is the Target

Everywhere you look, people are trying to sell you something. They tell you that if you use their products or services, you will be smarter, faster, more attractive, more secure. Companies pay advertising agencies and marketing firms billions of dollars every year to come up with the pitch that will pull in the most dollars for their company.

Marketing researchers are studying you to optimize how they pitch products and services to you. But you can outsmart ads and marketing by learning how to spot an advertising ploy the next time you're watching TV, searching the Internet, driving down the street, or listening to the radio. The PBS article "5 Ways to Promote Ad Savvy"[4] shares the following clues with teens:

1. **Ads thrive on making you feel like you're not good enough the way you are:** Ads that make you feel "unattractive" or "uncool" are trying to make you feel that way. If you feel insecure about yourself you might be desperate enough to go out and buy their product to feel better. These ads sell to an emotion or lifestyle. If you're tempted by ads selling you things like jeans, makeup, or electronics, ask yourself if it's the product you are attracted to or the models and lifestyle associated with the product.

2. **Actively be on the lookout for the next ad.** Have you ever watched a movie and noticed the brand placement on the side of the main character's soda can, on a truck driving down the street, or on an extra's T-shirt? These companies want you to associate their product with the movie, TV show, or video game you're engaged in. The next time you're watching something, see if you can spot any product placement and try laughing at it instead of buying into it.

3. **Know what they know.** Advertisers know more about you than you even know about yourself. Don't you think it's time you took an interest in you, too? Check out the Frontline special "The Merchant of Cool" to learn what teens think, get smart about media giants, and hear interviews from influential voices.

4. **Don't support commercialism.** PBS suggests checking out Adbusters and Commercial Alert or organizations like AlterNet and WireTap, which are only a few ways youth are fighting commercialism. If you're tired of ads, say goodbye to commercial products and hello to news, stories, and culture that aren't muddied with product placement.

5. **Take a stand!** You're probably thinking that you don't fall for advertising ploys—and so is the person next to you! Our society is so inundated with ads that they're not always easy to identify or realize. Get involved with groups like the New Mexico Media Literacy Project, and join a cause that's showing ads for what they are.

Advertisers know you and know that if they can convince you that their products will improve your relationships, give you control of your life, and somehow make you successful, you will buy those products.

But if you take the time to analyze those commercials, you will realize that no product can possibly do those things. However, those advertisers are counting on you being impulsive and not thinking. Just because your frontal lobe is not yet developed (Chapter 1), it doesn't mean you have to buy without thinking or let others take advantage of you. Prove those advertisers wrong and take control of your spending habits.

now you try it

INFLUENCE OF ADVERTISERS

1. List one purchase you've made that took some thought and may have required you to go outside your usual budget. Did advertising influence this purchase? How?

   _____

   _____

2. List one purchase that you made on a whim which may have caused you to go outside your usual budget. Did advertising influence this purchase? If so, how?

   _____

   _____

HOW CAN YOU BUILD A HEALTHY RELATIONSHIP WITH MONEY?

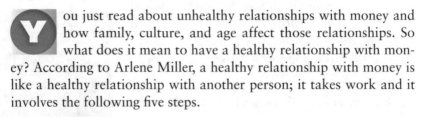 ou just read about unhealthy relationships with money and how family, culture, and age affect those relationships. So what does it mean to have a healthy relationship with money? According to Arlene Miller, a healthy relationship with money is like a healthy relationship with another person; it takes work and it involves the following five steps.

- **Build Honesty.** Don't lie to yourself about what you spend money on. Instead, keep a spending log. This log can be a piece of paper or a small spiral notebook that you keep with you at all times. This way, whenever you spend money, you can write down how much you spent and what you spent it on. Next to that, write down how you felt when you spent money on each item. At the end of the week, examine your purchases, the money you spent, and how you felt. Are there any surprises? Do you notice any trends in your spending habits? At the end of the month, examine your spending log again. Then stop buying things that you do not need or that make you feel confused or guilty. You'll be amazed how much better you feel and how much money you save.

> *"Like any other relationship, your relationship with money should be honest, living in the present, patient, be charitable, and be committed."*
>
> **ARLENE C. MILLER,** HOW NOT TO RAISE FUTURE GAMBLERS OF AMERICA

- **Live in the Present.** This is a way to budget your money without a lot of effort. When you see something you want to buy, notice how much it costs. Then ask yourself how many hours you would have to work to pay for it. Finally, decide if that item is worth your time and energy. For example, imagine that a video game you want costs $24. Now suppose you make $8 per hour at your part-time job. It will take you 3 hours to pay for the game. Is that game worth 3 hours of your life? If it is, buy it. If not, pass on it.

- **Build Patience.** If you are impatient and would rather spend without thinking instead of save money, remember this: Savings and investments take time to build and debt takes time to pay back.

- **Be Charitable.** Did you know that being generous can make you a happier person, especially when you're feeling down about your own financial luck? Gretchen Rubin, author of *The Happiness*

Project, says that when you give money away, you convince your-self that you're doing pretty well—well enough to give to others.[5]

- **Be Committed.** Come up with a financial plan and stick to it. In later chapters we will have exercises, tips, and resources to help you understand spending and saving, investments, and debt.

In a Junior Achievement poll of 1,512 students, 77.5 percent of stu-dents reported donating time, money, or both to the community.[6]

IT'S A FACT!
GUARANTEED

Think back to Shoshana and Denzel. Even though their par-ents had unhealthy relationships with money, both teens learned some ways to relate to money in a healthy fashion.

For example, Shoshana found a book on how to make a budget, how to open a savings account, and how to know where her money is going. The first step she took toward financial independence was opening a savings account where she put aside some of her earnings for college as well as big purchases.

Denzel searched online for a financial goals worksheet. He found one that helped him figure out how much he could spend on fun things, and how much he needed to save for college. He implemented his new budget right away so he could start getting ready for the future.

Both Shoshana and Denzel built their own unique, healthy rela-tionship with money.

Do you think your family influences your spending habits?

agardn16: I never thought about it until my friends commented on the amount of clothes I buy. I thought it was normal because my mom goes shopping every week, too.   5 minutes ago

JJ1997: Yes, of course they do. My parents are big on saving so they taught me at a young age to start putting money away.   12 minutes ago

Thunderbird67: My sister is really good with money and I'm not. She helps my parents with bills and grocery shopping but I think it's boring.   20 minutes ago

THE SOCIAL MEDIA FEED

FiNaNCiaL FoUL-UPS

LEARNING FROM THE MISTAKES OF OTHERS

Shawna was not a spoiled child. Her parents, in fact, were far from rich. But they worked incredibly hard to provide educational, athletic, cultural, and personal opportunities for Shawna. They didn't want to see her spending all her time on school and work.

Shawna got good grades, played sports, was a drummer in school band, and was looking forward to a vocational school path after high school. She did not have a part-time job, and her parents did not force her to do chores or pitch in with family work projects.

In her senior year of high school, Shawna's dad suffered a stroke and was forced to leave his job. Shawna's mom picked up a second job to make extra money, but now the expectations for Shawna changed. She was asked to get a 20-hour-per-week job to help the family meet expectations. She was asked to spend an hour per day doing basic household chores. She was urged to quit the school soccer team so she could take care of her younger brother in the afternoon.

Shawna felt alienated, and taken advantage of. She had her own life to live. How could she be expected to sacrifice her time and her own money for others? Why was life being unfair to her?

The relationship between Shawna and her parents deteriorated, and she moved out of the home to live with a friend. Without the daily guidance of her parents, she began making unhealthy decisions that affected her grades and attitude.

Shawna had never been asked to fend for herself financially. Money, though never plentiful, was always provided to her if she needed it. She did not know how to land a job, retain a job or save her earnings. She did not understand the demands of independence.

LET'S REVIEW

 ere's your chance to think about what you've learned in this chapter. Reviewing stimulates your brain to remember important facts.

To many people, money is an object. You get a job, you make money and you use that money to get what you want, whether it is a cup of coffee, a video game, a college education, a car, or a house. However, money is more complicated than that. Money is something that permeates every aspect of your life. Money is actually an energy exchange—you spend time to make money and only you can decide what your time is worth. Therefore you need to understand money and build a healthy relationship with it.

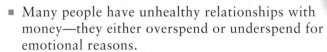

What Did You Learn?

- Many people have unhealthy relationships with money—they either overspend or underspend for emotional reasons.
- Your relationship with money is unique and is affected by several things: family, advertising, and the culture you live in.
- Building a relationship with money is like building a relationship with a person. You should be honest, live in the present, be patient, be charitable, and be committed.

New Terms

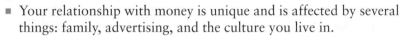

- Responsibility
- Option
- Consumerism
- Healthy

- Relationship
- Frivolous
- Status

- Necessity
- Frugal
- Success

END-OF-CHAPTER ACTIVITIES

Here's your chance to put your pen to paper, as well as discuss what you've learned with others. Doing activities and talking about them are great ways to make sure you really do understand the concepts you've read about.

Remember the Basics

1. Define responsibility and give examples of some things that you are responsible for.

_____

_____

_____

_____

_____

2. What is a "throw-away society"? When did this idea come about?

_____

_____

_____

3. Give an example of how you have been frugal and why. Then give an example of how someone you know has been frivolous and why.

_____

_____

_____

4. Did you learn anything about your parents when you interviewed them? If so, what?

_____

_____

_____

Work With a Team

Interview someone you respect about his or her relationship with money. Ask the individual the same questions you asked your parents or family.

1. How are their answers the same?

_____

_____

_____

2. How are their answers different?

_____

_____

_____

Put Your Math into Practice

Sometimes it's difficult not to be carried away by what others say and what you see on television when it comes to spending money. However, the more you can think for yourself and weigh the pros and cons of a purchase, the better. Think through the following example.

Lauren lives in a small, rented apartment with her mother, father, and brother. Both her mother and father work, and they constantly tell her how important it is to save money so they can eventually buy their own home. Lauren thinks it would be nice to live in a house, but sometimes she gets tired of always watching her spending, especially when her friends keep inviting her to go shopping at the mall.

Today she's at the mall with Kim and Angela when Kim suddenly stops at a store and points out a great outfit. Kim tells Lauren that she will look "so cool" if she buys it. Lauren knows that isn't really true— she's seen plenty of students at school who buy one item of clothing after another, in search of eternal popularity, and it never really makes a difference—except to their bank account. But the jeans, shoes, and purse on the store mannequin do look perfect. What should she do?

Help Lauren make the purchase decision by doing the math for her.

- Cost of jeans: $60.00
- Cost of purse: $25.00
- Cost of shoes: $45.00
- Lauren's wages: $7.50 per hour at the ice cream store (she works 10 hours per week)

1. How many hours will it take for Lauren to earn the money to pay for the jeans and purse?

_____

2. How many weeks will it take for Lauren to work those hours?

_____

3. Do you think she should buy the outfit? Consider how often Lauren might wear the items, whether she will outgrow them or get tired of them, how long they will stay in fashion, and how soon they will wear out.

- If you think she should buy them, why?

____

____

- If you think she should pass and not buy them, is there an alternative?

____

____

For more activities, assessments, and examples, visit www.lifebound.com.

SOLUTION:
\$60 + \$25 + \$45 = \$130 (total purchase)
\$130 ÷ \$7.50 / hour = 17.33 hours
17.33 hours ÷ 10 hours / week = 1.73 weeks
Is the complete outfit worth nearly 2 weeks of work?

Brought to you by . . .

Do you know how many advertisements you've seen in your lifetime? According to the market research firm Yankelovich, if you live in a city, you've already seen 5,000 ads today![7]

Many people are trying to change the policy on advertising because they believe ads make kids "want what they don't need." And this doesn't stop at entertainment, supplies, and accessories. Ads are being accused of playing a role in rising childhood obesity rates.[8]

. . . and now back to the show!

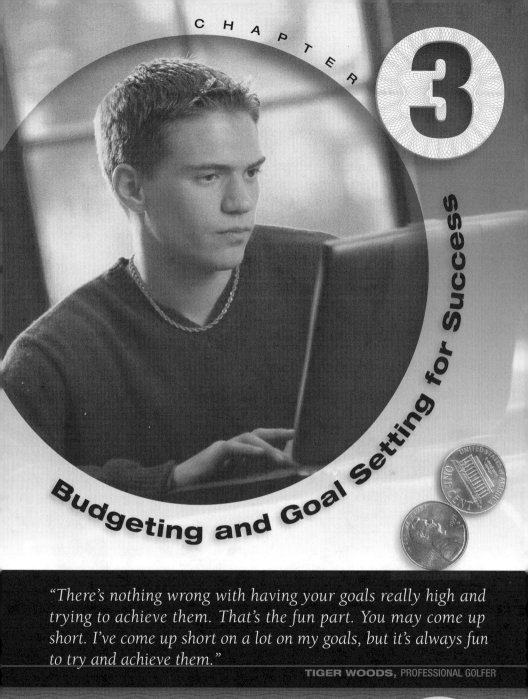

Budgeting and Goal Setting for Success

"There's nothing wrong with having your goals really high and trying to achieve them. That's the fun part. You may come up short. I've come up short on a lot on my goals, but it's always fun to try and achieve them."

TIGER WOODS, PROFESSIONAL GOLFER

Questions you will answer. . . .

1. What are your goals?
2. How do you create a spending log and a budget worksheet?
3. What does it mean to live a frugal life?

Test your financial skills with the Dollars & Sense chapter assessment at www.lifebound.com.

Meet Jack

Jack receives his first paycheck and thinks of all the things he can buy: a new iPod, the newest Seether CD, and a new book by Stephen King. But then Jack remembers he has bills to pay that interfere with his plans, including his cell phone bill and one-third of the car insurance premium for the family vehicle.

He also promised himself he would start a savings account once he got a job. He becomes overwhelmed and doesn't know how he can buy the things he wants, pay his bills, and save for the future. He asks his parents for advice.

His mother responds, "Jack, how about we sit down as a family to look at your income and expenses? We can even make a chart of your potential financial plans for the future. Sometimes a big task becomes less daunting when you get it on paper." Jack agrees. He feels relieved that he doesn't have to do everything on his own and can get some guidance from people he trusts.

get ready

Like Jack, what you want and need, how much you make, and what you plan to do in the future can seem overwhelming. But with some work and patience, you can learn to create and stick to a spending plan, as well as do some planning for your future.

WHAT ARE YOUR GOALS?

So, *what do you want to do when you grow up?* That's a question you have might have heard from people ever since you were a child. Your answer could be as specific as "marine biologist" or as general as "I want to help people." It might even be, "I don't know."

When you were younger, maybe you dreamed of becoming a firefighter, country singer, circus performer, or superhero. What-ever it was, you dreamed big. However, as you got older, you probably adjusted your career goal based on how people reacted to your big dreams. You might have scaled down your goal or changed it completely.

Goal, noun

The result or achievement toward which effort is directed; aim; end.

Fifty percent of college students will change their major; some as many as 2 or 3 times.[1]

IT'S A FACT! GUARANTEED

Goals are good because they help direct your efforts; they give you something to work toward; and they give you something to measure yourself against. It's still OK to dream big; it's just important to know that dreams and goals may change over time. The career that inter-ests you in high school may not be the career you eventually pursue.

In fact, the college major you choose may not be what you get your degree in. Many students end up chang-ing their majors several times, adjusting to changes in their interests based on new knowledge and experience. Life is full of changes, so even though setting goals for your future is important, it's OK if they change.

Getting to Know You

Before you think about your life goals, it's a good idea to think about who you are. What do you like to do? What have you always been good at? What have you learned to do well? What earns you praise from others?

Skills and Talents

First, consider your natural **talents**. These are things you are born with. Even if you don't practice them, they stay with you. Then think about your **skills**. These are things you have learned to do. However, without practice, you may forget how to do them.

For example, Jack, who appeared at the beginning of the chapter, is mechanically gifted—especially when it comes to cars. He intuitively knows what's wrong with any car and can fix anything. He's already restored several classic cars. Even though no one in his family is mechanical, he's a natural.

Talent, noun

An apparently natural power or gift in the learning or doing of anything.

Ability, noun

The power to do something, either physical or mental; skill.

Jack is also an excellent web developer and has been working on his own website and his friends' websites for years. He picks up programming languages easily: HTML, PHP, Ajax; it doesn't matter. However, whenever he stops working with websites for any period of time, he notices it's hard for him to get back into it because he's forgotten some of the languages. His programming ability is a skill, rather than a talent.

Likes and Interests

Next, consider what you like doing, whether you're good at it or not. Many people get pushed into a career because they are "naturally good" at something, even though they don't really like the job. Ultimately, you will be best at doing the things you like to do.

Finally, where do your interests lie? Interest often plays a more important role in career choice than skills; if you're interested and passionate about a job, you will probably do what it takes to gain the necessary skills and excel, even if you lack the natural talents to do so.

Let's take another look at Jack. He loves working on his own car as a hobby, but doesn't like the idea of working on other people's cars for a living. His real interest lies in car design, not repair. Even though he knows how to build websites,

Career, noun

1. *A profession or occupation chosen as one's life's work.*
2. *A path or progress through life or history.*

he doesn't want to do that for a living either. But because he is comfortable with programming languages, he's thinking about taking a computer-aided design (CAD) course so he can eventually become an industrial designer who designs cars online. Jake's combined his natural talents and learned skills to pursue a job that interests him.

Setting Goals

Once you have a better idea of who you are, it's time to research careers that might be a good fit. Remember, a career is not just about making money, it's about expressing who you are, doing something you like, and making a difference. If you're going to work for the next 30 or 40 years of your life, you should do something you enjoy. In fact, you may very well end up working at a variety of different jobs over the course of your career.

When you consider a career, you need to ask a lot of questions:

- Are there many job opportunities in the career you are looking at?
- Will you have to move to another part of the country to work?
- What kind of education will you need?
- What kind of money will you need to support yourself?
- Will the career allow you to express your skills and talents and allow you to do things you like or are interested in?

When setting a career goal, it is important to ask yourself all those questions. For example, Alice just graduated from James Madison University as a theater major. She loves performing in front of a live audience because she says she gets a lot from the audience's energy. She can't imagine acting in television or movies where she would only perform in front of a camera.

That's why her dream is to become a professional stage actress on Broadway. With this career choice, she realizes that her best option is to move to New York City for an opportunity in theater. Even though she will miss her family, there are more opportunities for her to go to auditions and find an agent in New York City who could help her fulfill her lifelong dream of becoming a star.

Like Alice, you may want to consider your family as you determine your future. When you start your career as an adult, would you like to live close to members of your family or spend some time apart from them? Depending on your relationship with your family, your family can be an excellent source of support. So don't be afraid to ask their opinion or personal experiences with their career choices.

now you try it

1. Make a list of your skills, talents, interests, likes, and dislikes. This will help you determine what you would be happy doing in a career.

Skills: _____

_____

_____

Talents: _____

_____

_____

Interests: _____

_____

_____

Likes: _____

_____

_____

Dislikes: _____

_____

_____

2. Find out which jobs match your specific skills and interests. This government website will help you:

   www.bls.gov/k12/index.htm

3. Find three potential careers on the website that look interesting to you:
   - What are they?

   _____

   _____

   - What kind of education is required?

   _____

   _____

   - What are the job prospects?

   _____

   _____

HOW DO YOU CREATE A BUDGET?

You just learned a number of things about yourself and planning for your future career. However, what about planning for the present by managing your money? As you become an adult, you go from your parents paying for most of your needs to you paying for them. The best way to prepare for your financial independence is to create a budget.

A good **budget** is a spending plan that includes everything you will spend money on, including purchases, expenses, and savings. These savings may be for a "rainy day," for large purchases, for donating, for education, or for investments for retirement. But no matter where the money is headed, you should always spend within your income.[2]

Budget, noun

An itemized summary of estimated or intended expenditures for a given period along with proposals for financing them.

Planning a budget usually involves two steps: 1) keeping a spending log and 2) using a budgeting worksheet.

Keeping a Spending Log

The first step in developing a budget is keeping track of what you spend your money on. A good way to do this is by keeping a **spending log**. As you learned in Chapter 2, this is a piece of paper or small notebook that contains a list of the money you spend each day. Carry it with you everywhere you go so that whenever you spend money on something or make money you can immediately write it down. Exhibit 3-1 shows you what a one-week spending log might look like.

EXHIBIT 3-1   Spending log

ITEM	$	DATE	TYPE OF PAYMENT
Latte and lunch with friends	-$12.00	1/21	Cash
Groceries	-$70.00	1/22	Debit card
New top and makeup	-$40.00	1/25	Credit card
Cell phone bill	-$75.00	1/28	Check
Paycheck	+$500.00	1/30	Auto-deposit
TOTAL:	+$303.00		

now you try it

1. Record everything you spend money on for two weeks.

Monday: _____

Tuesday: _____

Wednesday: _____

Thursday: _____

Friday: _____

Saturday: _____

Sunday: _____

Monday: _____

Tuesday: _____

Wednesday: _____

Thursday: _____

Friday: _____

Saturday: _____

Sunday: _____

2. On the list above, circle the purchases which were needs and draw a line through those that were wants.

It's important that you understand what you are spending money on before you can change your spending habits. The technique used is similar to people who keep a food log to lose weight. If you're going to change your diet, you need to keep a food log to find out what you are eating and when you are eating it. Only then can you see everything you eat over an extended period of time so you can get a realistic sense of everything that's consumed and where changes needed to be made in your eating habits. Writing seemingly elusive things down, like calories and expenses, helps keep them a priority when they could otherwise easily slip away.

After you've kept a spending log for a couple weeks, evaluate what you spend. Are you spending more money than you make? Are you spending your money on needs or wants? Do you tend to use cash or credit cards? Do you pay your bills on time? Are you spending money on the same types of things or different things? Are you an impulse buyer?

Now that you see where your money is going, you can create a budget to help you spend more wisely.

Using a Budgeting Worksheet

Creating a budget involves developing a worksheet that shows money coming in and money going out. The idea is simple: A successful budget ensures that you never spend more money than you make.

Some people like to create a monthly budget that shows what they plan to spend as well as what they actually do spend. Other people will create an annual budget that shows the same type of information for the entire year. Monthly budgets are usually easier to maintain.

Exhibits 3-2 and 3-3 show budgeting worksheets that allows you to calculate your monthly income. In Exhibit 3-2, record the amount you've budgeted for the month in the first column. In the second column, record the amount you actually earned, then subtract the second number from the first to see if you went over or under your budget.

In Exhibit 3-3, record all your monthly expenses, the amount you budgeted to pay them, the amount you actually spent, and find the difference. After you calculate your expenses, plug your answer from Exhibit 3-2 in the box **Income**.

EXHIBIT

3-2   Income worksheet for high school students

CATEGORY	BUDGET FOR THE MONTH	AMOUNT EARNED	DIFFERENCE
INCOME			
Jobs			
Family			
Miscellaneous			
INCOME SUBTOTAL:			

EXHIBIT

3-3   Expenses worksheet for high school students

CATEGORY	BUDGET FOR THE MONTH	AMOUNT SPENT	DIFFERENCE
EXPENSES			
Rent			
Telephone			
Car insurance			
Gas			
Food			
Entertainment			
Eating out			
Expenses subtotal:			
Total remaining (Income - Expenses):			

Did writing down your income and expenses produce surprising results? Did you have more money coming in or going out than you had expected? Is there an area you could cut back on? Take a few minutes and assess your results. Identify one area you would like to change, like eating out less, using less gas, or working more hours, and write it down. Start working toward your goal today and also share it with someone close to you who can help you be accountable to your financial goal.

Exhibit 3-4 shows an annual budgeting worksheet for college students. Even though it's aimed at college students, some of the income and expenses might be relevant to you right now. The categories also give you a good idea of the expenses you'll be responsible for paying when you become financially independent, whether or not you choose to attend college.

Your own worksheet might look different, based on your personal situation. It might have different items beneath **Income** and **Expenses.** You might choose to create sub-categories beneath **Income** and **Expenses.** However, the goal would be the same: to make sure that your remaining total (income minus expenses) is zero or greater. This indicates that you are NOT spending more than you make.

Negative numbers indicate that you spend MORE than you make. That's why it's important to look at the **Differences** column to see which items have negative numbers. These are the items to cut down on or eliminate.

EXHIBIT

3-4   School-year budget worksheet for college students[3]

CATEGORY	BUDGET FOR THE YEAR	AMOUNT EARNED	DIFFERENCE
INCOME			
From jobs			
From parents			
From student loans			
From scholarships			
From financial aid			
Miscellaneous income			
Income subtotal:			

EXHIBIT

3-4 School-year budget worksheet for college students, *continued*

CATEGORY	BUDGET FOR THE YEAR	AMOUNT EARNED	DIFFERENCE
EXPENSES			
Rent or room & board			
Utilities			
Groceries			
Telephone			
Internet			
Car payment/transportation			
Insurance			
Gasoline/oil			
Entertainment			
Eating out/vending			
Tuition			
Books			
School fees			
Campus parking			
Computer expense			
Miscellaneous expenses			
Expenses subtotal:			
Net Income (Income − Expenses):			

FINANCIAL FIGURES

LEARNING FROM THE EXPERIENCE OF OTHERS

Alina Laikola, *business owner, Cariño Coffee, Denver, Colo.*

Growing up in Panama, Alina Laikola practiced resourcefulness instinctively as a key for day-to-day family stability. "I guess that's where I picked up the habit of saving and not wasting things," says Laikola, now a successful business owner in Colorado. "Basically we used what we had. No food went uneaten, it was always reheated. Any outfit that didn't fit got changed into something else."

Sticking to a budget, and chasing her financial goals, has helped Laikola, who moved to the U.S. at age 8, transition from a very successful corporate career to the owner of a wildly popular coffee shop. "I left corporate America because I was working hard, but it wasn't fulfilling me," she admits.

Laikola and her husband saved relentlessly to plant the seed for Cariño Coffee, which serves up "coffee culture, Latin flavor" in the south Denver suburbs. Much more than a profitable business venture and a place for warm java, Cariño is a niche of arts, music, and culture. "The value the business had for us was more of the family lifestyle and filling a void for us to be together," Laikola says.

Laikola, who studied at Regis College, vaulted from an entry-level worker to vice president of marketing at Unipac, the second-largest student loan company in the nation. As a young adult, Laikola took a small bit from her regular paychecks and began putting money aside into a handful of savings accounts. More than two decades later, the accounts still exist and are a nice reward for those good habits. Laikola's savings allowed her to retire from her corporate career and pursue the dream of business ownership. She and husband Richard also have helped a daughter and son realize their college dreams with those carefully-set-aside savings.

"What I learned very early on is it's very difficult to accomplish any personal goals without having your financial life in order," Laikola says.

quick tip

HOW TO SAVE AND STILL HAVE FUN

Determine a set amount of money you will spend on entertainment expenses each month. Take this money out in cash. When the money runs out, you've run out of money to spend on going to the movies, seeing a show, eating out, etc. If there's something fun coming up on your calendar, make sure you adjust your spending accordingly so you have enough to fund your unexpected expense.

For example, Tina takes $100 of fun money out each month. She spends $25 a week on anything she wants. However, her favorite band is coming through town, and if she wants a good seat, she has to fork over $50.

She decides attending the concert is worth adjusting her usual spending schedule and takes the $50 out for the concert from her $100 of fun money. She's still left with $50 for the rest of the month, and adjusts her weekly fun allowance from $25 to $12.50 a week.

Planning your own budget and managing your own money exercises the skills you need to become a financially savvy and independent person. It also relieves you of a lot of worry—you know where your money is going and how much you have. You don't wake up in the middle of the night wondering how you are ever going to pay your bills.

HOW DO YOU LIVE A FRUGAL LIFE?

 When you first create a budget and try to stick to it, you may feel deprived. But after a week or two, you will be looking for ways to spend less. You might feel like there is no joy in daily life if you're not accompanied by a latte, new video game, vintage book, or whatever your poison may be. However, after controlling your spending becomes habit, you will start to feel in control of

Frugal, noun

Practicing economy; living without waste; thrifty.

your life because you actually know where your money is going and you start to see savings accumulate. You might even find the satisfaction of managing your hard-earned dollars is much more rewarding than throwing it away.

Want to learn more? Visit the Dollars & Sense page at www.lifebound.com

FiNANCiaL FoUL-UPS

LEARNING FROM THE MISTAKES OF OTHERS

Consider Diego, someone who never made a budget in his life and is paying for it now. Diego goes to community college and works full time. He makes decent money and never denies himself anything. He likes his cars and dirt bikes and is always making them faster and better. He likes eating out, going to movies, and buying his girlfriend whatever she wants. But when it comes time to pay his bills, he always comes up a little short.

He asks his mom for money and even though he's been out of the house for two years, she always gives it to him. She knows she's not doing him any favors by bailing him out time after time, but she feels responsible for his bad spending habits—after all, she never taught him any different. She and his dad were always impulse buyers too. They bought what they wanted, when they wanted it, and never worried about it until they got the bill. The funny thing is that they were always so surprised when they got the bill!

Diego's parents never wanted the kids to know about their money problems so they never involved them. Maybe if they had involved them and taught them about spending money, Diego wouldn't be experiencing the same problems that his parents always struggled with.

Have you ever had to make a budget? What tips do you have for developing a budget and sticking to it?

caroljcarter: Make a shopping list and make sure you stick to it. No impulse buys! 2 minutes ago

reneebrown: I make room for a little fun shopping in my budget. BUT I've learned to always wait 24 hrs and look 4 better deals b4 buying. 5 minutes ago

aj: Regularly review your budget and use online banking to monitor spending activity. about 1 hour ago

bfranklin: A penny saved is a penny earned. about 240 years ago

THE SOCIAL MEDIA FEED

Maintaining a budget and living a frugal life is easier than you think. Being frugal is about saving money and cutting back expenses, not about drastically reducing your quality of life. Start by looking at where you are spending the most money and make some small changes.

Food is usually a big part of everyone's budget. There are many different ways to cut back when it comes to food costs. Grocery stores have "store brands" that cost less than name brands. It's the same food, but it's cheaper because it doesn't have the expensive packaging and advertising that goes into name brands.

You might choose to avoid eating out by starting a weekly cooking club with your friends, where you all shop together, cook together, and then have food for a week. The Frugal-Living-Tips.com website provides some great recipe and cooking tips when you are on a budget.

REAL-WORLD MATH

Suppose you spend five dollars a day on lunch at a fast-food restaurant. You could easily pack a lunch to take with you, spending less money and eating food that is better for you.

Think what you could save by eating homemade lunches during the week:

- $5 per day x 5 days per week = $25 a week
- $25 per week x 52 weeks per year = $1,300 a year

You would save $1,300 a year by never eating out during the school week!

Even if you still ate out once a week, you would save money:

- $5 per day x 1 day per week = $5 a week
- $5 per week x 52 weeks per year = $260 per year

You would save $1,040 ($1,300 - $260) per year by eating out only 1 day a week.

- "Decide the three main meals of the day, even if lunch is a meal eaten away from home. This is especially important to avoid those expensive lunchtime buying habits it's so easy to get into."[4]

- "Stick to your weekly plan and pin it to the fridge as a constant reminder to you and everyone else as to what's on this week's menu."[5]

- "Freeze [your leftovers] and make them into another meal another day or refrigerate them and use them as lunches throughout the week. This second option is fantastic for saving time and also having far more exciting lunches than a sandwich."[6]

Food is not the only thing you can save money on. You can also save money with other lifestyle changes. Drive less by taking public transportation, carpooling, biking, or walking. Change phone plans so you are paying less for your cell phone. Make fewer calls and texts to save even more money.

Financial struggles are bound to happen here and there, so it never hurts to be prepared. Being a frugal person can be very rewarding. Just remember to have some fun along the way!

now you try it

Visit the Frugal-Living-Tips.com website or BeingFrugal.net website.

1. Navigate through the site to find tips that you feel might help you in your daily life.

2. What are five ideas you found for living a frugal life?

_____

_____

_____

_____

_____

3. If you live at home, how could your family put these tips into action?

_____

_____

_____

LET'S REVIEW

 ere's your chance to think about what you've learned in this chapter. Reviewing stimulates your brain to remember important facts.

What Did You Learn?

1. Keeping a spending log allows you to see your expenses and income on a small scale. You can use the information gained from keeping a spending log to make a personal budget.

2. Writing a budget allows you to estimate your income and expenses as well as propose the best way your money should be spent and saved.

3. Take a set amount of "fun" money out each month as a tool to monitor your spending on wants.

4. Living a frugal life is a balance between gaining control of your finances and leaving room for things you enjoy.

New Terms

- Talent
- Ability
- Career
- Goal
- Budget
- Spending Log
- Frugal

END-OF-CHAPTER ACTIVITIES

 ere's your chance to put your pen to paper, as well as discuss what you've learned with others. Doing activities and talking about them are great ways to make sure you really do understand the concepts you've read about.

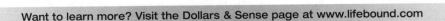

Remember the Basics

1. What does it mean to set a goal?

_____

_____

2. What are the benefits of having goals?

_____

_____

_____

3. What does it mean to budget?

_____

_____

4. What are the benefits of having a budget?

_____

_____

_____

5. How can frugal living help you financially?

_____

_____

Work With a Team

Brainstorm with your peers about your monthly bills.

1. What possible budget cuts do they recommend?

_____

_____

_____

_____

2. What things are in their budgets that are also in yours? What things are different?

_____

_____

_____

3. How do your friends stick to their budgets?

_____

_____

_____

Put Your Math into Practice

Shanna just moved into a new apartment with her roommate Amber. Their current monthly expenses are listed below:

- **Rent:** $700/month
- **Groceries:** $100/week
- **Utilities:** $75/ month
- **Cable & Internet:** $165/month
- **Total:** $1,040/month

They agree to split the expenses so each roommate pays $520 per month. Shanna currently makes $750 a month at her part-time job, so the situation is affordable for her.

1. What expenses could Shanna and Amber cut back on to budget more efficiently?

_____

_____

_____

2. What could they use this extra money for?

_____

_____

_____

For more activities, assessments, and examples, visit www.lifebound.com.

Beware of little expenses;
a small leak will sink a great ship.

                    —BENJAMIN FRANKLIN

What does this quote mean to you?

How can you apply this message to everyday spending habits?

4

Components of Personal Money Management

"*Learn from yesterday, live for today,
hope for tomorrow.*"

UNKNOWN

Questions you will answer. . . .

1. What is the difference between gross and net pay?
2. What are taxes?
3. What is personal finance planning?
4. What are personal documents?
5. How is your financial information protected by law?
6. What are different kinds of identify theft?

Test your financial skills with the Dollars & Sense chapter assessment at www.lifebound.com.

Meet Alisha

Alisha just started her junior year of high school and came to an agreement with her parents that it's time she start paying for some of her own expenses. She dropped off applications around her neighborhood and was excited when she got a job at one of her favorite clothing stores, working 20 hours a week and making $8.50 an hour. She calculates that when she gets her biweekly check, it will be for $340. That will allow her to save $100 a month and afford car insurance, gas money, and leave some extra for spending. But when payday rolls around and Alisha opens her paycheck, it's only for $296.08!

Alisha takes her paycheck to her mother because she doesn't understand where her money went. Her mother points out the information on the check stub: Alisha paid $22.75 in federal taxes, $12.43 in Social Security taxes, $5.16 in state taxes, and $3.58 in Medicare taxes. Alisha realizes she has to readjust her budget due to taxes.

LIVE AND LEARN

L ike Alisha, you're going to get a paycheck someday (or maybe you get one), and understanding where your money goes is important. That way you can make better decisions about what you want to do with your money.

WHAT IS THE DIFFERENCE BETWEEN GROSS AND NET PAY?

T here is a difference between what you earn and what you actually take home. **Gross pay** is the total amount paid to an employee each pay period, without any deductions. Gross pay includes regular pay, overtime pay, and other taxable earnings. You calculate it by multiplying the number of hours you worked per pay period by your hourly pay.

Net pay (or **take-home pay**) is what you take home after all deductions are taken out of your paycheck. These deductions include taxes and other withdrawals you have requested (for example, retirement savings).

REAL-WORLD MATH

You make $7.50 an hour as a hostess at a restaurant.

- Last week you worked 22 hours.
- This week you worked 18 hours.

What will be your *gross pay* on your next paycheck?

$22 + 18 = 40$

$40 \times 7.5 = 300$

Your paycheck before taxes: $300

WHAT ARE TAXES?

People pay taxes on the money they earn in most countries in the world. These taxes pay for government services and projects, like police and fire services, education, defense, bridges, and libraries. These are projects and services that no one has to pay for at the time they use them because they were already covered by their taxes. Deductions for taxes come out of your paycheck automatically.

Types of Taxes

The usual taxes taken out of your paychecks are Social Security tax and Medicare.

- **Social Security.** This tax provides benefits for retired workers and their dependents, as well as for disabled workers and their dependents. As of 2011, this amount is currently 4.2 percent of your income. Your employer must do more than match this amount by contributing 6.2 percent to the government.[1]

Do you think everyone should be required to pay taxes? It is illegal not to pay taxes in the United States.

IT'S A FACT!
GUARANTEED

- **Medicare.** This tax provides health care for people over 65 years of age and for disabled citizens. This amount is currently 1.45 percent of your income.[2]

Together, these two taxes are referred to as **FICA** taxes (Federal Insurance Contributions Act). Employers are required by law to pay a matching amount of FICA tax for each employee and contribute the money to a government fund. This is the fund that provides retirement income, disability insurance, and Medicare.

Deduction, noun

Something that can be deducted (or subtracted). An amount allowed by tax laws to be subtracted from income to decrease the amount of income tax due.

The amount of taxes you owe also depends on if you are married or single, and if you have any children or disabilities.

W-4 Form

When you get a job, you must fill out a form that your employer uses to calculate your taxes. This is called a **W-4 form.** In the form, you tell your employer if you are married or single, and if you have any dependents or children. Exhibit 4-1 shows you what a W-4 looks like.

Your employer can then take out the correct amount of taxes from your paycheck. Mistakes on the W-4 can be costly. If your employer takes out too little, you may owe more taxes at the end of the year. Consider what happened to Alisha's friend Yvonne.

When Yvonne got a job, she filled out her W-4 and claimed that she had six dependents (even though she was unmarried and had no children). She hoped that by claiming more dependents, fewer taxes would be withheld from her paycheck. Why? Because she felt she really needed all the money she could get.

Unfortunately, when she did her taxes the next year, she found out she owed the IRS $500. The problem was, by claiming she was married with children, her employer had withheld too little money from her paycheck because of the number of dependents she claimed. She hadn't saved any money along the way to pay for taxes because she thought she wouldn't owe any. As a result, she could not pay her taxes in full.

Yvonne managed to set up a payment plan with the IRS to take care of the taxes due. However, because she was paying over time, interest and late fees accrued,

EXHIBIT

4-1   Sample W-4 Form from the Internal Revenue Service

Form W-4 (2011)

Purpose. Complete Form W-4 so that your employer can withhold the correct federal income tax from your pay. Consider completing a new Form W-4 each year and when your personal or financial situation changes.

Exemption from withholding. If you are exempt, complete **only** lines 1, 2, 3, 4, and 7 and sign the form to validate it. Your exemption for 2011 expires February 16, 2012. See Pub. 505, Tax Withholding and Estimated Tax.

Note. If another person can claim you as a dependent on his or her tax return, you cannot claim exemption from withholding if your income exceeds $950 and includes more than $300 of unearned income (for example, interest and dividends).

Basic instructions. If you are not exempt, complete the **Personal Allowances Worksheet** below. The worksheets on page 2 further adjust your withholding allowances based on itemized deductions, certain credits, adjustments to income, or two-earners/multiple jobs situations.

Complete all worksheets that apply. However, you may claim fewer (or zero) allowances. For regular wages, withholding must be based on allowances you claimed and may not be a flat amount or percentage of wages.

Head of household. Generally, you may claim head of household filing status on your tax return only if you are unmarried and pay more than 50% of the costs of keeping up a home for yourself and your dependent(s) or other qualifying individuals. See Pub. 501, Exemptions, Standard Deduction, and Filing Information, for information.

Tax credits. You can take projected tax credits into account in figuring your allowable number of withholding allowances. Credits for child or dependent care expenses and the child tax credit may be claimed using the **Personal Allowances Worksheet** below. See Pub. 919, How Do I Adjust My Tax Withholding, for information on converting your other credits into withholding allowances.

Nonwage income. If you have a large amount of nonwage income, such as interest or dividends, consider making estimated tax payments using

Form 1040-ES, Estimated Tax for Individuals. Otherwise, you may owe additional tax. If you have pension or annuity income, see Pub. 919 to find out if you should adjust your withholding on Form W-4 or W-4P.

Two earners or multiple jobs. If you have a working spouse or more than one job, figure the total number of allowances you are entitled to claim on all jobs using worksheets from only one Form W-4. Your withholding usually will be most accurate when all allowances are claimed on the Form W-4 for the highest paying job and zero allowances are claimed on the others. See Pub. 919 for details.

Nonresident alien. If you are a nonresident alien, see Notice 1392, Supplemental Form W-4 Instructions for Nonresident Aliens, before completing this form.

Check your withholding. After your Form W-4 takes effect, use Pub. 919 to see how the amount you are having withheld compares to your projected total tax for 2011. See Pub. 919, especially if your earnings exceed $130,000 (Single) or $180,000 (Married).

Personal Allowances Worksheet (Keep for your records.)

A   Enter "1" for **yourself** if no one else can claim you as a dependent . . . .   **A** _____

B   Enter "1" if: { • You are single and have only one job; or
                      • You are married, have only one job, and your spouse does not work; or
                      • Your wages from a second job or your spouse's wages (or the total of both) are $1,500 or less. }   **B** _____

C   Enter "1" for your **spouse.** But, you may choose to enter "-0-" if you are married and have either a working spouse or more than one job. (Entering "-0-" may help you avoid having too little tax withheld.) . . . .   **C** _____

D   Enter number of **dependents** (other than your spouse or yourself) you will claim on your tax return . . . . .   **D** _____

E   Enter "1" if you will file as **head of household** on your tax return (see conditions under **Head of household** above)   . .   **E** _____

F   Enter "1" if you have at least $1,900 of **child or dependent care expenses** for which you plan to claim a credit   . . .   **F** _____
     (**Note.** Do **not** include child support payments. See Pub. 503, Child and Dependent Care Expenses, for details.)

G   **Child Tax Credit** (including additional child tax credit). See Pub. 972, Child Tax Credit, for more information.
     • If your total income will be less than $61,000 ($90,000 if married), enter "2" for each eligible child; then **less** "1" if you have three or more eligible children.
     • If your total income will be between $61,000 and $84,000 ($90,000 and $119,000 if married), enter "1" for each eligible child plus "1" **additional** if you have six or more eligible children   . . . .   **G** _____

H   Add lines A through G and enter total here. (**Note.** This may be different from the number of exemptions you claim on your tax return.) ▶ **H** _____

For accuracy, complete all worksheets that apply.   { • If you plan to **itemize** or **claim adjustments to income** and want to reduce your withholding, see the **Deductions and Adjustments Worksheet** on page 2.
• If you have **more than one job** or are **married and you and your spouse both work** and the combined earnings from all jobs exceed $40,000 ($10,000 if married), see the **Two-Earners/Multiple Jobs Worksheet** on page 2 to avoid having too little tax withheld.
• If **neither** of the above situations applies, **stop here** and enter the number from line H on line 5 of Form W-4 below. }

-   Cut here and give Form W-4 to your employer. Keep the top part for your records.   -

Form **W-4**	**Employee's Withholding Allowance Certificate**	OMB No. 1545-0074
Department of the Treasury Internal Revenue Service	▶ Whether you are entitled to claim a certain number of allowances or exemption from withholding is subject to review by the IRS. Your employer may be required to send a copy of this form to the IRS.	**2011**

1 Type or print your first name and middle initial. Last name		2 Your social security number

| Home address (number and street or rural route) | 3 ☐ Single   ☐ Married   ☐ Married, but withhold at higher Single rate.
Note. If married, but legally separated, or spouse is a nonresident alien, check the "Single" box. |
|---|---|
| City or town, state, and ZIP code | 4   If your last name differs from that shown on your social security card, check here. You must call 1-800-772-1213 for a replacement card. ▶ ☐ |

5	Total number of allowances you are claiming (from line **H** above **or** from the applicable worksheet on page 2)	**5** _____
6	Additional amount, if any, you want withheld from each paycheck	**6** $ _____
7	I claim exemption from withholding for 2011, and I certify that I meet **both** of the following conditions for exemption.
• Last year I had a right to a refund of **all** federal income tax withheld because I had **no** tax liability **and**
• This year I expect a refund of **all** federal income tax withheld because I expect to have **no** tax liability.
If you meet both conditions, write "Exempt" here . . . . ▶	**7** _____

Under penalties of perjury, I declare that I have examined this certificate and to the best of my knowledge and belief, it is true, correct, and complete.

Employee's signature
(This form is not valid unless you sign it.) ▶ _____   Date ▶ _____

8 Employer's name and address (Employer: Complete lines 8 and 10 only if sending to the IRS.)	9 Office code (optional)	10 Employer identification number (EIN)

For Privacy Act and Paperwork Reduction Act Notice, see page 2.   Cat. No. 10220Q   Form **W-4** (2011)

EXHIBIT

4-1 Sample W-4 Form, reverse side

Form W-4 (2011)   Page **2**

Deductions and Adjustments Worksheet

Note. Use this worksheet *only* if you plan to itemize deductions or claim certain credits or adjustments to income.

1	Enter an estimate of your 2011 itemized deductions. These include qualifying home mortgage interest, charitable contributions, state and local taxes, medical expenses in excess of 7.5% of your income, and miscellaneous deductions	**1**	$
2	Enter: $11,600 if married filing jointly or qualifying widow(er) $8,500 if head of household $5,800 if single or married filing separately	**2**	$
3	**Subtract** line 2 from line 1. If zero or less, enter "-0-"	**3**	$
4	Enter an estimate of your 2011 adjustments to income and any additional standard deduction (see Pub. 919)	**4**	$
5	**Add** lines 3 and 4 and enter the total. (Include any amount for credits from the *Converting Credits to Withholding Allowances for 2011 Form W-4 Worksheet* in Pub. 919.)	**5**	$
6	Enter an estimate of your 2011 nonwage income (such as dividends or interest)	**6**	$
7	**Subtract** line 6 from line 5. If zero or less, enter "-0-"	**7**	$
8	**Divide** the amount on line 7 by $3,700 and enter the result here. Drop any fraction . .	**8**	
9	Enter the number from the **Personal Allowances Worksheet**, line H, page 1	**9**	
10	**Add** lines 8 and 9 and enter the total here. If you plan to use the **Two-Earners/Multiple Jobs Worksheet**, also enter this total on line 1 below. Otherwise, **stop here** and enter this total on Form W-4, line 5, page 1	**10**	

Two-Earners/Multiple Jobs Worksheet (See *Two earners or multiple jobs* on page 1.)

Note. Use this worksheet *only* if the instructions under line H on page 1 direct you here.

1	Enter the number from line H, page 1 (or from line 10 above if you used the **Deductions and Adjustments Worksheet**)	**1**	
2	Find the number in **Table 1** below that applies to the **LOWEST** paying job and enter it here. **However,** if you are married filing jointly and wages from the highest paying job are $65,000 or less, do not enter more than "3"	**2**	
3	If line 1 is **more than or equal to** line 2, subtract line 2 from line 1. Enter the result here (if zero, enter "-0-") and on Form W-4, line 5, page 1. **Do not** use the rest of this worksheet	**3**	

Note. If line 1 is **less than** line 2, enter "-0-" on Form W-4, line 5, page 1. Complete lines 4 through 9 below to figure the additional withholding amount necessary to avoid a year-end tax bill.

4	Enter the number from line 2 of this worksheet	**4**	
5	Enter the number from line 1 of this worksheet	**5**	
6	**Subtract** line 5 from line 4	**6**	
7	Find the amount in **Table 2** below that applies to the **HIGHEST** paying job and enter it here	**7**	$
8	**Multiply** line 7 by line 6 and enter the result here. This is the additional annual withholding needed . .	**8**	$
9	Divide line 8 by the number of pay periods remaining in 2011. For example, divide by 26 if you are paid every two weeks and you complete this form in December 2010. Enter the result here and on Form W-4, line 6, page 1. This is the additional amount to be withheld from each paycheck	**9**	$

Table 1				Table 2			
Married Filing Jointly		**All Others**		**Married Filing Jointly**		**All Others**	
If wages from **LOWEST** paying job are—	Enter on line 2 above	If wages from **LOWEST** paying job are—	Enter on line 2 above	If wages from **HIGHEST** paying job are—	Enter on line 7 above	If wages from **HIGHEST** paying job are—	Enter on line 7 above
$0 - $5,000 -	0	$0 - $8,000 -	0	$0 - $65,000 -	$560	$0 - $35,000 -	$560
5,001 - 12,000 -	1	8,001 - 15,000 -	1	65,001 - 125,000 -	930	35,001 - 90,000 -	930
12,001 - 22,000 -	2	15,001 - 25,000 -	2	125,001 - 185,000 -	1,040	90,001 - 165,000 -	1,040
22,001 - 25,000 -	3	25,001 - 30,000 -	3	185,001 - 335,000 -	1,220	165,001 - 370,000 -	1,220
25,001 - 30,000 -	4	30,001 - 40,000 -	4	335,001 and over	1,300	370,001 and over	1,300
30,001 - 40,000 -	5	40,001 - 50,000 -	5				
40,001 - 48,000 -	6	50,001 - 65,000 -	6				
48,001 - 55,000 -	7	65,001 - 80,000 -	7				
55,001 - 65,000 -	8	80,001 - 95,000 -	8				
65,001 - 72,000 -	9	95,001 -120,000 -	9				
72,001 - 85,000 -	10	120,001 and over	10				
85,001 - 97,000 -	11						
97,001 -110,000 -	12						
110,001 -120,000 -	13						
120,001 -135,000 -	14						
135,001 and over	15						

and before she knew it, the IRS was taking money directly from her wages, barely leaving her enough to live on. All because she filled out her W-4 incorrectly!

How Much to Pay

Once a year, before the end of February, your employer is required by law to send you a **W-2 form.** This form states your total income before and after taxes, and lists the specific taxes you paid. This piece of information will help you fill out your annual income tax returns.

How much income tax you pay depends on a lot of things. But at the simplest level, it depends on your income. People fall into different tax brackets based on income and whether or not they are married. The amount of income changes every year. For example, Exhibit 4-2 shows the tax brackets in 2010 and 2011 for single people and for married people filing jointly (together).

The idea behind taxing people differently depending on the amount of income they make is this: People who make very little money should be taxed less because they have less money to live on; whereas, people who make a lot of money should be taxed more because they have more to live on and can afford to pay more taxes. The hope is that in the end, everyone's taxes will contribute to the services we all depend on.

EXHIBIT

4-2   2010-2011 tax brackets[3]

Tax Rate	2010		2011	
	Single	Married Filing Jointly	Single	Married Filing Jointly
10%	$0 - $8,375	$0 - $16,750	$0 - $8,500	$0 - $17,000
15%	$8,375 - $34,000	$16,750 - $68,000	$8,500 - $34,500	$17,000 - $69,000
25%	$34,000 - $82,400	$68,000 - $137,300	$34,500 - $83,600	$69,000 - $139,500
28%	$82,400 - $171,850	$137,300 - $209,250	$83,600 - $174,400	$139,500 - $212,300
33%	$171,850 - $373,650	$209,250 - $373,650	$174,400 - $379,150	$212,300 - $379,150
35%	Over $373,650	Over $373,650	Over $379,150	Over $379,150

Ways to Pay

Every year, you must submit a federal tax return by midnight of April 15, and most states require you to submit a state tax return as well. Several states base your state tax rate on your federal tax rate. Others base your state tax on a flat rate, flat fee, or earned interest.

Doing your taxes can be a confusing and time-consuming feat. If you're confused about the tax rate in your state or what number goes in which space, you're not alone. There are several tools today that can help you when tax season comes around to file your state and federal taxes.

- **Online.** Use an online service like TurboTax or TaxSlayer. Or go to the IRS website and file your taxes online. Many states have online tax filing as well.

- **Tax Preparer.** Use a tax preparer like H&R Block, Jackson Hewitt, or individuals who are certified accountants or tax preparers.

- **Print.** Pick up paper tax forms at your local library or post office, or download them from the IRS website. Then fill them out and send them in by mail.

If you decide to file your tax return on your own, either online or in print, make sure to file the correct tax forms. These forms include 1040, 1040A, 1040EZ, to name a few. For most teenagers, the 1040EZ will meet your tax needs. However, if you are a parent or an emancipated minor, you may have to fill out the 1040A, which has worksheets to help you maximize your refund.

WHAT IS PERSONAL FINANCE PLANNING?

Earning a paycheck and paying your taxes are only part of what it takes to be financially responsible. It's also important to create an overall balance sheet of your financial worth to find out where you are financially and help you plan for the future.

Balance Sheet: Assets vs. Liabilities

Big companies have financial balance sheets and so do individuals. A **balance sheet** identifies your financial position by showing both your assets and your liabilities.

- **Asset.** This is something that puts money *into* your pocket each month. Assets can include money you make from a job, money you get when friends pay back loans, money you get as a gift from relatives, or money you get when you sell something on eBay. It can also include investments, which we will discuss in Chapter 8. The most common asset that teens have is cash from jobs or relatives; the most common asset adults have is real estate.

- **Liability.** This is something that takes money out of your pocket every month. Whether you made money or not, the payment must still be made. Good examples of liabilities are your cell phone bill, your car insurance, your car payment, and groceries.

If you take your assets (for example, your income) and subtract your liabilities (for example, your bills and taxes), you have calculated your **net worth.** If your net worth is positive, you're in a good financial position; if it's negative, you're in debt.

now you try it

ASSETS VS. LIABILITIES

1. List all your assets:

   _____

   _____

   _____

2. List all your liabilities:

   _____

   _____

   _____

   _____

3. Are you in good or bad financial shape?

   _____

4. What is one thing you could do to improve your financial position?

   _____

   _____

REAL-WORLD MATH

Alisha is committed to saving $150 a month in a savings account for the next year. She also owns a car, her only other asset, that she estimates will be worth $3,000 in 12 months. She owes her parents $1,050, and will continue to make her monthly payments of $50 for the next year. At the end of 12 months, what will Alisha's estimated net worth be?

- Estimated assets: Cash = $150 X 12 = $1,800
  Car (estimated value) = $3,000
  Total assets = $4,800

- Estimated Liabilities: Loan from Parents = $1,050 – ($50 X 12) = $450

- Estimated Net Worth (assets – liabilities): $4,800 - $450 = $4,350

Managing Bills

Keeping a healthy balance sheet means paying bills on time and tracking your deposits and withdrawals. Many people do this electronically. For example, most banks or credit unions provide online banking for their customers. All you need is a user name and a password to log into your online account to check your balance and withdrawals. Some employers offer **direct deposit,** which lets them deposit your paycheck directly into your account. This saves you trips to the bank to deposit your check.

Automatic bill payment is the opposite of direct deposit. It allows the bank to automatically deduct money from your account and send it to the companies you specify. Most banks offer free online bill payment and will send checks to companies that don't accept electronic payment. Some people choose automatic bill pay because they want to avoid the hassle and paperwork that comes with their monthly bills. Other people use it because they are notorious for forgetting to pay their bills, and au-

Asset, noun

Owned items that can be sold and converted into cash, such as cash, inventory, machinery, tools, furniture, vehicles, or real estate.

Liability, noun

Money owed, financial obligation.

Net Worth, noun

The total assets of a business or individual total liabilities.

tomatic bill payments take the worry out of paying monthly expenses on time. Automatic bill pay is easy, but remember, computers have glitches and have been known to make mistakes. Even if you've given the bank control of distributing your money, it's still your money and your responsibility to periodically check and make sure the right amount of money is still going to the right place.

Online bill payment lets you pay, track, and manage your bills online. You typically go to your bank or credit union's website and look for "Online Bill Pay" or a similar title. The website usually guides you through the process of choosing who will get paid (such as the utility company, credit card company, phone company), how much they will receive, and when. The money is automatically deducted when the bill comes due.

Note: Always save your confirmation e-mail in case there is a problem.

Writing a Check

Money Order, noun

An order for the payment of money, issued by one bank or post office, and payable at another.

While they are convenient, not everyone uses automatic deductions, credit cards, or debit cards to pay for things—they also use checks. In fact, there are situations where you will have to write a check. When it comes to renting an apartment, townhouse, or home, landlords usually want a personal check or a money order. A **money order** is a more trusted method of payment than a personal check. This is because you must go to a bank or post office, pay the money up front (along with a service fee), and receive a money order in exchange. The money order looks just like a check, only it's payable by the bank or post office. Unlike a check that you can write whether or not you have money to back it up, a money order proves you have the money to pay the amount owed.

Did you know that retailers pay a "swipe" fee every time you use a credit card or debit card at their stores? In 2011, banks charged stores 44 cents on every debit card transaction, and even more for credit cards.[3]

Swipe fees can have a dramatic effect on small stores, where the fee for a $1.65 greeting card could be as high as $1.05.

If you've never written a check before, it's not very hard. It typically involves filling out the date and identifying who is receiving the money, the amount of money (in words and digits), and your signature. Exhibit 4-3 shows an example of a check a student wrote to Sandy's Prom Shoppe to pay for her prom dress.

EXHIBIT

4-3   Example check written by Tamara

Tamara Jones
123 Buttercup Lane
Townsville, State, 54321

2815

① Date 4/21/2012

② Pay to the Order of   *Sandy's Prom Shoppe*   ③ $ 300.12

④ *Three hundred and 12/100* ——————— Dollars

⑤ Memo *new prom dress*   ⑥ *Tamara Jones*

⑦ ⑆85871713 ⑆186358875711⑆ 11638 ⑧

①	**Date:**	Date you wrote the check
②	**Pay to the order of:**	Person or organization you are paying
③	**Total:**	Amount paid, in digits
④	**Amount:**	Amount paid, in words. Always specify the number of cents as "**xx/100**" and fill in the remaining space with a line (so no one else can add information)
⑤	**Memo:**	Note to yourself (may be the reason for the purchase or the last 4 digits of the account you are paying)
⑥	**Signature:**	Your signature
⑦	**Routing number:**	Number that identifies your bank (important for electronic transfers)
⑧	**Account number:**	Number that identifies your bank account

FINANCIAL FIGURES

LEARNING FROM THE EXPERIENCE OF OTHERS

Bobby Meacham, *Houston Astros baseball coach, Houston, Texas*

Want to experience a roller-coaster ride of salaries? Try life in professional baseball. Make the big leagues and you can reap millions. Languish in the minors and harsh financial realities weigh on you daily.

Bobby Meacham was a first-round draft pick in 1981 by the St. Louis Cardinals. He received a signing bonus of $100,000—a seemingly whopping sum, until his mom's laughter sent a warning. "I knew then that I had to take care of my money, that it wasn't going to last forever," says Meacham, who spent part of six seasons in the big leagues, including a stint as New York Yankees shortstop, before turning to coaching.

Guided by his faith and an instinctive ability to resist temptation, Meacham managed his money wisely during his playing days. That frugality proved crucial when he retired and joined the minor league coaching ranks, where salaries can be meager. Now, he's back in the majors, again at a higher salary, as a coach with the Houston Astros. Spending modestly, and knowing where his money is going, has kept Meacham on an even financial keel, allowing the family to put two daughters and a son through college.

"My wife and I have a budget book where we write down everything we spend," he says. "We figure out where we are, how much we can spend, how much we need to cut back on."

Known as a versatile, fundamentally sound ballplayer, Meacham has served as a role model for young ballplayers due to his personal and fiscal fundamentals. "You have to really believe in what you are doing," Meacham says. "When someone tells you this is a foolproof formula and you can't miss, you have to put up a warning flag. Nothing is foolproof. . . . Don't turn back if you believe in it. If you don't believe in it, if God's closing a door, it's closed for a reason. There's other doors out there."

When you write a check to pay for a purchase, most businesses require two forms of identification. Tamara uses her student ID and her driver's license when she buys the prom dress. Tamara could also use her debit or credit card, which we will discuss in Chapter 5.

If you typically frequent small stores, do them a favor and pay for your purchases with cash. That way they do not have to pay any swipe fees.

WHAT ARE PERSONAL DOCUMENTS?

With all this talk about paychecks and paying bills, it's easy to forget that a lot of "paper" accompanies money, and that paper contains important information. For example, bills and bank statements often have addresses and account numbers on them, and paychecks may have Social Security numbers on them.

Personal documents include your Social Security card, birth certificate, passport, bank account number, and credit card numbers. To keep these safe, it is a good idea to get a fireproof and waterproof safe box, so in case of fire or flood, your important documents won't be destroyed. Put the box somewhere you think it will be safe—a drawer or a closet. Some people even put their safe boxes in the freezer!

quickcheck

Why is your safe box important?

What would you put into your safe box?

Where would you put your safe box?

As you get older, other important things will need to go in your safe box, such as your tax forms, wills, deeds, automobile titles, and mortgage papers. It is never too early to keep your personal documents safe.

HOW IS YOUR FINANCIAL INFORMATION PROTECTED BY LAW?

Financial information is private, whether you store it in a box, on a computer, or somewhere else. But what happens when the storage of your financial information is not under your control—when someone else has the information, such as a bank or credit card company, or an online purchasing organization such as eBay or PayPal?

There are now a number of laws to protect your personal financial information from theives. Exhibit 4-4 summarizes four of 36 new laws relating to personal privacy.

EXHIBIT

| **4-4** | Personal privacy laws[5] |

Electronic Communication Privacy Act (ECPA)

The **ECPA** prohibits unauthorized access to computer records or stored electronic information. It also prohibits organizations that provide or maintain these records from releasing it without your legal authorization.

What if the government wants to access your personal electronic records in the case of a tax investigation or a divorce? The ECPA requires that you be notified and given a chance to legally contest the request.

Fair Credit Reporting Act (FCRA) and Consumer Credit Reporting Reform Act

The **FCRA** regulates the collection and use of personal financial information by credit reporting agencies. According to the FCRA, any access to your information must be for a legitimate business purpose. Additionally, individuals must give their permission to allow private or government agencies to access their records (or by court order).

The **Consumer Credit Reporting Reform Act of 1996** specifies that you have the right to a full copy of any credit report used in a decision to deny your application for credit.

Privacy Act and the Right to Financial Privacy Act

The **Privacy Act** regulates federal collection and distribution of personal data. It requires agencies to inform you whenever they are collecting information and show their authorization to do so. The Privacy Act also requires that agencies use the collected data only for the publicly announced purposes and maintain the safety and confidentiality of data in their possession at all times.

The **Right to Financial Privacy Act** requires that federal agencies inform you when they need to access your records and identify exactly what records they need. Those agencies can obtain a court order to access the records without informing you if they think you are going to flee or destroy evidence.

The Gramm-Leach-Bliley Act (Internet Privacy and Data Privacy)

The **Gramm-Leach-Bliley Act,** passed in 1999, requires financial institutions—companies that offer consumers financial products or services like loans, financial or investment advice, or insurance—to explain their information-sharing practices to their customers and to safeguard sensitive data.

The financial institution must send you a privacy notice that clearly states what information the company collects about its consumers and customers, with whom it shares the information, and how it protects or safeguards the information.

The financial institution must also send you an opt-out notice so that you can say "no" to having your information shared with certain third parties.

WHAT IS IDENTIFY THEFT?

Even with privacy laws and safe boxes, theft of personal and financial information is on the rise. This is called **identify theft** because thieves can use the information to pretend to be you and then make purchases, loan applications, credit card applications, and more, in your name.

Financial information belonging to teenagers is particularly valuable because most teenagers have not yet established a negative history. Someone who steals a teenager's financial identity hopes to gain a "cleaner" financial slate without debt, delinquent payments, or bankruptcy.

Personal and financial information can get stolen in a number of ways—some of them more personal than others.

Identity Theft, noun

Form of fraud in which someone pretends to be someone else by assuming that person's identity, typically to access resources or obtain credit and other benefits in that person's name.

In-Person Theft

This refers to someone physically taking your personal documents or money. For example, suppose you leave your wallet and bank statement on the seat of your car, forget to lock the door, and someone steals those items. The individual now has your license, credit cards, and bank account information.

To avoid theft. Never throw away bank statements, credit card bills, or anything that has your personal financial information on it (account information or Social Security number), along with your name, phone number, and address. Anyone can rifle through your trash or through a recycling bin to read the information and then use it. Instead, shred the paper and then recycle the shredded material. That way, no one can read the personal information and use that information to apply for loans or credit cards, join organizations, or make purchases in your name.

Statistics show the elderly are among the greatest risk of having their identities stolen because they are armed with little to protect themselves and commonly fall for identity theft traps.

When you carry your wallet, do not put all your credit cards inside (leave some at home). Never leave your purse or wallet in an unlocked car. Whenever you make a purchase, verify that you put your credit card or license back in your wallet. Finally, write down all your credit card numbers and phone contacts and store them in a safe place at home. That way, if your card is stolen, you can immediately contact the credit card company.

According to the FTC, in 2006, 5 percent of all identity theft victims were under the age of 18. Children are targets because they generally don't discover that their identity has been stolen until they turn 18 and try to apply for school, auto loans, or credit cards.

Hacking

This involves hacking into computer files, e-mail accounts, and chat rooms to look for user names, passwords, and account numbers. Hackers can also get into your Facebook, MySpace, and other social networking accounts that might hold a lot of personal information, like your phone number, address, names of family members and friends, and any other information you choose to advertise online.

How to avoid hacking. Do not store account numbers and passwords in a file on your computer. Do not include passwords and Social Security numbers in your e-mails or share this kind of information in chat rooms or social networking sites. A good rule of thumb is to consider what you feel comfortable with other people knowing about you, especially untrustworthy people, and adjust your settings and information accordingly. The information doesn't have to be blatantly posted either. Having a weak password can be just as bad as posting personal information. Ask your Internet service provider what you should do to create a secure password.

Phishing

This is an e-mail technique for obtaining private information. The phisher sends an e-mail that appears to come from a legitimate business, asking you to verify certain information: your Social Security number, your PIN number, or your account number. As soon as you click the link in the e-mail, you are taken to a fraudulent website. When you enter your personal information, the phisher steals it.

To avoid phishing. Be suspicious of seemingly illegitimate e-mails with these characteristics:[6]

- Has text that has poor spelling and grammar, or is poorly formatted and does not look professional.
- Mentions some type of terrible consequences if you do not respond. For example: "If you do not respond within 48 hours, we will close your account."
- Asks you to verify personal or private financial information. Real banks and credit cards already know this information; they would never ask you for it by e-mail.
- If you still aren't sure if the e-mail is legitimate, hover over the link in the e-mail to see the corresponding Internet address at the bottom of your e-mail. If the address does not look like it's related to the organization sending you the e-mail, it's probably a scam.

now you try it

GO PHISH

Go to your e-mail inbox and identify any seemingly illegitimate e-mails. If you have a strong filter on your account, you might have to go to your spam folder to find them.

1. How can you tell if these questionable e-mails could be potentially dangerous?

_____

_____

_____

2. What should or did you do with this "phishy" e-mail?

_____

_____

3. If you live at home, how could your family put these tips into action?

_____

_____

Vishing

This technique is similar to e-mail phishing. Instead of using e-mail as a delivery mechanism, it uses the interactive voice response (IVR) system on the phone. You typically receive an e-mail asking you to call the "bank" via a toll-free number to "verify" information. When you make the call, you encounter a series of recorded phone messages.

A typical vishing system asks you to enter your password or PIN (personal ID) several times. More advanced systems actually transfer you to the visher, posing as a customer service agent for further questioning. However, once you interact with a real person, you are entering the realm of "social engineering" (more about that next).

How to avoid vishing. Do not reply to any phone calls (especially automated ones) that ask you to say or enter your password, account number, or PIN number one or more times. No truly legitimate financial institution would ever ask you for this information over the phone.

Social Engineering

Social engineering does not depend on an e-mail, phone system, or fake website. It depends on a real person who knows how to

In the 2002 movie Catch Me If You Can, the star of the movie manages to successfully con millions of dollars out of people by posing as a Pan Am pilot, a Georgia doctor, a Louisiana attorney, and a parish prosecutor . . . all before the age of 21! Loosely based on the real-life story of Frank Abagnale Jr., this movie is an example of a modern-day social engineer or confidence artist ("con artist") who gained peoples' trust and then used lies and check forgery to steal from them.

gain someone's trust and manipulate his or her victim to give up important personal and financial information. The social engineer is a con artist who knows how to convince people to disclose private information they would usually never share.

FINANCIAL FOUL-UPS

LEARNING FROM THE MISTAKES OF OTHERS

Inner-city challenges never fazed Michael. An OK student with the ability to push drug temptations aside, Michael thrived on the baseball diamond. Fleet of foot, with a rocket for a right arm, Michael was the best centerfielder in the neighborhood. He was getting noticed. Enough to make the travel team. Then the high school varsity.

After connecting with an inspiring coach, Michael bulked up physically and elevated his game. All-state baseball honors led to college scholarship offers, but when he was selected in the third round of the Major League Baseball draft, he glimpsed a new financial reality. He was offered a $400,000 signing bonus if he accepted an assignment to the Class A farm team in the Carolinas.

Bonus check in hand, Michael and his buddy hit a local Cadillac dealership. The fully loaded SUV was $60,000, but man, was it sweet. He settled in with his minor league team, ponied up for a beachfront penthouse, and spent liberally, while meeting expectations on the playing field.

Two seasons into his minor league career, Michael's signing bonus was all but a memory. As was the Cadillac, which had been stolen the previous winter and was essentially a total loss due to insufficient insurance coverage. Worse, Michael tore an ankle tendon and was struggling to regain his foot speed. His batting average, and fielding, declined. He soon was released, and his baseball career was in doubt.

Michael signed on with an independent Florida league team for a minimum salary of $30,000 a season. That covered his monthly expenses, but not much more. Most of it went to pay off loans he had taken out during his Carolina high-roller days.

Michael was good at baseball. Paying taxes? Sticking to a budget? Forging a retirement plan? Those were foreign concepts. No strength coach or manager he'd ever encountered had offered him advice on how to be a solid money manager.

How to avoid a con. According to Kevin Mitnick, the world's greatest social engineer and hacker-turned-consultant, humans are the weakest link in any scam. Be suspicious of anyone who asks you for personal security information, including logins, passwords, or account numbers. A legitimate representative of a legitimate organization would never ask you these kinds of things—they already have the information. If you are being asked these questions in person or over the phone, then something is very wrong. Immediately report it to the organization.

Want to learn more? Visit the Dollars & Sense page at www.lifebound.com

What to Do If Your Identity is Stolen

If you do become a victim of some form of identity theft, take these steps to restore your personal security.

1. Immediately contact the companies associated with each of your credit cards so they can close your accounts. There is usually a "lost or stolen" phone number on the back of the card that you can call. Also contact your library, school, or any other organization for which you have some type of identity card. Contact the fraud department of the three major credit-reporting companies—Experian, Equifax, and TransUnion—so they can establish a fraud alert.

2. Report the crime to a local police department. Give them any evidence you have. Make sure to get a copy of the identity theft report. Keep the investigator's contact information (name, phone number, and e-mail address) and give it to your creditors.

3. Report the crime to the Federal Trade Commission (FTC) and include your police report number. Although the FTC does not investigate identity theft cases, it shares information with investigators nationwide who are fighting identity theft.[7]

Note: There are also several services to protect your identity online. Established companies like Lifelock, Identity Guard, or other services through credit bureaus can alert you when someone is trying to use your data without your permission.

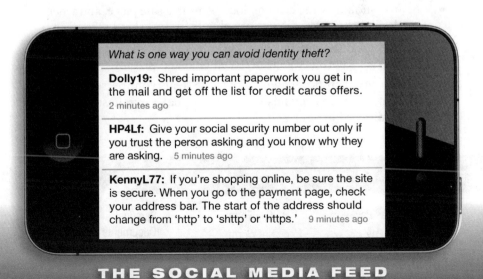

> **What is one way you can avoid identity theft?**
>
> **Dolly19:** Shred important paperwork you get in the mail and get off the list for credit cards offers.
> 2 minutes ago
>
> **HP4Lf:** Give your social security number out only if you trust the person asking and you know why they are asking.   5 minutes ago
>
> **KennyL77:** If you're shopping online, be sure the site is secure. When you go to the payment page, check your address bar. The start of the address should change from 'http' to 'shttp' or 'https.'   9 minutes ago

THE SOCIAL MEDIA FEED

LET'S REVIEW

 ere's your chance to think about what you've learned in this chapter. Reviewing stimulates your brain to remember important facts.

What Did You Learn?

1. Gross pay is the total amount of money you make, whereas net pay is what you actually take home after taxes and deductions have been taken out.

2. You must fill in a W-4 form when you become an employee so your employer knows how much money to withold from your paycheck for taxes.

3. Your employer must send you a W-2 form by the end of February indicating the wages paid to you during the year and the taxes you paid.

4. Your net worth is your personal financial value when you subtract your liabilities from your assets.

5. Many employers allow you to set up direct deposit for your paychecks and many banks allow you to set up online bill pay.

6. You should store personal documents in a safe place, and when you decide to get rid of them, you should always shred them first.

7. In the 1990s and continuing in recent years, many laws have been created to protect your personal financial privacy.

8. Identity theft occurs when someone steals your personal information and then pretends to be you, to make purchases or obtain a credit card in your name.

New Terms

- Gross Pay
- Net Pay
- Social Security Tax
- Medicare Tax
- W-4 Form
- W-2 Form
- Net Worth
- Direct Deposit
- Bill Pay
- Online Bill Pay
- Personal Documents
- Financial Privacy
- Identity Theft

END-OF-CHAPTER ACTIVITIES

Here's your chance to put your pen to paper, as well as discuss what you've learned with others. Doing activities and talking about them are great ways to make sure you really do understand the concepts you've read about.

Remember the Basics

1. What is your take-home pay?

2. How much are you paying in taxes?

3. What is your net worth?

4. Would you use online bill pay or write checks? Why or why not?

5. What personal documents would you put in a safe?

6. What do you do if you think you are a victim of identity theft?

Work With a Team

Taking your paycheck and using the Social Security (4.2 percent) and Medicare (1.45 percent) tax percentages from the beginning of the chapter, calculate how much your take-home pay will be on your next paycheck.

1. Were your calculations correct?

Sit down with some of your friends who work or your parents and compare their paycheck calculations to yours.

2. What do you think the difference is if someone is married or single?

_____

3. What do you think the difference is if someone has children?

_____

Put Your Math into Practice

Assume you made $1,000 this year in net pay. Using the Social Security (4.2%) and Medicare (1.45%) tax figures for taxes in the chapter, what was your net pay?

_____

SOLUTION: You need to pay 4.2% in Social Security taxes and 1.45% in Medicare taxes.

Social Security taxes = $1,000 x .042 = $42

Medicare taxes = $1,000 x .0145 = $14.50

Total deductions = $42+ 14.50 = $56.50

Net annual pay = $1,000 - $56.50 = $943.50

For more activities, assessments, and examples, visit www.lifebound.com.

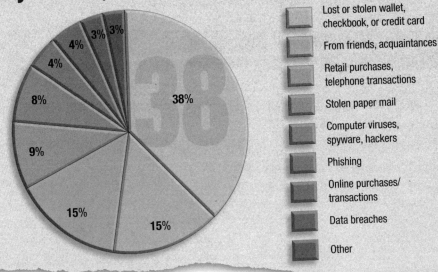

Identity Thieves, Still Reaching for Old-Fashioned Walle

- 38%
- 15%
- 15%
- 9%
- 8%
- 4%
- 4%
- 3% 3%

Lost or stolen wallet, checkbook, or credit card

From friends, acquaintances

Retail purchases, telephone transactions

Stolen paper mail

Computer viruses, spyware, hackers

Phishing

Online purchases/ transactions

Data breaches

Other

5

Balancing Credit and Debt

"Debt is like any other trap, easy enough to get into, but hard enough to get out of."

HENRY WHEELER SHAW

Questions you will answer. . . .

1. What is the difference between credit cards and debit cards?
2. How do you find the right card for you?
3. How can you be a responsible cardholder?
4. What happens when a credit card company makes a mistake?
5. How do you get a refund for a product or service you purchased?
6. What is your credit score and why is it important?
7. How do you get your credit report?

Meet Rebecca

When Rebecca was a junior in high school, her friends had credit cards, so she asked her mother if she could have a credit card too. Her mother didn't think she was ready for the responsibility of a credit card, so she took her to the bank and arranged for Rebecca to get a debit card. She said that if Rebecca could manage her money for six months, then she would consider helping Rebecca get a credit card.

When Rebecca first started using the debit card, she paid for things that she would normally buy with cash, things she could afford. But then she made a mistake: She spent too much money on an iPhone—with money she didn't have. The bank charged her a $30 overdraft fee and her mother had to loan her money to cover the iPhone expense.

Fortunately, Rebecca's mother sat down with her and helped Rebecca understand why she spent money she didn't have. It turns out that Rebecca's friends kept telling her she just had to have an iPhone, and she didn't want to admit to them she didn't have the money. She thought they would think less of her. Rebecca's mother explained that buying things to prove yourself is a losing game. There will always be someone who has more than you, and you will wear yourself out comparing yourself to others based on what you own. "You are who you are, whether or not you have a iPhone," said her mother. Rebecca thought about it and had to admit it made sense . . . especially when she thought of all the purchases she had made in the past to impress other people.

In the end, Rebecca's mother helped her keep track of her spending and showed her how to make a budget. Rebecca learned to be careful when she spent money and never overspent with her debit card again.

Later, Rebecca's mother helped her get an American Express card. Rebecca was required to pay off her monthly balance in full every month, rather than making minimum payments. As a result, she began to build good credit, credit that a lot of her friends did not have.

LIVE AND LEARN

ike Rebecca, learning the intricacies of credit is an important step to adulthood. Credit and debit cards may be handy, but they can easily get you in trouble if you don't understand how they work and how they affect your future financial standing.

WHAT IS THE DIFFERENCE BETWEEN CREDIT AND DEBIT CARDS?

ost purchases today are made with a card. You probably have been offered a credit card in the mail or a debit card when you opened a bank account. But what is the difference?

Credit card. A credit card can be an incredible lifesaver or a huge debt creator. A **credit card** allows you to make a purchase with money you don't have at the moment, money you are borrowing from the credit card company that you've promised to pay back at a later date. A

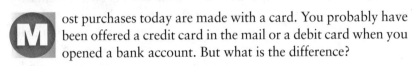

The average credit card debt in a household with credit accounts is $14,687. Typically, that debt carries a high interest rate.

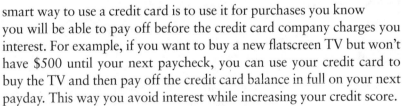

smart way to use a credit card is to use it for purchases you know you will be able to pay off before the credit card company charges you interest. For example, if you want to buy a new flatscreen TV but won't have $500 until your next paycheck, you can use your credit card to buy the TV and then pay off the credit card balance in full on your next payday. This way you avoid interest while increasing your credit score.

However, if you exercise poor credit card behavior your scenario would end differently. You would buy a flatscreen TV on your credit card without having the funds to cover it when your monthly bill comes around and have to pay anywhere

Credit Card, noun

People who qualify for a line of credit are issued a credit card that they can use to make purchases with the promise they will pay their balance back in full and on time.

from 11 percent to 24 percent interest as a penalty. That interest can really add up over time, especially if you keep making purchases. In fact, some people end up with so much credit card debt that their monthly payments barely cover their interest payments.

Debit Card, noun

A debit card looks like a credit card but is directly connected to your checking account. When you make a purchase with a debit card, you must have that amount of money in your checking account or you get penalized.

Debit card. This card is issued by a bank or credit union and is connected directly to your checking account. You can use the debit card at an ATM to withdraw cash or you can use it at the register to pay for your purchases. In the second instance, the card acts as a convenience because you don't have to carry cash around. When you use your debit card, the money comes out of your checking account, so every purchase made with your debit card appears on your bank statement. This helps you better track your purchases. If you use online banking, every transaction you make automatically posts to your online account, so you can log in to see the purchases you've made, cross-check to see if you were charged or returned the correct amount of money by someone, and evaluate your spending patterns all from your computer.

 **quick**check

What are two differences between a credit card and a debit card?

Should everyone have a credit card?

How can having a credit card help your credit score?

Exhibit 5-1 lists some differences between credit cards and debit cards and some perks included when using them.

HOW DO YOU FIND THE RIGHT CARD FOR YOU?

 hen you are shopping for a credit card, there are some important questions to ask yourself as you review the credit card contract:

- What are the interest and late fees?
- What interest rate is best for you?
- What's in the fine print?

EXHIBIT

5-1 Credit Cards vs. Debit Cards

TYPE OF CARD	CHARACTERISTICS
Credit	Lets you borrow money from the financial institution (bank or credit card company) that issued the card.
	The financial institution pays the vendor from whom you made the purchases and you pay back the financial institution, usually with interest.
	You sign an agreement to pay back the money that is borrowed.
	If you pay the credit card bill in full each month, you are not charged interest. If you make a partial payment, you are charged interest.
	You must at least make a minimum payment each month.
	If you do not pay on time, you are typically charged a late fee and your interest rate increases.
Debit	This card is aso known as an ATM card, allowing you to get cash from an ATM (Automated Teller Machine).
	The card is issued by your bank.
	It takes money directly from your checking account.
	Vendors treat it like a credit card; they swipe it when you pay for something.
	It is convenient to use because you do not have to carry cash around.
	It has a "PIN" number (Personal Identifcation Number) associated with it which you must use when withdrawing cash from an ATM, or sometimes, when making purchases.
	There are usually no fees or interest associated with the card unless you charge more money on the debit card than you have in your checking account.

If you don't understand something, don't be afraid to ask. A reputable credit card company wants you to understand the contract you are signing. If they refuse to answer your questions or try to overwhelm you with technical terms, go somewhere else. And one other thing you might think about: If the credit card company has lots of ads on television, consider how much that costs the company, and how it passes that cost on to you with interest rates and fees.

Examine the Interest Rate and Late Fees

Interest and late fees increase how much money you have to pay back. The **annual interest rate** is how much the credit card company charges per year to loan you money. You can estimate the monthly interest rate by dividing the annual rate by 12. If you miss a monthly payment, the interest rate increases and the credit card charges a late fee. These charges are added to the existing balance, making what you owe even greater.

Determine What Interest Rate is Best for You

Interest rates change based on what is happening in the economy. When the economy is strong, rates tend to be higher. When the economy is weak, the rates are lower. The average annual interest rate for a new credit card is 19 percent, which makes the monthly rate approximately 1.5 percent (19 percent divided by 12). The interest rate is higher for people who have not yet built up a credit history because banks and credit card companies do not know how financially responsible they are.

The average credit card interest rate is 12.83 percent. And yet, more than a third of respondents said they didn't know the interest rate on the card they use most often.

Several credit card companies have "deals" for students, with an introductory annual rate of 6 percent or 7 percent for the first six months. This allows you to build your credit at a low interest rate for a few months. However, once the deal is over, you suddenly have to pay the normal interest rate (10 percent or more) on all your purchases. It is always better to select a credit card with the lowest long-term interest rate, rather than the lowest "special deal" rate. That way there are no sudden interest increases.

When you do the math, you will realize that credit card companies make a lot of money off the interest they collect from millions of people who never pay off their credit cards and keep a running balance each month.

Fifty-one percent of Americans said that in the past 12 months, they carried over a credit card balance that was charged interest.

REAL-WORLD MATH

Imagine that you finally get a credit card with an introductory rate of 6 percent for six months. During that time you run up a lot of charges, rarely pay off your balance at the end of each month, and end up with balance of $450 by the end of six months. At that point, the interest rate changes to 19 percent.

1. What is the annual interest on $450?

   _____

2. What is the monthly interest?

   _____

3. If you make no more charges during the month, what will your new balance be next month?

   _____

Solution:

1. Annual interest = $450 x .19 = $85.50
2. Monthly interest = $85.50 ÷ 12 = $7.13
3. New balance = $450 + $7.13 = $457.13

Read the Fine Print

It is important to read the fine print found in each credit card offer. Although some of the legal language can be hard to understand, you can always ask questions. Study the fine print at the bottom of your credit card agreement to find this essential information:

- When your credit card bill is due
- How much your interest and late fees cost
- How much your minimum payments are

This information helps you keep track of where your money is going as well as saves you from late payment fees and bad credit reports.

HOW CAN YOU BE A
RESPONSIBLE CARD HOLDER?

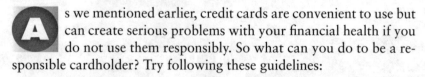

As we mentioned earlier, credit cards are convenient to use but can create serious problems with your financial health if you do not use them responsibly. So what can you do to be a responsible cardholder? Try following these guidelines:

1. **Do not purchase things you cannot afford.** Consider your credit card to be a convenience, not a way to get a quick loan. Suppose you have a $500 credit limit. If you have $200 in your bank account and decide you want to spend $350 on a new wardrobe, think again. Just because your credit limit allows, it does not mean you should charge that purchase. Besides, when you charge more than 30 percent of your available credit limit (in this case $150) and do not pay it off immediately, your credit score declines.[1]

2. **Pay off your balance in full each month.** Don't charge more than you can pay off at the end of the month. Why? Because of credit card interest rates. The more you charge and the more balance that you carry over from month to month, the more money the credit card companies make on interest. Think about it—19 percent interest? That credit card company is making a lot of money off of you, far more money than you could ever earn in your own bank account.

   Of course, there may be times when emergencies arise and you have to charge something that you cannot immediately afford. For example, suppose you have to buy two new tires for your car because your old ones have no tread left, and the bill comes to $200. If you don't have the money available, you will have to charge the purchase. However, if something like this happens, make a plan to pay off the purchase in two or three months, and budget enough money each month to make those payments.

3. **Never take a cash advance.** If you think the interest on your credit card purchases is high, wait until you see the interest on a **cash advance**. That's when the credit card company sends you "checks" that you can use to get cash. The interest on those cash advances is 2 percent to 4 percent higher than the interest on your credit card balance—we're talking 21 percent to 25 percent interest. So, if you get a $100 cash advance, you have to eventually pay $25 in interest in a year! If you had a $1,000 cash advance, how much would you eventually have to pay in interest over the span of a year?

4. **Make your payments on time.** Even if you are making minimum payments, make them on time. Nothing lowers your credit score and increases your interest rate faster than making late payments.

now you try it

TAKE AN INTEREST IN INTEREST

If you were offered two credit cards, one with an introductory rate of 6 percent and another at a fixed rate of 19 percent, which would you take? Why?

_____

_____

_____

What does an "annual interest rate" mean?

_____

_____

_____

WHAT HAPPENS WHEN THE CREDIT CARD COMPANY MAKES A MISTAKE?

When you make purchases with credits cards, problems may occur. For example, suppose you just received your credit card billing statement, and it shows that you used your card to purchase two pairs of shoes. It's news to you, because you know you bought only one pair of shoes. The credit card company clearly made an error, but you wonder how you will get the charge removed from the bill.

Don't panic. If you follow the rules established by the **Fair Credit Billing Act (FCBA)** created by the Federal Trade Commission, you will be able to clear your credit card bill of the duplicate pair of shoes.

FCBA Basics

T he **FCBA** is a law that protects consumers by setting clear rules for settling credit card disputes. The FCBA requires consumers to notify creditors of any errors. It also requires creditors to promptly investigate any disputed charges on billing statements and to fix any valid errors without damaging the consumer's credit rating. The law applies to open-end credit accounts, such as credit cards and revolving charge accounts ("charge cards"). The law does not apply to loans that have fixed payment schedules, such as car loans or payment plans.

Billing errors covered by this law include:

- Unauthorized charges against your card.
- Charges that list the wrong date and time.
- Charges for goods or services that you did not accept or were not delivered as agreed.
- Errors in calculating charges and interest.
- Failure to post payments, returns, and other credits.
- Failure to send a statement to your current address if you provided notice of your new address within 20 days.
- Charges that were already contested in writing and were not previously resolved.

Notification of Billing Error

If you suspect there is a mistake on your credit card statement, it's best to notify the credit card company as soon as you notice the mistake. The FCBA requires credit companies to tell consumers about their rights to report and resolve billing errors, so check your credit card contract to find out how many days you have to report the problem. In most cases, you must report the error within 60 days of receiving the statement.

When you report the error, follow these FCBA guidelines:

1. Send a paper notice of billing error within the specified number of days, to the address provided on your billing statement. Do not send an e-mail—it is unsafe to communicate your Social Security number and account number electronically.

2. Provide sufficient identification, such as your name and account number.

3. State the type, date, and the amount of the error and the reason(s) why you believe the error occurred.

According to the FCBA, once you notify the credit card company of the error, you are not required to pay the disputed amount or any related charges, such as interest.

Creditor's Response to the Notice

Once you notify the credit card company of the billing error, the company must follow these steps:

1. Acknowledge that it received a billing error notification from you.
2. Conduct a reasonable investigation to determine if the billing error actually exists.
3. Correct the error and related charges if the error is valid.
4. Send a correction notice to you.
5. Report the resolution to each credit agency notified of a delinquency.

Sometimes, when the credit card company investigates your billing error notification, it may find that no error exists or that another error happened. In that case, the credit company must do the following:

1. Correct any other errors.
2. Explain the new error or explain why the account is correct.
3. Provide documentation supporting this explanation.
4. Notify you of the amount owed and date the payment is due. (Response from a creditor if you send a second notice isn't required.)

As stated earlier, according to the FCBA, while the credit card company investigates a billing error, it cannot charge you interest on the disputed amount, nor can it report you to a credit reporting agency and say you are delinquent in your payment.

During this time, the company cannot send your bill to a collection agency. If it does, you simply need to indicate that you have a billing error under investigation. This usually involves showing your "paper trail": the erroneous credit card statement, the billing notification(s) you sent to the credit card company, and any responses you received (or the fact that you did not receive any response). If you believe the credit card company is violating the law, you can file a complaint with the Federal Trade Commission or talk to an attorney about filing a lawsuit in court.

WHAT CAN YOU DO TO GET A REFUND?

Sometimes the problem does not lie with the credit card company, it lies with the company where you bought a product or service. If that product or service is defective in some way, you may want to get a refund or replacement. The only way to get it is by writing a letter to the company, explaining the issue, and asking for what you want.

When you write such a letter, always ask yourself, "What is the outcome I want to achieve?" More than likely, what you really want is to get a refund or a replacement. Yet, many people end up writing complaint letters as if their main purpose was to get all their anger out in writing. Sure, you might feel better after writing an angry letter, but then what? When someone actually reads the letter, your words will probably only upset him or her, decreasing the chances of you getting what you want.

So what can you do to write an effective complaint letter? There is a fine art to writing a complaint letter, and it revolves around the idea of the "indirect approach." This means that you avoid stating the complaint at the beginning of the letter. Instead, you present your concern using the following structure:

1. **Begin with a buffer.** A **buffer** is a neutral message that does not make your reader angry and encourages them to read the rest of the message. For example, it usually explains who you are and why you shopped with the vendor.

2. **Outline the background.** Before you actually say what is wrong, outline the facts surrounding the purchase. For example, include when you made the purchase, what the purchase is, where you bought it, and any other details you think the vendor might need.

3. **Deliver the complaint.** Now you get to say what's wrong. It's best to position your complaint near the middle of the message. When you present it, avoid inflammatory and emotional language. Your goal is to explain what you want as clearly and unemotionally as possible.

4. **Ask for resolution.** Explain the resolution you would like—full refund, partial refund, or replacement.

5. **Provide a call to action and close positively.** Specify how long you will wait for a response. Then say something positive (if possible) at the end of your message to show that you are looking forward to resolving the issue and continuing to shop with the vendor (if you are).

Exhibit 5-2 illustrates a sample complaint letter using the suggested structure.

EXHIBIT

5-2 Sample Complaint Letter

Aiden Retuta
102 Trailridge Court
Estes Park, Colorado 80517
(970) 586-1111
Aiden.R@gmail.com   :

Your contact information.
Name, address, phone, e-mail

To: Customer Complaint Division   ← *Contact information for vendor*
       Ohms 'n Volts Electronics
       5312 S. Colorado Blvd.   *Brief description: Avoid the word "complaint"*
       Denver, CO 80222   *or "problem."*

From: Aiden Retuta   *1 Begin with neutral buffer*
Re: Voltmeter issue   *2. Provide background: Date of purchase,*
Date: August 12, 2010   *location, product, cost.*

Dear Customer Representative: *3. Deliver the complaint: Explain the problem.*

My name is Aiden Retuta and I have been buying electronics gear from your store for the past two years—usually to help me complete high school science assignments.

On August 1, I bought a Raleigh voltmeter, at your Colorado Boulevard store. The sales rep helped me choose the V-1023 Ultra-Light model because of its low weight and affordable cost.

Unfortunately, the voltmeter has not lived up to my expectations. Specifically, the needle moves around and will not sit still, as if there is a loose connection inside. As a result, I cannot get a decent reading. I am disappointed because I needed the voltmeter for my science fair project and because all the products I bought from your store in the past have always worked extremely well.

To resolve the problem, I would appreciate getting a replacement voltmeter that works properly. If one is not available, please send me a refund. To help you with the matter, I enclosed copies of the original receipt and warranty for the voltmeter.

I anticipate your reply and a resolution to me by the end of August, and I look forward to making more purchases in the future. If you have any questions, please contact me directly by phone, e-mail, or mail. My contact information is at the top of my letter.

Sincerely,

Aiden Retuta

Aiden Retuta

Enclosure(s): receipt, warranty

4. Ask for resolution: Suggest a solution and provide copies of supporting documents.

5. Provide a call to action and positive close: Suggest a day for resolution, say something positive, and mention your contact information.

List of enclosures: Remember, do not enclose originals, only copies

FINANCIAL FIGURES

LEARNING FROM THE EXPERIENCE OF OTHERS

Russell Wild, *financial journalist and author, Allentown, Pa.*

When that late-night, get-rich-quick infomercial airs, Russell Wild takes action—he changes the channel. An accomplished author and financial planner, Wild stresses that there is no magic wand for gaining financial security. Skepticism, patience, and reality can be your best friends as you ramp up your financial knowledge.

"The key lesson for teenagers who are embarking on a new financial life is to live below their means," Wild says. "There's no other way to avoid winding up in debt. There's no secret formula, no easy answers. At some point, you need to make more than you spend."

Wild urges college students to use credit cards responsibly. "[Credit card companies] come to college campuses and try to encourage the use of credit and make it very easy for college students to apply and qualify," Wild says. "It behooves us as parents and teachers to prepare our children and teenagers before they leave high school to realize what they're going to confront. Credit can be a good thing, but it also has a dark side."

Look for credit cards with reasonable interest rates and other favorable terms, such as low annual fees, Wild says. Even better, plan to pay back your balance at the end of each 30-day period to avoid interest. Check out bankrate.com and moneyaisle.com to brush up on interest rates. Comparison-shop for a bank or credit union that fits. And start investing early. Recent changes in the securities industry, Wild notes, "allow the small investor to invest like the big boys."

Wild has authored numerous books on investing, including *Bond Investing for Dummies, Index Investing for Dummies* and *Exchange-Traded Funds for Dummies*. "Even if you only have several hundred dollars to invest, go ahead and get your feet wet. Start learning about investing early," Wild says. "When you're young, you can be aggressive, especially if you're only investing a few hundred dollars, because if you lose it, it's not the end of the world."

WHAT IS YOUR CREDIT SCORE?

Using your credit card responsibly and clearing up billing errors is a good way to make sure you have a good credit score. Your **credit score** is a three-digit number that indicates your "creditworthiness." Companies look at this score to determine how likely you are to repay a debt and to discover whether or not you are a credit risk—the higher your credit score, the better the chances are that you will repay loans.

On-time payments account for 35 percent of your total credit score.

GUARANTEED · IT'S A FACT! · GUARANTEED

The formula to determine credit scores was developed by the **Fair Isaac Corporation** (FICO); hence the credit score is often called a **FICO score**. The score is calculated using a formula that takes into account the following information about you:

- Your payment history
- The amounts owed on different accounts
- The length of your credit history
- The type of credit you have
- The number of new credit accounts you have recently opened

FICO Score, noun

A debit card looks like a credit card but is directly connected to your checking account. When you make a purchase with a debit card, you must have that amount of money in your checking account or you get penalized.

Exhibit 5-3 shows you the breakdown of how those components contribute to your credit score.

Now that you know what goes into your credit score, you can understand why it might go up and down. In particular, any of the following actions would definitely cause it to decline:

- **Late payments.** For example, not paying your cable bill until two weeks after the due date.
- **Owing large amounts of money.** For example, student loans or mortgages.
- **Taking out many different kinds of credit at one time.** For example, applying for several credit cards at once, or applying for a personal loan and a home improvement loan at the same time.

EXHIBIT
5-3   What makes up your credit score?

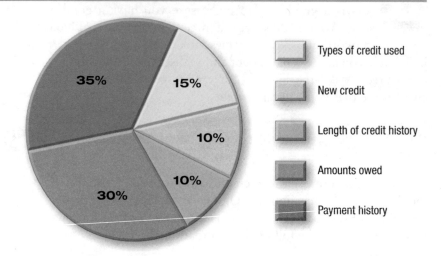

- Types of credit used
- New credit
- Length of credit history
- Amounts owed
- Payment history

How Do You Get Your Credit Score?

You don't have a credit score until you start establishing credit. Student credit cards or bills you pay yourself are good ways to build credit. Once you establish credit, there are a lot of reputable companies out there that can provide you with your FICO credit score, such as Equifax, Experian, and TransUnion. They all use the same credit reporting agencies to determine the score, but charge you different amounts. A few, like **myFICO** and **Credit Karma,** are free. However, many of the companies that charge have a free-trial period. You can sign up and then cancel before the trial ends so you don't get charged.

Credit scores generally vary from 300 to 800, where scores above 700 indicate low credit risk, and scores below 600 indicate high credit risk. Most people's scores fall between 600 and 700.[1] Higher credit scores accomplish a number of things for you:

- Lower your interest rate.
- Speed up credit approvals.
- Get you approved for apartments.
- Reduce deposits required by utilities.
- Get you better credit card, auto loan, and mortgage offers.

FINANCIAL FOUL-UPS

Credit cards are easy to misuse. Just consider what happened to Rebecca's friend Freddy. He got a job when he turned 15 and opened a bank account with a debit card rather than carrying the cash. He thought he'd be able to keep track of his spending better if he used his debit card whenever he bought something.

He had good intentions, but he just couldn't get into the habit of saving his receipts and writing them in his checkbook. He couldn't even remember to go to the bank's website and log in to his account and check his balance. As a result, he kept getting charged for using more money than he had in his account.

His solution was to get a credit card because then he would just pay the bill when it came in the mail, and he wouldn't have to keep track of anything. But when his bill came, it was a lot higher than he expected and he didn't have the money to pay it in full. Instead, he paid what he could, leaving a balance on his credit card.

The next month, the same thing happened again, except he now owed even more because of the interest on the previous balance and the interest on his new purchases. He really couldn't pay all of it now! This happened every month until he reached his credit limit and could no longer make any purchases with the credit card. He even got a late fee when he forgot to pay his bill on time when he was on vacation. Not only was he charged a late fee, but also his interest rate went up. He could no longer use his credit card and had no idea how he was ever going to pay off his huge credit card balance!

In **Chapter 7, Avoiding Debt and Staying Out of Debt,** you will learn what causes lower scores and how to improve a low score.

How Do You Get Your Credit Report?

There is more to your credit rating than your score. There is also a detailed **credit report** that creditors, insurers, employers, and other businesses use to evaluate your applications for credit, insurance, employment, or renting a home or apartment. It includes the following:

- Personal identification information. This includes your name, Social Security number, address, and phone number.

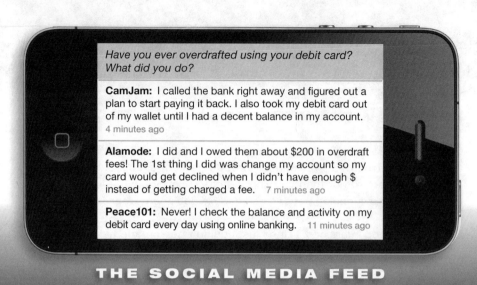

- List of all your credit card accounts. This includes the date opened, your credit limit, your account balance, and your payment history (Did you pay on time? Did you make minimum payments?).

- Number of inquiries made about your credit. Some of these might be inquiries you made, while others might be from individuals or companies that accessed your credit report in the last two years.

- Amount of overdue debt. This information is usually provided by collection agencies. It may include bankruptcies, foreclosures, and lawsuits.

The **Fair Credit Reporting Act** (FCRA) guarantees that the three national credit reporting agencies, Equifax, Experian, and Trans-Union, must allow you to access your credit report for free—every 12 months. In the past you actually had to pay for it. According to the Federal Trade Commission, there is only one authorized source where you can get your credit report for free under federal law:[1] **www.AnnualCreditReport.com.**

Check that Report

Once you get your report, check it carefully. If you see accounts you don't recognize or information that is inaccurate, immediately contact the credit reporting agency and the company that provided the information. For example, suppose you notice that your credit report shows you have a Target credit card, but you know you closed that account. You need to contact both the credit reporting company that provided the credit report (Experian, Equifax, or TransUnion), as well as the vendor, Target. And you need to contact them in writing.

The Federal Trade Commission provides an excellent, easy-to-read report on how to deal with credit report errors. You can access the report online at: **www.ftc.gov/pcp/edu/oybs/consumer/credit/cre21.pdf**

LET'S REVIEW

 ere's your chance to think about what you've learned in this chapter. Reviewing stimulates your brain to remember important facts.

What Did You Learn?

- Credit and debit cards are different. Credit cards are a loan you are borrowing against what you will have to pay back with interest. Debit cards take the money right out of your checking or savings account, so there is no interest.

- It's important to understand your credit card contract, especially interest rates and late fees the credit card company will charge you.

- The Federal Credit Billing Act sets clear rules for settling credit card disputes.

- It's important to know what your credit score is, and to check your credit report for errors at least once a year.

- The Fair Credit Reporting Act guarantees that you can get a free credit report, once a year, from the three national credit reporting agencies.

New Terms

- Credit Card
- FCBA
- Debit Card
- FICO Score
- Interest Rate
- FCRA

END-OF-CHAPTER ACTIVITIES

ere's your chance to put your pen to paper, as well as discuss what you've learned with others. Doing activities and talking about them are great ways to make sure you really do understand the concepts you've read about.

Remember the Basics

1. What are the benefits of having a debit card and where do you get one?

   _____

   _____

2. What are the benefits of having a credit card? What are the risks?

   _____

   _____

3. How do you get your free credit report?

   _____

   _____

4. Why might companies want to look at your credit report?

   _____

   _____

Work With a Team

Go to **www.AnnualCreditReport.com** and request your free credit report.

1. Have you established any credit?

   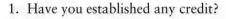

2. If you have established any credit, is all of the information correct?

   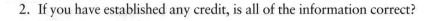

3. What is your credit score?

_____

4. Compare your information with your friends or classmates. What differences are there? Why?

_____

_____

_____

5. Compare your information with your parents? What differences are there? Why?

_____

_____

_____

Put Your Math Into Practice

You decide to establish some credit, so you get your first credit card. Because you don't have any credit established, your interest rate is pretty high (19 percent) and the credit card company gives you a modest credit limit of $600.

You initially use the credit card to buy things you would normally purchase with cash, so you can pay off the card in full every month to build good credit. But your prescription glasses break and you have to buy new ones. This is an unexpected expense and you have no choice but to buy new glasses because you can't see without them. The new glasses cost $300 and you have to charge them because you don't have enough money in your checking account to pay cash or pay by check.

1. If you don't pay the balance in full, how much interest will you be charged on your next bill if your total purchase is $400 (cost of the glasses plus other purchases)?

_____

2. What is your new balance?

_____

SOLUTION:
Annual interest = $400 x .19 = $76
Monthly interest = $76 ÷ 12 = $6.33
Total balance = $400 + $6.33 = $406.33

For more activities, assessments, and examples, visit www.lifebound.com.

Numbers Talk

What does it say to you that the amount of debt rises instead of lowers as people get older?

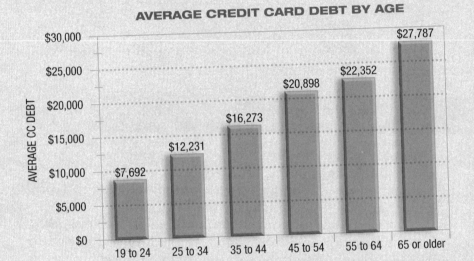

AVERAGE CREDIT CARD DEBT BY AGE

AGE OF DEBTOR	AVERAGE CC DEBT
19 to 24	$7,692
25 to 34	$12,231
35 to 44	$16,273
45 to 54	$20,898
55 to 64	$22,352
65 or older	$27,787

Avoiding Financial Pitfalls

"*The most important thing for a young man is to establish credit—a reputation and character.*"

JOHN D. ROCKEFELLER

Questions you will answer. . . .

1. What is wrong with carrying a large balance on your credit card?
2. What is a payday loan?
3. What is a pawnshop loan?
4. What is the alternative to high-interest loans?
5. What is bankruptcy?
6. What are additional ways to prevent identity theft?

Test your financial skills with the Dollars & Sense chapter assessment at www.lifebound.com.

123

Meet Kevin

Kevin applies for a job. He knows he is qualified because of his previous experience in the field, and the interview goes very well. Kevin feels confident he will get it. But when he comes back for a second interview, the prospective employer tells Kevin that he is not eligible for the job because of his credit report. The report shows a long history of late payments, large balances, cash advances, and lots and lots of credit cards. As a result, Kevin's credit score is very low. Given his poor credit history and low credit score, the company believes that Kevin lacks the level of responsibility required to do the job.

LIVE AND LEARN

L ike Kevin, you may find that your own bad financial habits come back to haunt you in the form of a poor credit report and a low credit score. Both of those could prevent you from getting something you want or need, like a job. The best way to avoid Kevin's predicament is to recognize your bad financial habits and drop them now.

This chapter is a little different from the rest of the chapters because it talks about what you should NOT do. As you read, think about whether you or members of your family practice any of the bad financial habits that are mentioned. If so, now would be a good time to replace them with good habits.

What's Wrong with Carrying a Large Balance on Your Credit Card?

In Chapter 5, Balancing Credit and Debt, you learned how credit card companies charge you interest on the money you spend using the card. You also learned that if you do not pay off the card at the end of the month, the remaining balance accumulates interest, along with any new charges you make. If you recall the story of Freddy at the end of Chapter 5, you know that interest can really add up.

The bigger your balance, the more interest you are charged, and the more money the credit card company makes at your expense. Not only that, when your balance exceeds 30 percent of your credit card limit, or your credit card debt exceeds 37 percent of your income, you credit score will decline. And when your credit score declines, you become a high-risk borrower. This means you will have a harder time getting a mortgage or car loan and sometimes even a credit card.

As you learned in Chapter 5, when you miss a payment, your interest also increases and you are typically charged a late fee, which means your balance gets even bigger. If you are consistently late making payments, the credit card company considers you **delinquent**. This means they consider you at risk of not paying that money back and may turn your account over to a collection agency. As a result, your credit score drops even lower. You may not care about your credit score now, but it can make a big difference to your financial options in the future.

Over the last year, 15 percent of American adults (34 million people) have been late making a credit card payment and 8 percent (that's 18 million people) missed a payment entirely.

If you or your parents have a lot of credit cards with large balances, consider cutting up the credit card with the largest balance to stop using it. Then try making more than the minimum payment each month. When the card is paid off, close the account. Or, you might find the card with the smallest balance and pay it off as quickly as possible. The basic idea is to:

- Stop using your credit card to keep the balance from increasing.
- Pay down your balance with more than the minimum payments to stop interest from building.

If neither of these ideas will work because you or your family is too short on cash, consider visiting a free debt counselor—most city or county agencies have someone you can talk to. You will learn more about getting your debt under control in Chapter 7.

What is a Payday Loan?

A **payday loan** is a high-interest, short-term loan that usually must be paid back within two weeks. Its name comes from the fact that people think of this type of loan as a cash advance to tide them over until the next payday. A scenario in which you might use a payday loan is if you ran out of money before your next payday but needed groceries for the week.

Payday Loan, noun

Small, short-term, high-interest loan intended to cover the borrower's expenses until the next payday. The payback period is typically two weeks and the annual percentage rate is usually 390 percent.

With a payday loan, you generally pay $15 up front to get a $100 payday loan. If you cannot pay it off in two weeks, you are charged the same $15 fee again for the next two weeks, which will continue until you pay it off.

A big mistake that families make when they find themselves in financial trouble is getting a payday loan. If you thought credit card interest rates were too high, think again. Interest rates on payday loans are even higher—generally 15 percent over a two-week period, though they vary from state to state. Considering there are 26 two-week periods in a year, that's 15 percent x 26 or 390 percent annual percentage rate (APR). This is 20 times more than a credit card advance. Exhibit 6-1 shows you this shocking evidence.

EXHIBIT 6-1   Cost of borrowing $300 over 30 days (in dollars)

REAL - WORLD MATH

Let's look at the real cost of the payday loan. Suppose you need $300 for an emergency car repair. You know you won't be able to pay it off until the end of the month. So, you take out a $300 loan for a typical two-week period and pay 15 percent interest or $45. Because you cannot pay it off for another two weeks after that, you have to pay another $45. By the time you pay off the loan at the end of the month, you have paid $90 of interest on a $300 loan.

- 15% = .15
- $300 x .15 = $45 in interest in 2 weeks
- $45 + $45 = $90 in interest in 4 weeks

Now let's figure out the annual interest rate and how much you would pay if you kept taking out $300 loans every two weeks for a year.

- 15% for 2 weeks ÷ 2 = 7.5% interest rate for 1 week
- 7.5% x 52 weeks = 390% interest rate for 1 year
- 390% = 3.90
- $300 x 3.90 = $1,170 of interest paid in 1 year

The 390% annual interest rate (APR) is 20 times the interest rate on a credit card advance.

The sad thing about payday loans is they are designed to keep people in debt. According to "Springing the Debt Trap":

- 60 percent of payday loans go to borrowers with 12 or more loans per year.
- 24 percent of payday loans go to borrowers with 21 or more loans per year. If you assume a typical two-week loan, that equates to 10 months of indebtedness.

You might be thinking, "Why would anyone get a payday loan? It sounds like such a horrible idea!" People get payday loans when they need a helping hand. A payday loan can be a good idea if you know you're going to be able to pay the loan back on time, like in a scenario where you need to buy groceries, pay the electric bill, or fill your car up with gas before payday.

What Is a Pawnshop Loan?

Pawnshops are often a last resort for getting funds. A **pawnshop loan** is a high-interest, short-term loan that requires you to provide collateral. The interest rates are not as high as payday loans, but the pawnshop requires you to put up something you own as collateral in exchange for a 30-day loan. This might be a ring or a guitar or personal item you think is valuable. The pawnbroker will then assess a "fair" market value for that item and give you the money, which is usually half the item's retail value. The pawnbroker keeps your personal item and gives you a ticket for it. The ticket contains information such as: pawnshop name and address, your name and address, item, the amount loaned, the interest rate, and the date the loan is due.

Pawnshop Loan, noun

Small, short-term, high-interest loan requiring collateral that the pawnbroker holds. The pay back period is typically 30 days and the annual percentage rate is usually 195 percent.

Interest rates on pawned items usually run 10 percent to 20 percent for 30 days. At the end of the 30 days, you must pay back the loan with interest to reclaim your personal item. If you do not repay the loan within a certain grace period, the personal item becomes the property of the pawnshop and the pawnbroker can sell it to recover the loan money.

quickcheck

What is a payday loan?
What is a pawnshop loan?
What is the difference?

What's the Alternative to High-Interest Loans?

When you or your family starts thinking about payday loans and pawnshop loans, things are probably pretty bad, financially speaking. So what are some alternatives to those high-interest loans that are almost guaranteed to keep you in debt?

REAL-WORLD MATH

As we did with the payday loan, let's examine the actual annual interest rate (APR) charged by a pawnshop. Imagine it's winter and you need $300 to pay your gas and electric bill. You go to a pawnshop and pawn a ring that belonged to your grandmother. It is worth more than $600, but you get $300 for it. The pawn ticket indicates you have 30 days to pay off the loan at 15 percent interest. Luckily, you work some overtime and get a bonus, so you have no problem repaying the loan within the 30 days. Let's calculate the interest.

- 15% = .15
- $300 x .15 = $45 of interest paid in 4 weeks

Now let's figure out the annual interest rate and how much you would pay if you kept taking out $300 loans each month for a year. Compare this to the payday loan example earlier.

- 15% for 4 weeks ÷ 4 = 3.75% interest rate for 1 week
- 3.75 % x 52 weeks = 195% interest rate for 1 year
- 195% = 1.95
- $300 x 1.95 = $585 of interest paid in 1 year

That is half the cost of a payday loan, but it is still 5 times the annual interest rate (APR) on a credit card advance.

Here are some suggestions:

Work out extended repayment plans with creditors. This is by far the best action to take. Contact each creditor. Explain that you want to pay off the debt in regular payments, on time. Explain that you will no longer use your card. Ask if the creditor can drop your interest rate so you can pay off the debt. Most creditors would rather get their money and will work with you to make sure that happens. In fact, some credit card companies will help you build a budget so you spend more wisely if you have trouble meeting your obligations on a continual basis.

Get a loan from friends and relatives. Depending on the financial situation of your friends and families, and how well you get along with them, this might be a possibility. They probably won't charge you interest and will give you more time to pay back the money. Be aware, though, that not paying back a loan could cost you a relationship with your friend or family member.

Salary advances from employers. Some employers will advance you money based on how much you will be working the following week or month (however long the pay period is) and charge you no interest. Check your employee handbook to find out if your employer will do this. Since it's money you are going to earn anyway, there is no interest. However, you typically need to write a letter requesting the advance, explaining what it is for and indicating that you understand the advance will be deducted from your next paycheck. This is generally an option only for an emergency and employers are not likely to provide salary advances on a repeated basis.

Employer Salary Advance, noun

A short-term, 0 percent loan provided by an employer to help you meet work-related or personal expenses. The amount of the loan will be deducted from your next paycheck.

Credit card advances. In Chapter 5, Balancing Credit and Debt, you learned that credit card companies often send you "checks" that you can cash. Credit card companies also let you swipe your credit card in an ATM to withdraw cash. These are both examples of credit card advances. The value of the check or the swipe at the ATM will be charged to your credit card. The interest you pay on the credit card advance will be 2 percent to 4 percent higher than the normal credit card interest rate. That means if your credit card company normally charges you 19 perxcnt APR on purchases, it will charge you 21 percent to 23 percent APR on a cash advance. But if you compare that to 390 percent APR (payday loans) or 195 percent APR (pawnshop loans), it is definitely more desirable.

Credit Card Cash Advance, noun

A sum of money that can be withdrawn by using your credit card at an ATM or using a credit card check. The money is money you do not have, that is charged on your credit card.

Get a raise or take on another part-time job. Another option to consider for paying off mounting debt is something you or your family may not have thought of—make more money. You might be asking, "Hey, if I were making more money, would I be in this mess?" But the truth is, the best way to get out of debt is to stop using your credit card and make more money. This might take the form of a part-time job, a second job, or a better job. The extra money you make must go to paying off your credit card debt, not making more purchases. If you start making more money, but do not change your spending habits, you'll find yourself in even greater debt.

now you try it

Pretend you are considering asking a family member or friend for a loan of $100 over getting a payday or pawnshop loan. How would you go about asking them for the favor?

_____

_____

Pretend you need to ask your employer for an advance. What information would be important to include in your letter requesting your cash advance?

_____

_____

REAL-WORLD MATH

Think back to the $300 payday loan and pawnshop loan. The payday loan company charged you $90 interest at the end of the month; the pawnshop charged you $45. If a credit card company charges 22 percent for cash advances, what would it charge you at the end of a month for a $300 cash advance?

- $300 x .22 = $66 per year
- $60 ÷ 12 months per year = $.50 interest per month

$.50 interest at the end of the month for a cash advance is a lot more affordable than $45 interest for a pawnshop loan or $90 for a payday loan.

LEARNING FROM THE EXPERIENCE OF OTHERS

Judy Lawrence, *bestselling author, Albuquerque, N.M.*

Five jars steered a teenage Judy Lawrence down a wise financial path. Today, tools such as the Monthly Budget Worksheet help solidify the bestselling author's reputation as "The Money Tracker."

As a Wisconsin schoolgirl, Lawrence worked at a cheese factory, and with an instinctive knack for discipline, she developed a terrific savings habit. She stashed her weekly earnings into five glass jars in her bedroom, labeled College, Clothes, Savings, Spending, and Car.

"Visually, I wanted to see my money growing," says Lawrence, author of *The Budget Kit: Common Cents Money Management Workbook*, which has sold nearly half a million copies. "I learned that I could have what I wanted; it would just take time. Also, that I have control over my money. I learned the model and value of working and generating money."

Self-reliance is crucial to learning sound financial behavior, Lawrence says. "Teenagers who learn problem solving, resourcefulness, creativity, and working out difficult situations will have a future advantage."

Without supportive parents, Lawrence says, teens might lack "a core way to think and be around money. Without having core financial knowledge, skills, and mindset, they don't have a lot of defense or skills against the bombardment and temptation of media around them ... everything around them that tempts them and tells them this is where they need to spend their money."

Technology and social changes might make the jar system obsolete, but Lawrence's five jar labels would apply for most teens today. And even with online banking and a shift to virtual money, teens need a budget and a plan. "Whether it's cash, old-fashioned checking, a virtual account, a debit card, or smart phone account," she says, "it's still important to have some system where you're staying mindful of spending."

What is Bankruptcy?

Ongoing bad spending habits, especially with credit cards, and excessive loans can lead to a situation where you have too little money, too much debt, and have no way to pay the money back. In this case, the only alternative is bankruptcy. **Bankruptcy** is a federal court procedure that helps people wipe out their debt or establish a plan to repaying that debt. There are two typical forms of bankruptcy: **reorganization** and **liquidation**.

"According to the 2010 Fiscal Year statistics from the Administrative Office of the U.S. Courts, the number of bankruptcies filed between October 1, 2009 and September 30, 2010 increased from 1,402,816 to 1,596,355, an increase of 13.8%."

Reorganization: Chapter 13 Bankruptcy

Chapter 13 bankruptcy deals with reorganization. The goal of Chapter 13 is to give you a chance to reorganize your debt so you can pay it off. This involves a court-approved plan for paying off your debts, interest-free. The plan identifies the details of all the transactions that will occur to pay off the debt, and when they will occur. The details are based on how much money you make and how much you owe.

The repayment must begin within 30 to 45 days after you file for Chapter 13 bankruptcy. You typically have three to five years to pay off all your creditors. This type of bankruptcy does not require you to sell any of your assets, such as property or belongings. However, it does require that you be employed or have an income at the time you file for bankruptcy.

NOTE: You cannot file for Chapter 13 bankruptcy if you have already done so within the past six years.

Chapter 13 Bankruptcy, noun

A financial reorganization supervised by a federal bankruptcy court that allows income-receiving debtors to pay off their debts over three to five years with no interest, provided they fulfill a court-approved plan. This type of bankruptcy stays on a credit report for seven years.

Liquidation: Chapter 7 Bankruptcy

Chapter 7 bankruptcy deals with **liquidation**. The goal of this type of bankruptcy is to liquidate or sell off your assets to pay back your creditors. In this case, some of your property can be seized and sold to repay the debt. The rules about what property is exempt (cannot be seized) vary from state to state. Exempt property often includes your home, professional books and tools, life insurance, Social Security, prescription health aides, and veterans or disability benefits. Of course, many people who file for this type of bankruptcy have no assets to liquidate. In this situation, the debts are discharged, and you start afresh with no debt.

Chapter 7 Bankruptcy, noun

A liquidation bankruptcy that allows a debtor with or without income to sell non-exempt assets to pay off part of a debt, and have the rest of the debt discharged to provide immediate, complete relief from overwhelming debt. The record of a Chapter 7 bankruptcy stays on a credit report for 10 years.

NOTE: You cannot file for Chapter 7 bankruptcy if you have already done so within the past eight years.

How to Avoid Bankruptcy

Bankruptcy is an unpleasant experience and stays on your credit record for seven to 10 years, depending on the type of bankruptcy you declare. Once your debts have either been discharged or paid, your outstanding credit card balances are wiped clean in your credit report. However, the bankruptcy is noted in your credit report, which could make it harder to rent an apartment or get a credit card at a low rate of interest. It might also make it difficult to get a home mortgage loan or insurance. This is because future lenders know you went through a bankruptcy and may be concerned that you will have difficulty repaying your debts in the future. Because they see you as a high risk, they may charge you higher interest rates or refuse to extend you credit. However, over time, you can rebuild your credit.

It is much better to avoid bankruptcy than to have to go through it. Exhibit 6-2 lists effective ways to avoid bankruptcy. You'll notice that a few of the methods were already mentioned in earlier chapters as ways to reduce credit card debt in the first place.

now you try it

What are the differences between Chapter 7 and Chapter 13 bankruptcy?

_____

_____

_____

What are three easy ways you could avoid bankruptcy?

_____

_____

_____

EXHIBIT

6-2   10 ways to avoid bankruptcy

METHOD	DESCRIPTION
Budget	Trim your budget, including cable TV or satellite services, cell phone, coffee, and expensive nights out.
Sell things	Consider selling any valuable possessions. This is a quick way to get out of any financial distress. Consider big and small assets.
Ask for help	Credit companies, banks, and other institutions can help troubled clients by putting them on their "hardship programs." They can help reduce some of your stress when you find yourself financially burdened.
Refinance	Refinancing a loan on a car or a house may cost you a fee, but it could help reduce your monthly payments if you are currently paying a high interest rate.
Settle your debts	Contact your collection agency to see if the agency can lower your debt.
Ask for government assistance	You might want to consider assistance from local, federal, and state agencies. You may be able to get assistance with basics like rent, heat, electricity, and groceries.
Work with creditors	Talk to creditors about possible options for renegotiating your interest rate or your payments. This might save you from filing for bankruptcy.
Get credit counseling	This can help you get a lower interest rate and might get your payments lowered. The law requires you to get credit counseling before you can file for bankruptcy.
Increase your income	Ask for more hours at work (especially overtime), consider another job, or get a part-time job.
Request write-offs	Contact the creditor and ask for written proof of the debt. If there is no written proof, you might be able to write off the debt.

Revisiting Identity Theft

In this chapter, you have walked through a lot of financial pitfalls and learned what *not* to do when it comes to being financially responsible. The last pitfall is identify theft, something you learned about in **Chapter 4, Components of Personal Money Management.** This might be a good time to review a few additional ways to avoid identity theft, since it can result in unwanted purchases in your name and increased debt that has nothing to do with you. Ultimately, it can give you a bad credit score.

Exhibit 6-3 lists a number of excellent methods to employ to avoid identify theft. These methods were devised by Frank Abagnale, the gentleman you learned about in Chapter 4. He is a reformed con artist and thief, a respected authority on identity theft, and the inspiration for the movie *Catch Me If You Can.*

EXHIBIT

6-3   More ways to avoid identify theft

METHOD	DESCRIPTION
Avoid giving out personal information	This includes your Social Security number or the last four digits of your Social Security number.
Shield your personal information	Cover up your debit or credit card and account information while you stand in line. Someone could be taking photographs and use that information to scam you.
Watch your mail	Don't leave your mail out freely. Someone could easily look through it for your financial information.
Carry less	Don't carry personal information, like your Social Security card, passport, and credit cards, when you don't need them.
Use the post office	Do not mail your bill payments from home. Checks can be stolen from your mailbox, wiped clean with chemicals, and have new amounts and names entered.
Monitor important information	Monitor your credit reports and statements for any suspicious activity. Thieves will often wait long periods of time before they use your information.

FiNaNCiaL FouL-UPS

US TREASURY

LEARNING FROM THE MISTAKES OF OTHERS

Remember Kevin at the beginning of the chapter? He had a friend, Lisa, who never had good judgment when it came to men. She fell in love with her high-school sweetheart, Ricky, the bad boy. He was very good looking and had a motorcycle but had no plans for college or a career. She didn't care; she loved him anyway.

After they graduated from high school, they moved in together. They were able to get a loan to buy a cute little house because Lisa had good credit. Over the next two years, they also took out loans on a couple of cars and managed to charge up some large balances on Lisa's credit cards.

One day Ricky ran off with another woman, leaving Lisa with the mortgage, two car payments, and three credit card bills. Plus, she just found out she was pregnant. Even with both their salaries, they were barely paying their bills, so how was Lisa going to pay the bills on her own with a baby coming? She didn't even have health insurance any more, since it was through Ricky's work, not hers.

Lisa eventually moved back in with her parents, lost her house to foreclosure, and had her cars repossessed. Foreclosures and repossessions did not mean she didn't owe money anymore. Lisa was still responsible for paying the loans on the cars and house. Ricky's name wasn't on those loans because he never had good enough credit to get a loan, so she was stuck with all the debt.

Lisa's phone rang constantly from creditors demanding their money. Her good credit was ruined and she couldn't get back on her feet until she fixed that credit. But it would take her a lifetime to pay back all of the money she owed. Filing for Chapter 13 bankruptcy was out of the question because Lisa had too much debt to be paid off in five years. Instead, she filed for Chapter 7 bankruptcy. Because she was living with her mother, she had few assets to sell, so the court discharged all her debt.

Lisa had a clean financial slate, but her bankruptcy was recorded on her credit report and it would remain there for at least 10 years while she tried to build up her credit again. Ten years was a long time to have to wait to start over. Lisa wished she never got mixed up with a loser like Ricky who left her in such a bad situation. Next time she would be more careful about who she got involved with and who she shared her money with.

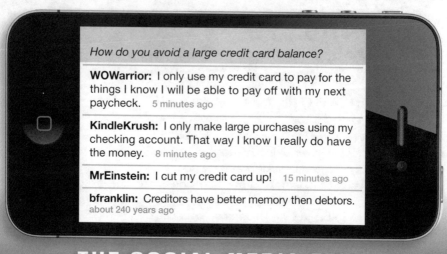

How do you avoid a large credit card balance?

WOWarrior: I only use my credit card to pay for the things I know I will be able to pay off with my next paycheck. 5 minutes ago

KindleKrush: I only make large purchases using my checking account. That way I know I really do have the money. 8 minutes ago

MrEinstein: I cut my credit card up! 15 minutes ago

bfranklin: Creditors have better memory then debtors. about 240 years ago

THE SOCIAL MEDIA FEED

LET'S REVIEW

H ere's your chance to think about what you've learned in this chapter. Reviewing stimulates your brain to remember important facts.

What Did You Learn?

- Large balances on your credit card lead to big interest payments and lower credit scores.

- Interest rates for payday loans and pawnshop loans are unusually high: payday loans charge up to 390 percent APR and pawnshop loans charge about 195 percent APR.

- The interest rate on credit card advances is typically 2 to 4 percent higher than normal card interest, which often runs about 19 percent APR.

- There are alternatives to high-interest loans, such as loans from friends and family, salary advances, and even a second job.

- There are two types of bankruptcy: Chapter 13 and Chapter 7. The first deals with reorganizing your debt and paying off your creditors over three to five years with no interest. The second deals with selling what you have to pay your creditors what you can, and then having the rest of the debt wiped clear. Chapter

13 bankruptcy stays on your credit report for seven years and Chapter 7 remains for 10 years.

- There are additional ways to avoid identity theft that involve watching and monitoring mail and personal information.

New Terms

- Delinquent
- Pawnshop
- Credit Card Advances
- Chapter 13 Bankruptcy
- Payday Loan
- Salary Advance
- Chapter 7 Bankruptcy

END-OF-CHAPTER ACTIVITIES

Here's your chance to put your pen to paper, as well as discuss what you've learned with others. Doing activities and talking about them are great ways to make sure you really do understand the concepts you've read about.

Remember the Basics

1. What does it mean to be delinquent or a high-risk borrower?

   _____

   _____

2. What is a payday loan? How does a $15 charge on a typical $100 two-week payday loan become 390 percent annual interest?

   _____

   _____

3. What is a pawnshop loan? How does a $15 charge on a typical $100 one-month pawnshop loan become 195 percent annual interest?

   _____

   _____

4. What happens if you can't pay back your pawnshop loan?

_____

_____

5. What is a cash advance and how much interest is usually charged on it?

_____

_____

6. What is the difference between Chapter 13 and Chapter 7 bankruptcy?

_____

_____

_____

_____

_____

7. What are some additional ways to prevent identity theft?

_____

_____

_____

_____

_____

Work With a Team

Read through this scenario with several friends. Then discuss and answer the questions at the end.

Shandra's mom lost her job two months ago and has been looking for another job ever since. After her last interview, she finally landed a new job. However, it won't start for another week—at the beginning of next month. Rent and utility bills have to be paid before then. Her mom has some money left, but she is still $300 short. Her mom thinks about ways she could get the money:

She could ask her brother for the money and pay him back after she starts her job. She's pretty sure he would help, but she feels really embarrassed asking. He always says she has no head for finances.

She could pawn her wedding ring (she's divorced).

She could get a payday loan and pay it back as soon as she gets her first paycheck in about three weeks.

She could get a cash advance on her credit card, which currently has a $2,500 balance and an interest rate of 19 percent.

1. Work with your friends to write down the pros and cons of each action.

_____

_____

_____

_____

_____

2. As a team, which action do you recommend and why?

_____

_____

_____

Put the Math Into Practice

Lamar's dad got injured and can't work for a month. In the meantime, the family is short on cash and Lamar's mom decides to get a payday loan for $400 to help with groceries. She knows her husband will be back on the job in four weeks. Assume the normal payday loan fee is $15 per $100, to be paid back in two weeks.

1. What is the normal interest rate on a payday loan for two weeks?

_____

2. How much interest will accumulate on $400 after two weeks? After four weeks?

_____

3. How much money will Lamar's mom owe at the end of the month to pay off her loan?

_____

4. What is the annual interest rate for the entire year (remember, a year consists of 52 weeks)?

_____

For more activities, assessments, and examples, visit www.lifebound.com.

SOLUTION:

$15 ÷ $100 = .15 = 15% interest every two weeks

.15 x $400 = $60 interest after two weeks

$60 + $60 = $120 interest after four weeks

$120 + $400 = $520 to pay off the loan

.15 interest rate per 2 weeks x 26 interest periods per year = 3.9 = 390% per year!

When you make a mistake, don't look back at it long. Take the reason of the thing into your mind and then look forward. Mistakes are lessons of wisdom. The past cannot be changed. The future is yet in your power.

—HUGH LAWSON WHITE (1773–1840)

What does this quote mean to you? How can you apply it to moving on from a financial mistake?

Avoiding Debt and Staying Out of Debt

> "Some debts are fun when you are acquiring them,
> but none are fun when you set about retiring them."
>
> **OGDEN NASH**

Questions you will answer. . . .

1. What is smart spending?
2. How much should you be saving?
3. Why give to charity?
4. How do you fix your credit score?

Test your financial skills with the Dollars & Sense chapter assessment at www.lifebound.com.

Meet Corina

Corina was recently laid off from of her part-time job. Now she has to figure out how to pay her $200 cell phone bill without any income. While she was employed, she never worried about how long she talked on her phone. In fact, some of her friends used to joke that her phone was permanently connected to her ear. And now her addiction to checking her Facebook every minute, mass-texting her friends, and talking well into the night was coming back to haunt her.

She managed to borrow the money from her cousin to pay the phone bill, but before she handed it over to the phone company, her friends invited her to go shopping at the mall. Next thing she knew she was spending her borrowed money to buy a new outfit. Then, she was going to the movies with her friends, where she was notified her debit card was declined for insufficient funds. In desperation, she asked her brother for the money and he reluctantly agreed. Now she owes money to both her brother and her cousin. They're both asking her when she's going to pay them back, but Corina doesn't have the money. She's in trouble.

get ready

Corina's situation is not unique—anyone can fall into debt. In this chapter, you will learn tips for avoiding debt in the first place, saving money, and getting out of debt if you happen to already be in it. While it's true that you may not always be able to avoid debts like student loans and mortgages, you need to be smart about what type of debt you are getting into and what it costs to get out. If you are lucky enough to know people who avoid debt and are smart with their money, you will probably learn how to do the same.

PICK A GOOD ROLE MODEL

You have many influences in your life; some may be obvious and some subtle. Perhaps you set out to dress like your favorite celebrity, volunteer like your best friend, or have a career like your parents. Maybe you have the same mannerisms as your sibling or best friend. Guess what? If you know people who influence your attitude, style, and behavior, you probably know people who influence your spending and the way you think of money.

People whom you admire, who influence you, are your **role models**. Who are your financial role models? They might not be the people closest to you. You might think your parents display poor financial skills and prefer Bill Gates as a role model for your financial future. Consider what steps you need to take to achieve your role model's financial status. Are you taking any of those steps now? What are some of your role model's traits and habits that you can practice today to be financially fit tomorrow?

Role Model, noun

Someone you admire, look up to, or who influences you.

PRACTICE SMART SPENDING

Part of thinking about your financial fitness is thinking about your spending habits. At this time in history, the United States is very much a consumer nation and citizens are constantly bombarded with messages from the media to "buy, buy, buy," whether they need the products or not. However, you can learn to say "no" to unnecessary purchases, as well as learn how to make smart decisions about the necessary ones. Use the following tips to learn how to take advantage of your choices and start spending smart.

Differentiate Between Needs and Wants

You already learned about needs and wants in Chapter 1, but it doesn't hurt to review the difference. People often make the mistake of thinking they absolutely have to buy something because they want it. A **want** is simply a personal desire; it is not a necessity. A **need** is something you must have to survive.

For example, suppose you go to the mall with your friends and see a new cell phone with all the latest "bells and whistles." You already have a cell phone that has the capabilities to text and call, but it doesn't have a touch screen, Internet access, or a GPS. You decide you've just got to have the new one because "everyone else has one" and you feel left out.

FINANCIAL FIGURES

LEARNING FROM THE EXPERIENCE OF OTHERS

Kimberly Palmer, *author and personal finance columnist for U.S. News & World Report, Washington, D.C.*

The scooter collecting dust in her parents' garage reminds Kimberly Palmer of her high school spending habits. "I was wasting money on really silly purchases," says Palmer, a personal finance columnist for *U.S. News & World Report* and author of *Generation Earn: The Young Professional's Guide to Spending, Investing, and Giving Back.* "I wish I had skipped some of those trendy purchases."

Responsible spending, Palmer admits, is more difficult today than ever before. Blame technology. "It is so much easier to compare ourselves to our friends," Palmer says. "With things like Facebook and social media, there is more pressure on consumer spending, because people are constantly comparing themselves. When a friend buys the latest iPhone, you want it also. It's even more tempting to play that game, keeping up with what your friends are buying."

Palmer, who also pens an insightful daily blog, Alpha Consumer, advises high schoolers to take the spending diary challenge. "Write down everything you spend money on for two weeks, even if you are spending your parents' money," Palmer says. "It can be shocking how all the little things we buy add up. That can be a good way to gain insight into how much you are spending and where you can cut back and practice savings."

Teens' best financial advisors might be sitting at their dinner table, Palmer says. "Most parents feel awkward talking about money. A lot of parents feel they made financial mistakes growing up and aren't perfect. But they will love it if you sit down and ask them about how you budget, how you save. It can be such a good way to get conversation going. Parents are always looking for any chance to talk to their teenagers."

If you took time to think about it, you would realize that: a) you do not need a new cell phone and b) you cannot afford one. Your current phone works fine, you can make the calls you need to make, text when you want to, and take pictures. You barely have money for lunch for the next week, and buying a new phone is going to clean you out or put even more debt on your credit card (which you can barely pay off as it is). Eating lunch is a need, but purchasing a new phone is nothing more than a desire to make your ego feel good; it would only hurt you in the end.

Avoid Impulse Buying

You've probably been guilty of impulse shopping in your life. Have you ever gone into a convenience store for a pack of gum and walked out with a pack of gum, a 16-ounce soda, a candy bar, and a new pair of sunglasses?

Impulse buying is simply buying without thinking. This type of buying, whether big or small, is a serious problem for many people. Whether you leave with an unplanned bag full of goodies from the convenience store or stop in at the mall for a $500 leather jacket on a whim, these impulse buys don't have a place in your budget and will only make you stray beyond your means and spin into overwhelming debt.

According to a 2009 survey by Seventeen *magazine, working teens are saving up for the three C's: clothes (57 percent), college (54 percent), and a car (38 percent).[1]*

IT'S A FACT! GUARANTEED

If impulse buying not only has the potential to put you into debt but also make you feel bad about yourself, why do people do it? That's easy. Impulse buying gives you instant gratification—you feel great immediately. However, like a high from drugs, the feeling quickly fades, and the instant gratification quickly turns to guilt as you ask yourself: "Why did I buy that?" The impulse buy comes back to haunt you when it's time to pay your bills and you don't have the money to do so. So, what can you do? Here are some good tips to avoid impulse buying.

Avoid unplanned purchases. To fight impulse buying, never allow yourself to buy an item you have not planned for. For instance, if you take a trip to the mall and a new hoodie catches your eye, don't buy it on this trip. If you're still thinking about it in a week, go back and get it. Chances are you'll only remember it if you really needed it and you'll avoid feeling guilty because you took the time to think it through.

Too many impulse purchases can put you in debt.

EXHIBIT

| 7-1 | Your paycheck and expenses |

Paycheck:	$500
Monthly expenses:	
Phone bill	$ 60
Monthly gasoline	$100
College savings	$100
Lunch money	$150
Total expenses:	$410
Money remaining:	$ 90

Avoid shopping on payday. When you get a surge of money on payday, it's easy to think you can afford to spend more because you have a big balance in your bank account. Instead of thinking about your paycheck as your spending money, look at it in terms of the money you owe. Whether you owe money to yourself in a savings account or to bill collectors, it's money you don't really have. For high school students, a typical paycheck and the amount of money you owe (expenses) might look like Exhibit 7-1.

Do not buy anything from the checkout line. Do you ever stand in line at the grocery store reading a magazine while you wait, and then find yourself buying it? Do you ever stare at all the candy by the checkout stand and find your hand reaching out on its own to buy something you never planned to buy? The checkout line is designed to tempt you into making additional purchases as you wait with nowhere else to go. So, the next time you're staring at the taunting sign, "3 candy bars for $1," or placing a magazine on the conveyer belt so you can finish reading it at home, remember that you are falling victim to a marketing ploy.

If you have a hard time fighting the urge to buy in line, take your mind off the wire racks dripping with candy and gossip and look at your grocery basket. Calculate the prices of the items in your head and try to figure how much your bill will be with tax. If that doesn't work, bring your own paperback book to read or just people watch.

The next thing you know, you will be at the head of the line and it will be time to check out.

Shop consciously. This tip comes in three parts: 1) Always be prepared with a list when you go shopping. 2) Always stick to your list when you go shopping. 3) Never grocery shop when you are hungry. If you have a hard time resisting items at the checkout lane, you are likely to have a really hard time resisting items when you're free to roam an entire store without a plan. Worse, who knows what you will grab when you're hungry. Everything will look too good to pass up. Making a list in your head doesn't count. Commit yourself to a physical list and you won't walk away with things you don't need or forget the things you do need.

Consult a professional. Sometimes overspending habits are serious enough to warrant intervention in the form of a professional counselor. For example, "shop-a-holics" are compulsive buyers who get a high from spending money. Their feelings are similar to what gamblers feel when making bets or what addicts feel when taking drugs. They spend money, not necessarily because they want to, but because their brains tell them they have to so they can feel good. Their behavior is considered **impulsive** because the person doing it acts without thinking about the consequences.

Compulsive Buyer, noun

Someone who feels they must buy things.

Impulsive Buyer, noun

Someone who doesn't think before they buy.

Compulsive and impulsive spenders have an especially hard time breaking their negative spending cycle. However, this kind of overspending behavior can put people in serious financial turmoil that piles on stress and can ruin their future. If you think you're an extreme impulsive or compulsive spender, consider getting psychological or financial help from a professional.

Compare Prices

Once you get your spending behaviors under control, it's time to think about what things cost. Where do you do your shopping? Do you go to a retail store to buy a new pair of running shoes or do you go online and find them at a wholesale price? Do you buy only new electronics or do you look at what people are offering for a discounted price on eBay, Amazon, and Craigslist? Smart spending often requires more work and foresight to compare prices so you can save money.

now you try it

DIFFERENTIATE BETWEEN NEEDS AND WANTS

1. List the last few impulse buys you made. What influenced you to make these purchases?

_____

_____

_____

2. Do you have a technique you use to battle the urge to impulse buy? What is a new technique, either from the book or that you make up, which you can implement?

_____

_____

Did you know you can buy name-brand supplies at the dollar store and save over 50 percent instead of buying them at a commercial grocery store? Shop Smart Magazine recently conducted a study involving 100 consumers who shopped at 100 stores to find the best bargains. The consumers chose the following items as their best bargains to purchase at the dollar store.[2]

- Party supplies
- Cleaning supplies
- Paper products

- Candles
- School supplies

Note: The article did go on to say that many of those items did not cost exactly one dollar, and that other types of items were not necessarily a good buy in terms of quality.

Shop at Thrift and Consignment Stores

Not everyone wants to buy from a dollar store or can find what they want there. However, there are other alternatives to retail stores: thrift and consignment stores that sell pre-owned (used) goods. According to a poll by Harris Interactive and eBay, 70 percent of adults said it is more socially acceptable now to shop at a thrift store than it was five or 10 years ago.[3] That could account for sales at retail stores going down 7.3 percent from 2008–2009, while sales at used goods shops have continued to increase by 7 percent every year.[4]

Shoppers beware: Impulse buying is not only a problem when buying new items; it's just as great a problem when buying used items. Some people can't resist a deal, whether they need the thing or not.

When you buy used, you are not only saving money, you are saving resources. New items cost money and resources to manufacture; used items do not. Additionally, when you shop at thrift stores like Goodwill and The Salvation Army, you also give back to the community. For example, in 2010 more than 74 million people donated to Goodwill. Approximately 84 percent of those Goodwill sales went to making it possible for people with disabilities, a lack of education or job experience, or other employment challenges to get back into the workforce after undergoing job training.[5]

Use Coupons

Another way to save a lot of money is with coupons. When you hear the word "coupon," do you picture your grandmother cutting the week's deals out of the paper or someone with a handful of coupons holding up the line at the grocery store? If so, think again. These days, you're less likely to have a newspaper at home from which to cut your coupons, and are more likely to find coupons and savings online.

Groupon and Living Social

If you live in a major city, you can sign up for daily deals from Groupon or Living Social that will show up in your e-mail or Twitter and Facebook feeds. Fill in your gender, location, and age to get deals designed for you, such as entertainment, eating out, grocery shopping, hot-air balloon rides, and more. Some cities, big or small, offer similar online services that are only available locally. **Note:** Vendors who offer Groupon coupons usually provide a discounted price for trying out a particular product or service. However, once you try it and like it, you often have to pay full price if you purchase it again.

eCoupons

Do you have a customer discount card for your local grocery store? You can get even more savings if you visit sites like Cellfire.com before you head out for groceries. Go to the site, plug in your location and download the coupons directly to your customer discount card.

Websites

You can even get great savings advice and coupons on the web. For example, the Mrs.MoneySaver.com blog gives advice and money-saving coupons every day. The blogger even lists her top coupon databases. All you have to do is go to the site, visit the **Coupons** page, select any of the databases below, and print your coupons.

- Coupons.com
- RedPlum
- Smart Source
- Betty Crocker

- Eat Better America
- Coolsavings
- Grocery Coupon Network

now you try it

DO YOU SHOP SMART?

Here's your chance to evaluate your own spending. Look back over the smart spending tips.

1. Which tips from this chapter do you currently follow?

_____

_____

_____

2. Which tips would you like to try?

_____

_____

_____

3. Where are your problem areas?

_____

_____

_____

4. What are you going to do about them?

_____

_____

PRACTICE SMART SAVING

T aking care of your finances isn't just about managing your spending; it's also about managing your savings. Of course, if you have out-of-control spending, you probably have no money left to save. So your first priority is to get your spending under control. But once it's under control, it's time to think about saving money.

When you're in high school, it may be hard to imagine your future 10, 20, or 30 years down the road. What will you be doing? Where will you be living? Where will you be working? Even if you have a hard time picturing the future, it doesn't hurt to start saving money to be prepared for whatever the future holds. Let's look at different types of savings you can start building now to be ready for a variety of life's curve balls and pleasures.

Emergency Savings

No matter how well you plan, emergencies happen. Perhaps you have to buy a special book for a school project or an expensive uniform for a sports activity. Maybe you have to help pay for auto repairs when someone hits your car in a parking lot. Or what if your mother or father gets laid off from a job and you have to help out financially?

That's where emergency savings come in handy. These savings need to be in **liquid form**. This means you can gain access to them easily and they are already in the form of money (unlike investments or property, which have to be sold to be converted to money).

The easiest way to build up an emergency savings fund is to open a savings account at your bank and invest a small amount of money in it each month. Ideally, you should save 10 percent of what you make. However, people in the U.S., compared to others around the world, have been having a difficult time saving and have put themselves into serious debt. In the late 1990s, the average savings in the U.S. hovered around zero (no savings at all), but due to a shaky economy, it has actually risen to about 5 percent (as of 2011).[6] Examine Exhibit 7-2 to see how personal savings have varied over the last 50 years in the U.S.

EXHIBIT

7-2   Average personal savings in the U.S. (as a % of disposable income)

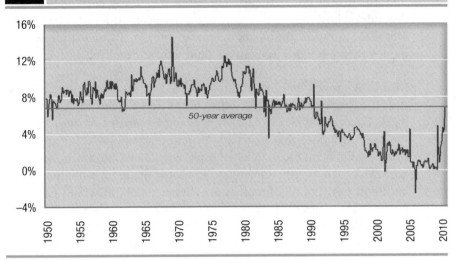

If you cannot afford to save 10 percent of your earnings, try saving 5 percent, and if you can't do that, just save something. In fact, if you already have a part-time job and a checking account, you might even consider an automatic transfer from your checking account into your savings account every time you deposit a paycheck. People often like this approach because the money never touches their checking account balance, which means they never have the opportunity to spend the money before it's whisked away into their savings account.

You can also use your savings account as a place to save up money for Christmas, a holiday where impulsive spenders often rack up a lot of debt. When Christmas arrives, you can use the money in your savings account to buy gifts, rather than use a credit card and spend money you don't have.

Short-term Savings

Imagine you want to save money to take a trip across the country to visit your older sibling. Where do you put money you're planning to spend in a year or so and that you want to keep safe from being spent on anything else? There are two good options you might consider as you think about saving for your trip or other short-term savings goals like college, a car, or an apartment. Both options are usually available through your bank.

CD (6, 12, 60 months). Certificates of deposits (CDs) are bank investments for your savings. The interest rate you earn on your CD depends on how long you keep your money invested with the bank. The longer the duration, the higher the rate of interest. If you withdraw your money before it matures, your account will be penalized with interest.

MMA. A money market account (MMA) offers competitive interest yields, easy access to ATMs, plus checks and a debit card. A money market account typically earns higher interest than a savings account but has restrictions that a savings account does not have. For example, there are limits on the number of times you can withdraw money from an MMA each month. Sometimes you must maintain a minimum balance and pay monthly fees that are higher than you would pay for a traditional savings account. When you talk to a bank about an MMA, make sure to ask questions about interest, restrictions, balance, and fees. Read the account terms and conditions carefully before signing an agreement.

Long-term Savings

Finally, it's important to consider **long–term savings**; savings that won't be touched for decades—usually after you retire. You probably won't be involved in this type of savings until you are working or living on your own. With long-term savings, the money in your account is not only growing from what you put in it; it's growing from the interest that is accumulating.

Exhibit 7-3 shows you the formula for calculating simple interest.

A bank is a good place to start for short-term savings plans.

EXHIBIT

7-3   Calculating simple interest

$I = P \times r \times t$	
I = Interest	*The additional money earned on your principle; it depends on the interest rate and the amount of time your money is invested.*
P = Principle	*The amount of money you invest.*
r = Interest rate	*The percentage used to calculate interest.*
t = Time	*The amount of time the money is held in the bank.*

However, this formula does not accurately reflect the fact that money in your account is growing each month and the interest earned should be based on the new monthly amounts. This is why banks calculate **compound interest** instead of simple. Compound interest is based on the principle, the rate of interest, and the interest that has accrued so far. The formula for compound interest depends on whether the bank compounds annually, quarterly, or monthly. Monthly is most common.

Exhibit 7-4 shows the formula for calculating compound interest. The formula is complicated, so it's best to use a compound interest calculator. This type of calculator is typically found online or in printed tables.

EXHIBIT

7-4   Calculating compound interest

$I = P \times (1 + r)$	
I = Interest	*The additional money earned on your principle; it depends on the interest rate and the amount of time your money is invested.*
P = Principle	*The amount of money you invest.*
r = Interest rate	*The percentage used to calculate interest.*
t = Number of time periods	*This could be the number of years if interest is compounded annually, the number of quarters if interest is compounded quarterly, or the number of months if interest is compounded monthly.*

REAL-WORLD MATH

Compound interest always beats simple interest, as you can see in the following example.

Imagine that you manage to save $50 a month throughout high school. After four years, let's look at how much money you would earn if you deposited the money in an account that compounded interest monthly.

Simple interest

- Interest = $50 per month x .03 interest x 48 months = $72.00
- Amount invested = $50 per month x 48 months = $2,400
- Total amount (using simple interest) = $72.00 + $2,400 = $2,472.00

Compound interest

- Interest = $50 per month x $(1 + .03)^{48}$ = $50 x $(1.03)^{48}$ = $50 x 4.132 = $206.60
- Amount invested = $50 per month x 48 months = $2,400
- Total amount (using compound interest) = $206.60 + $2,400 = $2,606.60

IRAs

Interest adds up over the years, and the most common form of interest-bearing, long-term savings is an individual retirement account (**IRA**). The power behind the IRA is that the money you put into it has years and years to increase in value due to interest. Most people don't open up this type of account until they are working at their profession. There are two kinds of IRAs: traditional and Roth. The one you choose depends on whether you want to be taxed before or after retirement.

Traditional. This is a special type of account that you cannot draw money out of until you retire, where the retirement age set by the U.S. government is 59½ years. If you draw the money out early, you pay taxes on the withdrawal, plus a 10 percent penalty. Exceptions to the early withdrawal penalty include hardships such as large medical expenses, college expenses, home purchase, or sudden disability.

The money you put into a traditional IRA is **tax-deductible**; it is deducted from your annual income at tax time, which may put you in a lower tax bracket. The interest you earn on it each year is also not taxed. All taxes are deferred until you retire; then the IRA is considered income and you are taxed on the money that you withdraw from the IRA. The idea behind a traditional IRA is that prior to retirement, when your earning power is higher, you will benefit from the tax deductions. After retirement, when you have less income, you will be in a low enough tax bracket that the taxes on your IRA distributions should be relatively low.

quickcheck

What is compound interest?

What is a short-term savings account for?

What are the two types of IRAs?

Roth. This type of IRA is the opposite of a traditional IRA. The money you put into it is not tax-deductible; it is still considered part of your earnings and you are taxed on it. However, it is **tax-exempt**—you are not taxed on the interest as it accrues, nor are you taxed on the money you withdraw from the Roth account after you retire. The idea behind a Roth IRA is that some people would prefer to pay taxes on their investment while they are earning money, and then never have to worry about taxes when they start to withdraw that money after retirement.

Note: You will be penalized if you withdraw the money before retirement age (59½) and before money has been in the Roth IRA for five years. The exceptions to the early withdrawal penalty are the same as for the traditional IRA.

Home

In the future, when you purchase a home, it will become a type of savings account. The longer you own it and pay a mortgage on it, the greater its equity. That is because **equity** is the difference between how much the home is currently worth and how much you owe on the mortgage. You can then borrow money against that equity to deal with emergencies and home improvement projects, as well as medical or business issues. Over time, your home actually becomes a wonderful investment that you can borrow against.

TRY CHARITABLE GIVING

Up to this point, you've probably been thinking a lot about yourself—how much are you spending, how much can you save, and where should you store your savings? But have you ever considered that the money you make can help others as well?

If your spending is under control and you have some savings, you might consider using some of those savings to make a **charitable donation**. This is a gift to an organization, charity, or private organization. You can make a cash gift or you can donate clothing, household goods, vehicles, or securities. Donating to charity is a way to help others, to expand your awareness of the world around you, and to realize that you are part of the community. However, before you make a contribution to your favorite charity, make sure you know what you can afford to donate. After all, you must take care of your own finances before you can help others with theirs.

Once you know what you can afford to give, the next step is to decide who should receive your contribution. This may seem difficult when you have limited funds and there are so many worthy organizations asking for help. To help make the decision, ask yourself these questions:

- What issues do I feel strongly about?
- Am I more concerned with people, things, ideas, animals, or the environment?
- Where can my contribution make the greatest difference?
- Do I want to contribute at the local, national, or international level?
- Do I want to contribute once a year, or contribute a smaller amount each month?

After you do your research and make a decision, you'll feel good knowing that your contribution is making a difference. Plus, that contribution is tax-deductible if it is not associated with a political organization.

now you try it

TRY CHARITABLE GIVING

1. What is one issue you feel strongly about that you would be willing to contribute to that would make a difference?

_____

2. What is one thing of value you could give as a charitable donation?

_____

FIX YOUR CREDIT SCORE

Watching your spending, managing your saving, and reaching out to others through charitable donations are all ways to become financially responsible. But there's more. Like you learned in Chapter 5, another part of being financially responsible is knowing your credit score, because that score is going to affect you in the future in terms of getting a job, getting a loan, or buying or renting a place to live. Remember a credit score is three-digit number that indicates your "creditworthiness." The formula to determine credit scores was developed by the Fair Isaac Corporation (FICO); hence the credit score is often called a **FICO score**.

FiNaNCiaL FOUL-UPS

LEARNING FROM THE MISTAKES OF OTHERS

Jeremy was thrilled. He had just spoken by phone with a potential new employer for his dream job and they wanted him to come in for a second round of interviews. Since graduating from college, Jeremy had been concerned about landing a job at all. He couldn't believe he was only one interview away from landing his dream job!

On the morning of the interview, Jeremy was nervous but felt completely prepared. He was dressed in a pressed suit with polished shoes, had his main selling points memorized, and was running 15 minutes ahead of schedule. He arrived at the office in a good mood and ready to land a job that would mark the starting point of his career.

The interviewer opened the door to his office and greeted Jeremy, inviting him to come in and take a seat. They exchanged some small talk and then the interviewer got serious.

"Jeremy, you had a great interview and you would be an excellent fit for our company, but we won't be hiring you today." Jeremy's heart sank. The interviewer saw his reaction and continued to explain the company decision. "We feel your low credit score is a potential liability for our team."

The unpaid cell phone bill from high school, the broken lease in college, and the late credit card payments all came spiraling back.

"I wish you luck in raising your credit score and hope you'll come back in the future."

He thanked the interviewer for his time and left feeling embarrassed and shocked. He never knew his credit score would be standing between him and his dream job.

How Can You Increase Your Credit Score?

Now that you know how a higher credit score can help you in your personal and professional life, how can you increase your score if it's low? Here are a few ways:

- **Pay your bills on time—even if you can only make a partial payment.** Late payments increase your interest rates and lower your credit score. The longer you pay your bills on time, the better your score.

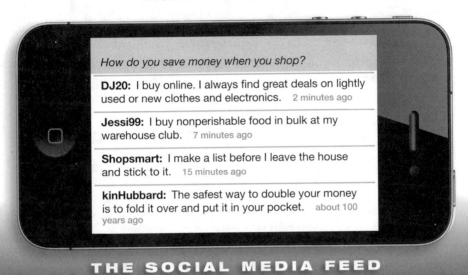

How do you save money when you shop?

DJ20: I buy online. I always find great deals on lightly used or new clothes and electronics. 2 minutes ago

Jessi99: I buy nonperishable food in bulk at my warehouse club. 7 minutes ago

Shopsmart: I make a list before I leave the house and stick to it. 15 minutes ago

kinHubbard: The safest way to double your money is to fold it over and put it in your pocket. about 100 years ago

THE SOCIAL MEDIA FEED

- **Do not use your entire line of credit every month.** Credit cards should be for emergencies only or special purchases; not everyday use.

- **Pay off your debt.** There are a number of ways to do this: Stop using the credit card with the highest interest rate. Pay off the credit card with the lowest balance. Stop using your credit card completely and pay only with cash; that way you do not increase your debt.

- **If you get into trouble, ask creditors to work with you.** Creditors would rather have some money from you than none at all. Maybe you can work out a partial payment schedule if you can only make partial payments.

- **Ask a friend or relative if they would put you on one of their accounts.** If that person has a high credit rating, the fact that your name is also on that account automatically raises your score. However, if you abuse the account, you destroy that person's credit rating as well.

- **Apply for new credit cards only when you need them.** Having too many credit cards can actually lower your credit score.
- **Get help.** If you're not sure what to do, contact your local consumer credit counseling organization. It's usually a nonprofit organization with counselors who can provide you with free assistance.

How Long Does the Record Remain?

Your credit score changes every time your information changes at the credit reporting agency. This could be due to a new credit card, a late payment, or a closed credit card. That's why it's important to check your credit report regularly for any errors or omissions. Then contact the creditor and credit reporting agency immediately to get those mistakes corrected. This is particularly important because bad debts can remain on your credit report for 7½ years after the delinquency that caused the account to go bad. That's a long time!

LET'S REVIEW

Here's your chance to think about what you've learned in this chapter. Reviewing stimulates your brain to remember important facts.

What Did You Learn?

- Smart spending includes thinking about what you need versus what you want and making a shopping list, then sticking to it.
- You should be saving enough to cover emergencies.
- Giving to charity not only improves your community, but also improves your relationship with money. If you believe you have enough to share, you feel better about your circumstances.
- Fixing your credit score takes time and patience, but it can be done. One of the best ways to increase your credit score is to pay your bills on time.

New Terms

- Role Model
- Smart Spending
- Charitable Giving

- Smart Saving (emergency, short-term, and long-term)
- Compulsive or Impulse Buying

END-OF-CHAPTER ACTIVITIES

Here's your chance to put your pen to paper, as well as discuss what you've learned with others. Doing activities and talking about them are great ways to make sure you really do understand the concepts you've read about.

Remember the Basics

1. What is smart spending?

_____

_____

_____

2. What is impulse buying? What are some ways to avoid it?

_____

_____

_____

3. Are you or is anyone you know an impulse buyer?

_____

_____

_____

4. What is liquid money?

_____

_____

_____

5. How much should you be saving?

_____

_____

_____

6. What is the difference between long-term and short-term savings?

_____

_____

_____

7. Why give to charity?

_____

_____

_____

8. How do you fix your credit score?

_____

_____

_____

Work With a Team

Compare shopping tips with your friends or relatives.

1. Where do they find the best deals?

_____

_____

_____

2. What stores do they avoid?

_____

_____

_____

Put Math Into Practice

This exercise helps you determine the amount of money you have available to put into savings. It also demonstrates how different interest rates affect your savings, and how simple and compound interest differ.

1. Currently, how much money do you earn each month?

   _____

2. How much money do you spend each month? (Think back to your budget in Chapter 3.)

   ▪ What is left over?

   _____

   ▪ Of that leftover amount, how much could you realistically put into savings for an emergency fund?

   _____

3. Imagine that you put that amount into a savings account every month. Use the table below to do the following:

   ▪ Calculate how much interest you would earn at the end of the year under the following circumstances. **Note:** Use a physical calculator or go online and find a compound interest calculator to determine the compound interest.

   _____

   ▪ Then, determine the total amount of money you would have in your account at the end of the year.

   For more activities, assessments, and examples, visit www.lifebound.com.

   _____

	SIMPLE INTEREST	COMPOUND INTEREST (monthly)
Interest Rate: 3.5%	$I = P \times r \times t$	$I = P \times (1 + r)\, t$
	Total amount $= I + P$	Total amount $= I + P$
Interest Rate: 5.0%	$I = P \times r \times t$	$I = P \times (1 + r)\, t$
	Total amount $= I + P$	Total amount $= I + P$

Plant the Seed for an Excellent Credit Score

What are three things you can do to help your credit score grow?

_____

_____

_____

730+ = excellent credit!

700-729 = good/above average

670-699 = good credit

585-669 = fair credit

584 or below = poor credit

Investing for the Future

> *Money is like manure. . . .*
> *You have to spread it around or it smells.*

J. PAUL GETTY, AMERICAN INDUSTRIALIST

Questions you will answer. . . .

1. What is investing?
2. What is return and risk?
3. What is the stock market?
4. What are the three most typical types of investments?
5. What are other types of investments outside the stock market?
6. How do you research investments?
7. How do you purchase securities?

Test your financial skills with the Dollars & Sense chapter assessment at www.lifebound.com.

Meet Eliza and Hannah

Hannah's grandmother, Eliza, worked for AT&T in the 1960s. As part of the company's retirement plan, Eliza faithfully invested 3 percent of her salary each month into AT&T stocks, and the company matched her contribution. Over the years, her investment grew, but Eliza always worried that if anything ever happened to AT&T, the stocks might lose their value and her retirement fund would be in serious trouble.

As she received promotions and her salary grew, she decided to open another retirement account and invest on her own. She started with some certificates of deposit (CDs), a few socially responsible mutual funds, and then purchased some individual stocks in a new high-tech firm and a wind energy company.

In the 1980s, when Eliza's granddaughter, Hannah, was born, Eliza decided to open an investment account for Hannah and start buying stocks and bonds for her college fund. When Hannah was a teenager, her grandmother visited her on weekends and they would look at the business section of the paper to see how her stocks and bonds were performing. By doing this, Eliza taught her granddaughter how to research potential investments, read a prospectus, and go online to look at performance charts. By the time Hannah turned 18, she had quite a college fund and a strong foundation in the art of investing, thanks to her grandmother.

LIVE AND LEARN

You may not have a grandmother like Hannah's who successfully invests and takes time to teach you to do the same. However, you can still learn how to make money work for you. That is what investing is all about and what you will learn in this chapter.

WHAT IS INVESTING?

You have probably done some investing in your life without knowing it, especially when it comes to emotions. For example, did you ever take a risk and tell someone you liked him or her before you knew if that person felt the same way? You were investing your emotions, hoping they would pay off. If the person did not reciprocate your feelings, you probably felt bad, like you lost something; if the individual did reciprocate, you probably felt terrific, like you gained something. But if you had never taken the risk at all, you would never have known the outcome, good or bad.

Investing your money is a lot like investing your emotions—you hope that it will pay off in the end. Strictly speaking, **investing** means putting your money toward something so that it can grow. You invest when you buy securities such as stocks, bonds and mutual funds (more about these later), hold on to them for some time, and then sell them—hoping their value has increased over time so that you make some money. However, there is always the risk that their value may not increase and you will actually lose money.

Invest, verb

To put (money) to use, by purchase or expenditure, in something offering potential profitable returns, as interest, income, or appreciation in value.

WHAT IS RETURN AND RISK?

When it comes to investments, **return (or yield)** refers to the amount of money an investment generates over a given period of time. The **rate of return** (ROR) is a percentage value calculated by dividing the yield by the total investment. You can think of an ROR like an interest rate because it indicates the rate at which the value of your investments are growing (or shrinking).

Return, noun

The change in the value of a portfolio over an evaluation period, including any distributions made from the portfolio during that period.

Whether you invest time, energy, or money, return and risk always go hand in hand. **Risk** measures the uncertainty of your investment, the likelihood that the investment's return will be less than expected, or possibly nothing at all.

Risk-return Tradeoff

Typically, investments with potentially high returns have a greater risk, and investments with potentially lower returns have less risk. For example, suppose you are a risk taker and decide to invest in a new, unknown, high-tech start-up company. If the company fails, you stand to lose everything (high risk); if it succeeds and does well, you *may* make a lot of money (higher return). If you prefer to play it safe with your money, you might decide to invest in an established, well-known, conventional firm. The company is not likely to fail (low risk), but you probably won't make as much money (lower return).

Exhibit 8-1 illustrates how return and risk are related.

Risk, noun

The uncertainty associated with any investment. That is, risk is the possibility that the actual return on an investment will be different from its expected return.

The risk-return tradeoff could be called the "ability-to-sleep-at-night test." While some people can handle the equivalent of financial skydiving without batting an eye, others are terrified to climb the financial ladder without a secure harness. Deciding what amount of risk you can take while remaining comfortable with your investments is very important.[1]

EXHIBIT

8-1   Risk vs. return

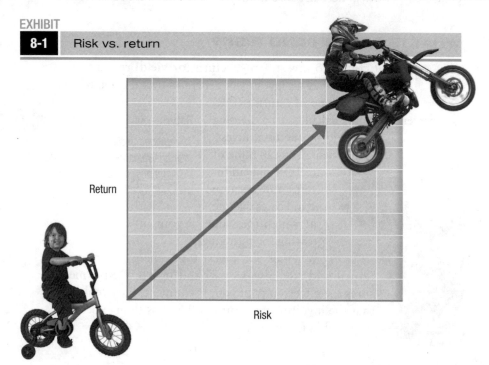

Return

Risk

As an example of the risk-return tradeoff, let's revisit Hannah's grandmother, Eliza. In the 1990s, Eliza invested in Boo.com, a new global online fashion store. The stock price was low at the time, so Eliza could buy a lot of shares for relatively little money, but the risk was high—the company was unknown and online retail stores had not been around very long. However, Eliza reasoned that if the store took off, and people all over the world started buying fashions online, the stocks would be worth a lot (potential high return). As it turned out, the company went bankrupt in 2000 and Hannah's grandmother lost all the money she had invested in Boo.com. Such was the plight of a high-risk/high-return stock that didn't return as expected.

How Much Risk Can You Take?

Knowing your risk tolerance is very important before you invest. Are you a person who likes taking risks and can afford to lose some money? Or are you someone who prefers safety and cannot afford to lose money? How you feel about risk affects the type of investments you will feel comfortable making.

For example, with insured bank investments, such as CDs, you face **inflation risk**, which means that you may not earn enough over time to keep pace with the increasing cost of living. Exhibit 8-2 is a visualization of how costs have risen over the last 50 years.

Inflation, noun

Inflation is a persistent increase in prices, often triggered when demand for goods is greater than the available supply or when unemployment is low and workers can command higher salaries.

EXHIBIT

8-2	Rising prices over the years	
ITEM	**1950**	**2010**
Home	$12,700	$249,500
Car	$2,600	$29,217
Gas	$0.25/gallon	$2.90/gallon
Income	$5,315	$50,000

If you examine the average income, you can see that the dollar went a lot further in 1950 when a new house cost just a little more than twice someone's annual income and a car cost about one month's salary. By 2010, a new house cost at least five times someone's annual income, and a car cost about five times someone's monthly income. Now imagine what might happen to prices over the next 30 years or so while your investments are growing. Will the value of your investments keep up with those price increases? That's a risk.

With **uninsured investments**, such as stocks, bonds, and mutual funds, you face the risk that you might lose money if the price falls and you sell for less than you paid to buy. It's important to remember that stock prices are based solely on peoples' perceptions of the companies that issue the stocks (more about this later when we discuss stocks). There is always a risk associated with investing in a stock that people think is "hot" or a stock that's receiving a lot of hype. You know how quickly the latest fashion and music goes out of style. Consider your stocks like one of these trends; people might be into it now, but the stock might suddenly fall when the company falls out of favor or doesn't live up to its reputation.

now you try it

Take the following quizzes to find out what kind of financial risk taker you are. Use your results to evaluate what kind of investments you could potentially make.

- **Rutgers** Investment Risk Tolerance Quiz:
  www.njaes.rutgers.edu/money/riskquiz/
- **MSN Money Central** How Much Will My Savings Be Worth Calculator:
  www.money.msn.com/saving-money/savings-calculator.aspx
- **CreditCards.com** What's Your Tolerance for Financial Risk:
  www.creditcards.com/credit-card-news/quiz/whats-your-tolerance-for-financial-risk.php

WHAT IS THE STOCK MARKET?

efore we get too deep into talking about stocks, bonds, and mutual funds, it's important to explain the **stock market**. This is where stocks and bonds are bought and sold. The

FINANCIAL FIGURES

LEARNING FROM THE EXPERIENCE OF OTHERS

Robin Wise, *CEO of Junior Achievement-Rocky Mountain, Denver, Colo.*

As president and CEO of Junior Achievement-Rocky Mountain, Robin Wise has a front-row seat to the high school maturation process. "It's just so much fun to watch how light bulbs go on, whether it's a class I teach for of one our programs like Business Week, or interviewing a kid for a potential Junior Achievement scholarship. I know JA has had an impact on their lives."

Through a volunteer network, Junior Achievement provides in-school and after-school programs for students that focus on entrepreneurship, financial literacy, and work readiness.

In the popular JA Stock Market Challenge, students learn about investing and trading in a hands-on simulation of the New York Stock Exchange. "It's fun to see the metamorphosis, even in just a couple of hours," Wise explains. "Kids come in, they're 'too cool for school,' but 45 minutes later after the game has started, they're standing on chairs yelling, whooping. You can see the panic in their eyes because something is happening with one or two of their stocks. It's just a blast."

Other JA offerings include Banks in Action, Capitalism with a Conscience and Be Entrepreneurial. JA Finance Park is an interactive expo that teaches eighth-graders financial planning and serves up challenges such as parenting, health care, and job hunting. Imagine the board game Life, super-sized.

"You've got to understand what it means to be financially literate, understanding the elements that go into not only protecting yourself, but what you can do to build wealth," Wise says. "So often, financial literacy is taught by fear—don't let this happen to you, beware of evil business. That's only a piece of being financially literate. The other piece is knowing how to build your own wealth and how to protect your assets."

stock market is not a physical location like a grocery store, because people can buy and sell investments by phone and over the Internet from anywhere in the world.

However, there are actual **stock exchanges**, real organizations with physical locations, where buyers and sellers get together to trade during certain hours of the day. You may have heard of some of these exchanges: the New York Stock Exchange (NYSE), Tokyo Stock Exchange (TSE), and London Stock Exchange (LSE). Perhaps you have seen movies about the New York Stock Exchange, with images of hordes of people running around, shouting, and making gestures with their hands to indicate what they want to buy or sell. Luckily, you can make investments without ever stepping foot in a stock exchange. You'll learn how later.

Despite the New York Stock Exchange's notoriety, it was not the first stock exchange in the United States. That distinction belongs to the Philadelphia Stock Exchange, which was founded in 1790.[2]

WHAT ARE TYPICAL INVESTMENTS?

he most typical investments that people buy and sell are stocks, bonds, and mutual funds. As a group, these different types of investments are referred to as **securities**.

Stocks

A **stock** is a unit of ownership in a company. When you buy stock in a company you become a **shareholder** and actually own a piece of the company. Companies issue stocks to raise money for things like product research, purchasing or repairing buildings and equipment, or hiring more employees. When you own stock, you share in the company's profits. If the profit goes up, so does the price of the stock and your investment is worth more than you initially paid for it. If the company's profits go down, so does the price of the stock and your investment is worth less than you initially paid for it.

As mentioned earlier, the price of the stock does not necessarily reflect the true value of the company—it merely represents people's perception of the company or its reputation. For example, think about what students say about one another, and how those words affect the reputations of other students—whether they are true or not. Just because a stock's price goes down, it doesn't mean the company is no good. If the company still has its employees, its equipment and buildings, and good products, it's still worth investing in—even if the stock price is low. In fact, if you already own stock in such a company, you might consider buying more while the price is low, so that you could potentially get more for your money.

Securities, noun

A document—historically, a physical certificate but increasingly electronic—showing that one owns a portion of a publicly traded company or is owed a portion of a debt issue. Securities are tradable. At their most basic, securities refer to stocks and bonds, but the term sometimes refers to derivatives such as futures and options.

Bonds

A **bond** is a different type of investment than a stock. Instead of buying ownership in a company, you are lending money in exchange for interest. Here's how it works. Entities, such as corporations, municipalities (cities, counties, and states), or the federal government, issue bonds to raise money. When you buy a bond, you are lending money to an entity for an agreed amount of time, usually called the **life of the bond**. In return, the entity promises to pay a specified amount of interest AND repay the **face value** of the bond (what it's worth) when it's due. Some bonds pay in-

terest throughout their lives, rather than at the very end. You can think of the bond as an IOU that must be paid off, with interest, within a specific amount of time.

Some bonds are issued by municipalities to raise money to build or repair schools, roads, libraries, and other public structures. Others are issued by corporations to buy new equipment or pay for research and marketing. Finally, U.S. Savings Bonds are issued by the federal government to help pay off government debt. These are the safest kind of bonds.

There are two types of U.S. Savings Bonds you can buy:

EE bonds. These are discount bonds. You buy these for half their face value, they accumulate interest over time, and when they come due, they are worth their face value. For example, suppose you pay $500 for a $1,000 EE savings bond that earns 1.5 percent interest a year (on the $500) and comes due in 20 years. This means that over the next 20 years you are guaranteed to receive $15 per year or $300 in interest over the life of the bond. At the end of the 15 years, you can cash in the bond for its face value of $1,000.

I bonds. These are non-discounted bonds. You buy these bonds for their face value. They accumulate interest over time, and when they come due, they are worth more than their face value. Their interest rates are usually higher than those of discounted bonds. For example, suppose you spend $1,000 on a bond that pays 4.5 percent interest annually and matures in 20 years. This means that over the next 15 years you are guaranteed to receive $45 per year or $900 in interest over the life of the bond. At the end of the 20 years, you can cash in the bond for its face value, $1,000.

Figure 8-3 illustrates the difference between discounted bonds (EE) and non-discounted bonds (I).

With bonds, you are not looking for their value to go up, like stocks; instead, you are looking for steady interest over time. Bond prices typically remain more stable than stock prices, so they are considered safer investments than stocks. This is especially true with U.S. Treasury bonds that are backed by U.S. government and municipal bonds that are insured. For example, a family might invest in U.S. Treasury bonds when their children are born and then cash them out to pay for their children's college education.

quickcheck

What is a stock?

What is a shareholder?

What are the two types of U.S. Savings Bonds?

FiNaNCiaL FouL-uPS

LEARNING FROM THE MISTAKES OF OTHERS

Ever since Jacqueline and her mom, Janice, had a "financial talk" she's been worried about her mother aging and not having the means to retire from the hard work she's done her entire life.

At school, Jacqueline learned about setting aside a percentage of her wages in a savings account and she wanted to know if her mom was saving for anything. Janice tries to explain that she's wanted to set up a savings since her business started taking off, but she can't seem to get on top of it. She pays a lot of taxes on her business come tax time, but she doesn't put money away throughout the year to pay them off, so she's constantly on a payment plan with the IRS to pay off back taxes.

Since she works for herself, she's opted to not pay for a personal health insurance plan so doctor's visits come directly from her pocket. She also has never invested in the stock market, has no 401K, or even a life insurance policy.

Janice admits she's concerned about retiring. Her friends are already talking about retirement, how they've paid off their homes, and their next vacation. Janice has no retirement savings, is still renting, and hasn't had a vacation in years. She fears it's too late to start saving and investing, but she really fears Jacqueline never learned the financial skills she needs to not end up in like her.

EXHIBIT

8-3   Two types of U.S. Savings Bonds

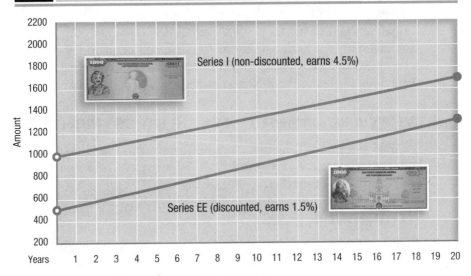

Series I (non-discounted, earns 4.5%)

Series EE (discounted, earns 1.5%)

Amount

Years   1   2   3   4   5   6   7   8   9   10   11   12   13   14   15   16   17   18   19   20

○ Purchase price   ● Face value plus interest

179

Mutual Funds

If you think stocks are too risky, and bonds are too safe, you might try a mutual fund. This is a fund that consists of a wide variety of stocks, bonds, and money market assets. This type of fund is considered **diversified** because it consists of a variety of securities.

A full-time, experienced, and dedicated fund manager researches investments and decides what goes into the fund. As a result, you don't have to pick and choose the stocks. When you buy shares of a mutual fund, you are actually buying shares in lots of different companies. The benefit of a mutual fund is that even if one or two investments in the fund do not do well, as long as others do well, you don't see big losses.

Short-term Investments

You can also invest in the money market accounts and CDs that you learned about in Chapter 7. These are good when you want to tie up your money only for a year or so and want your investment in liquid form. People tend to use these types of investments as a way to save for emergencies or for a particular purchase, such as a vacation, car, or new computer.

Why Diversify?

When we talked about the mutual fund, we mentioned that it was a diversified fund because it contained a variety of securities, not just one stock. As a result, if one stock in the fund does poorly, its losses may by offset by gains in another stock. Remember Hannah's grandmother, Eliza, and the fiasco with Boo.com? Luckily, Eliza had only a small amount of her money invested in Boo.com; her other money was invested in a wide variety of stocks in different industries. So, when Boo.com went bankrupt, Eliza had plenty of other stocks that were doing well and the loss did not hit her finances that hard.

WHAT ARE OTHER TYPES OF INVESTMENTS?

 o round off the discussion of investments, we'll take a look at a variety of investments that you might make outside of the stock market.

401K Plans

Remember when we talked about "painless" saving in Chapter 7 and suggested automatic transfers to your savings account? Here is another

REAL-WORLD MATH

Here is an example of how 401K accounts work. Remember Hannah? Suppose she gets a job as a part-time bagger at her local supermarket when she's 18 years old, making about $883 a month or approximately $8,400 a year before taxes. The company she works for offers a 3 percent 401K contribution option, with employer matching. This raises the contribution to 6 percent.

- Each month, Hannah contributes $26.49 to her 401K account (.03 x $883).
- Her company contributes another $26.49.
- Her total invested is $26.49 + $26.49 = $52.98 per month.

The predicted rate of return for the investment is 8 percent. Hannah works out that if she retires at age 67 and never gets a raise or another job (highly unlikely since she works hard and plans to get better full-time positions as she gets more education and experience), she will have close to $390,000 for retirement!

"painless" and effortless way to save that makes you even more money. A **401K plan** is a retirement plan offered by many companies that allows you to contribute a percentage of your paycheck into a retirement fund, while the company matches that contribution. For example, if you contribute $100 per paycheck, the company contributes another $100, and you end up investing $200 every time you get paid. The 401K fund is handled by an investment management firm that decides what to invest in.

Because the investment is automatically deducted before you even receive your paycheck it's easy to save money because you do not even realize that something is missing.

Don't Forget!

When you leave your job, your 401K money stays with the investment firm that manages the 401K fund. The fund will continue to grow (hopefully) and you will be able to withdraw money when you retire. However,

because the fund is managed by an investment firm, you will not have a say in how the money is invested. Plus, if you change jobs several times, you may end up with a lot of 401K funds hanging around. If you want to consolidate your retirement savings and have some control over where they get invested, consider rolling over the funds from a 401K plan into your own IRA when you leave a job. That way you have the freedom to choose your own investments and choose what kind of IRA you want—a Roth or a traditional IRA—both of which you learned about in Chapter 7.

Real Estate

If you prefer to see and touch your investments, you might consider real estate. As we mentioned in the previous chapter, a home is an investment because it acquires equity the longer you own it, and you can borrow money against that equity. Your home is also an investment because it can increase in value over time and be worth more than you paid for it. Some people purchase rental properties so they can collect rent from the tenants to pay the mortgage on the properties. They hope that the rental properties will eventually increase in value so they can sell them for a profit.

Like the values of stocks, the values of real estate are often based on perceptions, not necessarily on reality or actual value.

For example, in the late 1990s, earthquake damaged ranch-style homes with three bedrooms and two baths in less than 1,200 square feet were selling for more than $500,000 in the Bay Area. But by 2010, the real estate bubble had burst and the same homes were suddenly worth about half that much. The value of real estate can be quite volatile. You cannot predict its future value, so it can be a very risky investment.

Life Insurance

Finally, let's look at life insurance, a different type of investment. It provides a sense of security in the case of death, rather than in the case of retirement. Instead of protecting your retirement funds, it protects your dependents. If you die, your husband or wife and any children you have will receive the full value of the insurance policy to help them deal with the loss, pay for medical expenses, make the house payments, and have something to live on.

In general, most single people don't need life insurance because no one depends on them financially. But there are exceptions. For instance, some single people provide financial support for aging parents or siblings and others may be carrying significant debt that they don't want to pass on to family members who survive them.

If you decide to get insurance, what kind should you purchase? **Term life insurance** is the cheapest type of life insurance. It is considered temporary insurance because it provides coverage for a specific number of years. This period of time is called a **term** and you get to pick how long you want the term to last: 10 years, 20 years, 25 years, etc. You pay a fixed monthly premium that never changes for the duration of the term. At the end of the term, you can terminate the insurance (in which case your dependents are not covered), or you can renew it for another term. However, the payments will now be higher because you are older, and therefore more likely to need life insurance than when you were in your youth.

As you get older, it makes more sense to purchase **whole life insurance**. Whole life insurance is permanent insurance because it lasts for your lifetime. The monthly premiums are higher, but they never change. Plus, as you get older, the premiums become lower than what you would pay if you kept renewing term insurance.

Regardless of what type of insurance you choose, the higher the value of the policy, the higher the monthly premium. As long as you continue to make the payments regularly for term or whole life insurance, your dependents are covered.

Although you think you are too young to be thinking about life insurance, it's good to know what it is. And who knows, you may need it sooner rather than later, depending on your life circumstances. Consider this scenario: Hannah is now in college. While attending a poetry slam at a local coffee house, she meets Luz and they hit it off. Although Luz is only in her late 20s and unmarried, she already has a life insurance policy. Her mother died several years ago and Luz has been taking care of her disabled brother. Luz just took out a life insurance policy because she wants to make sure that if something happens to her, her brother will be taken care of.

now you try it

INVESTIGATE INVESTING

Thinking about so many different investments probably makes your head spin. Here's you chance to take a break and ask yourself a few questions.

1. What kinds of investments do your family members have?

_____

_____

_____

_____

_____

2. If they don't have investments, why not?

_____

_____

3. If they do have investments, how did they choose the investments they have?

_____

_____

_____

4. Does anyone you know have life insurance?

_____

_____

5. If they do not, why?

_____

_____

6. If they do, what type is it and what is the policy worth?

_____

_____

HOW DO YOU RESEARCH INVESTMENTS?

If you did the activities in Chapter 7, you probably have a pretty good sense of how much money you have available to save or invest. Based on the questions raised earlier in the chapter, you should also have an idea of how comfortable you are with risk. Now it's time to research the specific investments you would like to make.

Books

If you enjoy relaxing and reading books at your leisure, here are several books that will help you understand investing and how to make good investment decisions:

- *Generation Earn: The Young Professional's Guide to Spending, Investing, and Giving Back,* by **Kimberly Palmer.** This book helps you understand not only where you should invest your money, but also what kinds of life decisions you can afford, such as what kind of job to get or if you can afford a baby.

- *Piggybanking: Preparing Your Financial Life for Kids and Your Kids for a Financial Life,* by **Jeff D. Opdyke.** This book is for parents (or future parents) who want to raise their children to be comfortable and confident managing the daily finances of life.

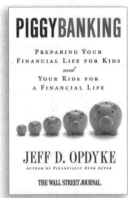

- *The Money Book for the Young, Fabulous and Broke,* by **Suze Orman.** This book is for people in their 20s and 30s who are working hard, struggling to make ends meet, and are buried in credit card debt and student loans. It offers a clear introduction to practical investing and money management techniques that can turn around the most dismal financial situations.

Magazines and Newspapers

If you're someone who likes flipping through magazines and newspapers to find good articles, here are several periodicals with the latest investment tips and trends. All appear in print and online.

- *Forbes.* Contains articles for CEOs and individual investors. Articles include profiles of companies and private investors, as well as helpful statistics. Famous for its lists, such as: 50 Most Powerful Women in Business, 400 Richest Americans, Best Paid Celebrities Under 30.

- *Kiplinger's.* Magazine and newsletter that provides professional advice about personal finance, investing, and retirement. Excellent source of information to help you make financial decisions now and in the future.

- *The Wall Street Journal.* Great source of the latest global and financial news. Written for serious investors and business people. Some of the articles may be overwhelming (and boring) for those just learning about investments. Most famous for its daily, detailed list of stock market quotes.

- *The Economist.* Provides a global perspective on what is going on in terms of world news, politics, economics, and finances. Some of the articles may be a little over your head, but others may improve your understanding of the economy of the whole world, not just the United States.

Websites

If you prefer scanning the Internet, here are several websites with tutorials, forums, and real-time market updates for investors.

- **Investopedia.** Comprehensive investing dictionary with a stock simulator and lots of tutorials for learning about how investing works.
  www.investopedia.com

- **Scottrade.** Commission-free online trading site for stocks, bonds, and mutual funds.
  www.scottrade.com

- **TDAmeritrade.** Commission-free online trading site with educational and research materials available.
  www.tdameritrade.com

- **The Motley Fool.** Amusing site with lots of humor and plenty of tips and instructions for investing wisely.
  www.fool.com

For more financial references and tools, refer to the appendices in the back of the book.

now you try it

OPTIONS FOR INVESTING

1. Use the resources you just read about as a jumping-off point to research what investments you could make.

    _____

    _____

    _____

2. Organize your research in two lists: a) what you can invest today and b) what you can invest in the future.

    Today: _____

    _____

    _____

    Soon: _____

    _____

    _____

Prospectus

The most important part of your research involves studying the prospectus for any investment you are considering buying. The **prospectus** acts much like a job candidate's résumé acts for potential employers. It is legal document that provides relevant information to help investors make decisions about whether or not to purchase shares of the stock, bond, or mutual fund. This relevant information includes:

- Structure and goals of the company or fund
- Terms of purchase
- Amount of load (extra cost for buying or selling shares)
- Investment strategy
- Historical financial statements[4]

The **U.S. Securities and Exchange Commission (SEC)** requires every publicly owned company or mutual fund to file a prospectus and make it available to all potential and existing investors. This is because the primary mission of the SEC is to protect investors. Because stocks and bonds are not guaranteed by the federal government, they can lose value, which can dramatically affect the lives of the people who purchase them. These are often people who depend on those investments to pay for college or retirement. By reading the prospectus, potential investors have a chance to study the company's financial information before deciding to invest.

Exhibit 8-4 shows a few pages from a sample prospectus.

EXHIBIT

8-4   Sample prospectus

Hypothetical Summary Prospectus – Prepared By SEC Staff – For Illustrative Purposes Only

THE XYZ BALANCED FUND   SUMMARY PROSPECTUS
(Class A and Class B Shares)   November 1, 2007

Before you invest, you may want to review the Fund's prospectus, which contains more information about the Fund and its risks. You can find the Fund's prospectus and other information about the Fund, including the statement of additional information and most recent reports to shareholders, online at [Web address]. You can also get this information at no cost by calling 1-800-000-0000 or by sending an e-mail request to [e-mail address]. The Fund's prospectus and statement of additional information, both dated April 27, 2007, and most recent report to shareholders, dated June 30, 2007, are all incorporated by reference into this Summary Prospectus.

Investment Objective: Income and capital growth consistent with reasonable risks.

Fees and Expenses of the Fund: The tables below describe the fees and expenses that you may pay if you buy and hold shares of the Fund. You may qualify for sales charge discounts if you and your family invest, or agree to invest in the future, at least $25,000 in XYZ Funds.

Shareholder Fees (fees paid directly from your investment)	Class A	Class B
Maximum Sales Charge (Load) Imposed on Purchases (as percentage of offering price)	5.75%	None
Maximum Deferred Sales Charge (Load) (as percentage of the lower of original purchase price or sale proceeds)	None	5.00%

Annual Fund Operating Expenses (ongoing expenses that you pay each year as a percentage of the value of your investment)	Class A	Class B
Management Fees	0.66%	0.66%
Distribution (12b-1) Fees	0.00%	0.75%
Service (12b-1) Fees	0.23%	0.23%
Other Expenses	0.28%	0.46%
Total Annual Fund Operating Expenses	1.17%	2.10%

Example
The Example below is intended to help you compare the cost of investing in the Fund with the cost of investing in other mutual funds. The Example assumes that you invest $10,000 in the Fund for the time periods indicated. The Example also assumes that your investment has a 5% return each year and that the Fund's operating expenses remain the same. Although your actual costs may be higher or lower, based on these assumptions your costs would be:

	1 year	3 years	5 years	10 years
Class A (whether or not shares are redeemed)	$687	$925	$1,182	$1,914
Class B (if shares are redeemed)	$713	$958	$1,329	$1,974
Class B (if shares are not redeemed)	$213	$658	$1,129	$1,974

HOW DO YOU PURCHASE SECURITIES?

ou've done all the research, reading, and thinking. You are ready to take action and make some investments. If you are under 18 (or under 21 in some states), you will not be able to open an investment account in your own name, because you are legally not old enough to sign a contract. So you will need help from an adult.

There are several ways to open an investment account and purchase securities.

In Person

To open an account in person, you must visit a broker or investment adviser. These people are typically listed in the phone book. However, before you make any investments, make sure that the broker, investment adviser, or investment firm meets the following criteria:

- **Is licensed or registered.** This is required by federal and state laws. If you do business with an unregistered securities broker or firm that later goes out of business, there may be no way for you to recover your money.

- **Has not had any problems with regulators or complaints from other brokers.** You don't want to make the mistake of sending your money to a con artist, a bad financial professional, or disreputable firm.

How do you find out if the broker, adviser, or firm is licensed, has received any complaints, or has done anything illegal? Here two great sources of information:

- Information concerning brokerage firms and individual brokers is publicly available through **FINRA's Broker Check Program.** This program provides information about brokerage firms and individual brokers, such as the address, legal status, owners and officers, felony charges and convictions, investment-related misdemeanor charges and convictions, courts actions, and more. The contact information for FINRA is as follows:

    Website: www.finra.org/Investors/ToolsCalculators/
    BrokerCheck/index.htm
    Phone: 800-289-9999

- You can also find out information about certain investment adviser firms through the SEC's **Investment Adviser Public Disclosure (IAPD)** program. Search for a firm or adviser to view professional background and conduct, including current registrations, employment history, and disclosures about certain disciplinary events.

Website: www.adviserinfo.sec.gov/%28S%28beelzxfz
uae4zkscxgiwvyjy%29%29/IAPD/Content/IapdMain/
iapd_SiteMap.aspx

When it comes to working with a financial adviser, there is no such thing as asking a dumb question. It's your money at stake. You are paying for the assistance of a financial professional.

Online

You don't have to go to a financial adviser to open an account. You can open the account online and do your own research to decide what to buy and sell. There are more than 100 online brokers to choose from. Most charge you nothing to open an account, but all charge a fee for buying or selling shares. Whenever you buy or sell shares, you are performing a **transaction**.

Some online brokers charge as little as $7 per transaction, others charge a percentage based on the value of what you are buying or selling. For example, suppose an online broker charges a 1 percent transaction fee and you decide to shell 100 shares of a stock worth $10 a share. The total value of the transaction is $1,000 and you have to pay a fee of 1 percent or $10. Often, online brokers charge lower fees as your transaction increases in value.

What's your favorite investment tool for your phone or computer?

LissyLu: I use the Forbes app on my phone. I like it because I get free information from a recognized investment source.   4 minutes ago

Bobo: I like being able to trade from anywhere I am so I use the E*trade Mobile Pro app on my phone.
7 minutes ago

TrumpGold: I've used Kiplinger's "Which Online Tool Is Best for You?" tool to find trusted companies to invest in.   10 minutes ago

THE SOCIAL MEDIA FEED

Online trading can save you time and money, but it forces you to do all the research and make all the decisions about your investments. You may be able to make a trade with a click of the mouse, but making wise investment decisions takes time. Before you trade online, take time to study your investments and their performance so you can make an educated decision about whether to buy or sell.

Investment Clubs

One other way to invest is through investment clubs. An **investment club** is a group of people who research and pool their money to make investments. Of course, the club will probably do its investing online. The benefit of the club is that you do not have to pay a financial advisor to help you, nor do you have to do your investing alone. Instead, members of the club study different investments and share what they learn with each other. The club decides what to buy or sell based on a majority vote by the members. By joining an investment club you meet other investors, gain an education, and actively participate in investment decisions.

LET'S REVIEW

This chapter presented a lot of financial information and many new terms. But the overall message is simple: Investing is about making your money work for you over time; it's not about getting rich quick. If you start thinking about and researching investments while you are still in high school, you will be better prepared to invest early so your money has time to grow. You will also feel more comfortable making your own financial decisions, rather than handing those decisions over to someone else.

What Did You Learn?

1. There are no guarantees in investing, which is why you need to evaluate risk beforehand.
2. Investing is something anyone can do.
3. Different kinds of investments have different levels of risk.
4. There are many different resources to help you understand and choose your investments.
5. You can invest in person or online.

New Terms

- Investment
- Risk
- Stocks
- Bonds

- Mutual Funds
- Money Market Funds
- CDs
- 401K Plans

- Life Insurance
- Real Estate
- Prospectus
- SEC

END-OF-CHAPTER ACTIVITIES

H ere's your chance to put your pen to paper, as well as discuss what you've learned with others. Doing activities and talking about them are great ways to make sure you really do understand the concepts you've read about.

Remember the Basics

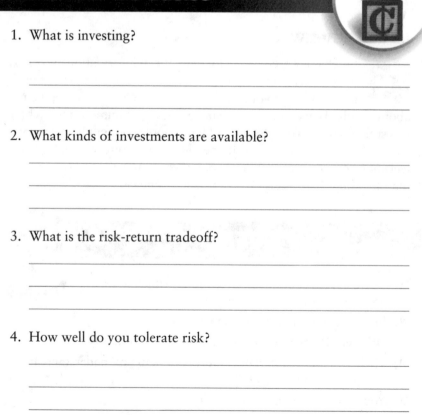

1. What is investing?

2. What kinds of investments are available?

3. What is the risk-return tradeoff?

4. How well do you tolerate risk?

5. What kinds of investments should you invest in, considering your comfort level with risk?

_____

_____

_____

_____

_____

6. What is the difference between stocks and bonds?

_____

_____

_____

7. Why is diversification a good idea?

_____

_____

_____

8. What is the difference between a discounted and non-discounted bond?

_____

_____

_____

9. Why is the SEC important to investors?

_____

_____

_____

10. What is the benefit of having a 401K? How is it different than other savings plans?

_____

_____

_____

Put Math into Practice

Hannah is thinking about investing in some stocks for her future. She asks her grandmother for advice. Eliza suggests that Hannah invest in a mutual fund rather than an individual stock so that her investment is more diversified, and safer. Together they research promising mutual funds. Hannah finds a green energy fund that has been doing well for the past five years. It invests in companies associated with wind energy, solar energy, and biofuel. The energy fund requires an initial investment of $5,000 and earns an average of 7 percent a year.

1. Assume the energy fund is currently trading at $10 a share.

    a. How many shares will $5,000 buy?

    _____

    b. If the fund performs as expected, how much money will Hannah earn at the end of the year on her $5,000 investment? (use the simple interest calculation you learned in Chapter 7)

    _____

    Answer: $5,000 / $10 per share = 500 shares

    $5,000 x .07 = **$350 earned**

2. Suppose the value of the fund increases to $20 a share several years after Hannah buys it.

    a. Assuming Hannah still owns the same number of shares, what will be the value of her investment?

    _____

    b. Now how much interest will her investment earn in one year? (use the simple interest calculation you learned in Chapter 7)

    _____

    Answer: 500 shares x $20 per share = $10,000

    $10,000 x .07 = **$700 earned**

Work With a Team

Start your own investment club where you research and track investments without actually buying or selling.

NOTE: If you have any questions about starting an investment club, visit Better Investing Community, a non-profit, volunteer-based educational group dedicated to providing "sound investment information, education and support that helps create successful lifetime investors."[5]

- Visit: **www.betterinvesting.org/public/default.htm**
- Go to the **Getting Started?** link to find out how to start an investment club, the things you need to look out for, and who to contact if you have questions.

1. Discuss the following criteria with the members of your group:
   - **Risk tolerance.** Are you comfortable taking risks for potentially higher returns or do you prefer safer investments?
   - **Diversity.** Do you want to purchase individual stocks and bonds or mutual funds? What industries are you interested in?
   - **Investment period.** Do you plan to hold on to your investments less than a year, a year, more than a year?

2. Research companies that fit your group's criteria. This may involve reading articles in newspapers, magazines, or online, or ordering a prospectus from each company.
   - Decide how much money the group could afford to invest if it were using real money.
   - Decide which investments to purchase and how many shares to buy.

3. For the next two months, track the performance of your investments each week to note whether you are losing or gaining. Notice how prices fluctuate.

4. At the end of the two months, discuss the performance of your investments and decide whether to stick with the same investments or make some changes.

5. On page 179, what is one thing Jacqueline could take away from her mom's financial regrets?

_____

_____

6. What can Janice start doing today to take back control of her finances? Is it important that she get financial control? Explain.

_____

_____

_____

_____

_____

For more activities, assessments, and examples, visit www.lifebound.com.

Dummies.com . . . Making Everything Easier

Go to www.dummies.com and watch the tutorial video "How to Read Stock Tables."

What do the following investment terms mean?

52-week high

52-week low

Stock symbol

Dividends

Volume

Yield

P/E ratio

Closing price

Net change

Financial Planning in High School

"*The importance of money flows from it being a link between the present and the future.*"

JOHN MAYNARD KEYNES, ECONOMIST

Questions you will answer. . . .

1. How can you start saving early with part-time jobs and bank accounts?
2. How do you set short-term, medium-term, and long-term goals?
3. How do you research colleges and their costs?
4. What types of financial aid are available for college students?
5. How do you find and apply for financial aid?
6. What is work study?

Test your financial skills with the Dollars & Sense chapter assessment at www.lifebound.com.

Meet Andrew

Andrew lives on the coast and has always loved the beach and the ocean. No wonder he wants to become a marine biologist. He knows he'll have to get a degree to become a marine biologist, so he's currently looking at different colleges that he might want to attend when he graduates. He just started his junior year in high school, so he feels he has time to find out what kind of colleges are out there that offer a degree in marine biology.

Andrew does have some money put aside for college from his part-time job, as well as savings bonds his aunt has given him for his birthday every year. But he has no idea how much different colleges cost, or what his parents can afford.

That's why he's doing the research early and figuring out a plan. He knows that if he picks the right school, saves his money, and gets all the financial aid he can, he should be able to go to college without "breaking the bank."

LIVE AND LEARN

Like Andrew, many teenagers have a general idea of what they want to do after graduating from high school. But even general ideas require some funding, whether they involve going to college, backpacking through South America, or buying a new car. That's why it's important to start saving and investing for your future while you're still in high school.

HOW DO YOU START SAVING EARLY?

It's never too early to start saving for your future. In chapters 1 through 8, you learned how to wisely spend, save, and manage your money. With your understanding of budgets, you can see how saving a portion of your income means having money for emergencies and the future. And with your understanding of interest and investments, you will realize that a little bit of money can grow to a lot of money if you just give it time. But what can you specifically do in high school to ensure that you will have money for college and beyond? Let's explore some useful strategies.

Get a Part-time Job

A part-time job that does not interfere with your schoolwork can help you earn money for day-to-day needs, as well as for the future. A part-time job is generally any type of work you do that takes up less than 20 hours per week. This could be working for a company, for people you know, or for your family. Exhibit 9-1 lists some common part-time jobs for teenagers.

Thinking about loading up on work hours in high school to get ready for college? You might want to think again. A study involving 1,800 middle-class teens in grades 10 and 11 found students who work more than 20 hours a week during the school year are more likely to have academic and behavior problems than those who work less.

IT'S A FACT! GUARANTEED

EXHIBIT
9-1 Typical teenage part-time jobs

JOB	DESCRIPTION
Fast-food worker	Prepare food, serve food, run cash register, clean up
Retail clerk	Run cash register, help customers, stock shelves
Pet sitter	Feed, water, groom, and clean up after pets
Office worker	File, enter data, and answer phones
Gardener	Plant flowers and bushes, water them, and trim them
Babysitter	Care for small children (may include food preparation and trips)
House cleaner	Do weekly cleaning such as vacuuming, floor washing, bathrooms, dusting, and laundry
Errand runner	Shop for others or take them wherever they need to go
Grocery clerk	Stock shelves, bag groceries
Recreation worker	Teach swimming, supervise children at playgrounds, and teach arts and crafts
Lawn mower	Mow and trim lawns

With a part-time job, you can pay for little things like food, special clothes, outings, or games. However, if you spend all your part-time earnings on eating out, cell phone bills, gasoline, and CDs, there won't be anything left to help you later when you need that money in college. That's why you should regularly put aside a percentage of those earnings for college or other investments.

If you are concerned that a part-time job will interfere with your studies in high school, take advantage of the summer and work as much as you can. When you work over 40 hours a week at a job that allows overtime, your employer must pay you time-and-a-half for any hours over 40. Your employer might also offer overtime wages if you have to work on a national holiday. The more overtime you work during the summer, the faster your savings will grow, and the fewer hours you will have to work during the school year.

Open a Bank Account

No matter how few hours or how many hours you work during high school, you need a place to store that money. Sure, you could put it in a jar or hide it under your mattress, but then it would never earn any interest.

Choose the Right Bank

Choosing the right bank is an important part of saving the money you earn. Here are some things to consider:

1. If you plan to be making your own deposits, choose a bank that is near your home or school. The more convenient the better. If you can easily walk or bike to the bank, you're more likely to make those deposits. After all, if it takes 30 minutes to drive across town to make a deposit, you just might not take the time to do so.

2. If your parents, grandparents, or guardians will be making the deposits, consider choosing their current bank so they can conveniently make the transactions. Or you might consider a national bank that has locations near them and near you.

3. Make sure the bank's Automated Teller Machines (ATMs) are located near your home or school. When you use the bank's ATMs, there is no transaction fee. When you use "foreign" ATMs not owned by your bank at restaurants, stores, or gas stations, you are typically charged a service fee. These fees add up if you use ATMs a lot.

4. Visit several banks and credit unions and talk to a representative about the different financial products they offer. These products

typically include checking accounts, savings accounts, online accounts with bill-pay options, credit cards, and student loans. Find out the fees associated with those products.

To keep your banking fees low, you might consider choosing a bank that lets you do all your banking online. This means you can log in and check your balance anytime, receive online bank statements, and use ATMs to deposit and withdraw cash. However, a few banks with "no-fee" online banking may charge you when you walk into the bank to perform a transaction in person. Find out this information ahead of time.

According to bankrate.com, in 2007 consumers paid more than $4 billion in ATM fees.[2]

If you still can't decide which bank to use and which financial products are best for you, ask your parents, siblings, or friends where they bank, and what they like or don't like about the bank.

Select a financial institution that has the products you need, not necessarily the institution with the most products. For example, Andrew visits several financial institutions in his city. He decides to go with a credit union because it is an easy biking distance from school, has an ATM machine in its outside lobby that is available 24/7, and offers free online checking and savings accounts with a $25 minimum balance to maintain. Andrew likes the idea of being able to log on and see his account balance anytime he wants to, and he likes the idea of not paying a monthly fee for the account. He's also glad to find out that even if he signs up for online banking, the credit union will not charge him if he comes into the bank to make the deposits in person.

REAL-WORLD MATH

Suppose you use an ATM outside your bank's network because it happens to be close to your school. Unfortunately, the ATM's owner charges you a $1.50 service fee each time you use the ATM, and your bank charges you an additional $1.50. This means you get charged $3 every time you use the ATM, and you use it at least four times a month. What will these fees add up to over the years?

- $3 fee per transaction x 4 times a month = $12 a month in service fees
- $12 per month x 12 months = $144 in ATM fees per year
- $144 per year x 4 years = **$576** in fees during your four years of high school

Just think what would have happened if you had selected a bank with ATM branches close to your home or school, and only used its ATMs. You could have put those fees in a savings account or investment. At the end of four years of high school, you would have saved at least $576, and that does not include interest!

Open the Right Account

When you're ready to open an account, call the bank to find out if you have to make an appointment with a personal banker ahead of time, or if you can simply drop by. Then collect the information the bank will need. This usually includes the following:

- Full name and birth date
- Driver's license
- Social Security number
- Passport (optional)

Types of Bank Accounts

When you visit the bank, a personal banker will probably ask you what type of account you want to open. You can open one account or multiple accounts, depending on your needs. The most common accounts are checking, savings, and money market, shown in Exhibit 9-2.

EXHIBIT

9-2   Different types of bank accounts

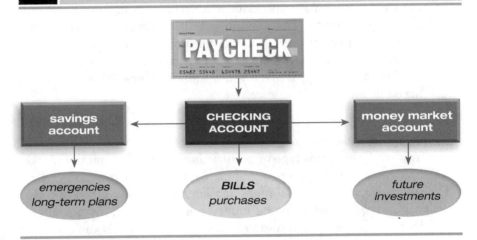

Checking account. This is an account where you deposit money regularly and then withdraw it as you need it.

You will typically deposit your paycheck into a checking account and then write checks or use a debit card to pay for purchases. You can also withdraw cash from the account using an ATM.

With online banking, the technology allows you to get money directly deposited into your checking account and deducted for automatic payments. Employers who offer automatic deposit directly deposit your check in your checking account so you don't have to. A lot of companies now offer automatic payments for things like car insurance, phone bills, Internet, or donations, which allows you to make your payment on time every month without you ever writing a check.

Checking accounts rarely pay interest on what you put in them, and if they do, the rate is generally the same as what savings accounts pay. The advantage of a checking account is that you can take money out of it anytime. The disadvantage is that you usually don't earn any interest. Plus, some banks require a minimum account balance, and if your account drops beneath that amount, you have to pay a fee.

Savings account. This is an account where you typically deposit money, but do not make many withdrawals. The purpose of the account is to accumulate money and interest for the future. Savings accounts usually pay interest between 1 percent and 3 percent, but the interest rate does fluctuate according to economic conditions.

The advantage of a savings account is that it allows you to put money aside in a separate account where you are not likely to withdraw the money. You may decide to keep only enough money in your checking account to cover monthly bills and regular expenses, and then have a fixed amount of money automatically transferred to your savings account. This is a great way to accumulate savings.

The disadvantage is that if you withdraw money on a regular basis, the bank will charge you a fee.

Money market checking account. This is an account that you set up at the bank, just like a checking account, but it earns more interest. You read about this type of account in Chapter 7. A money market account is a great place to accumulate funds so that you can purchase stocks, bonds, or mutual funds at a later date. The advantage is that you earn more interest on the money you deposit. The disadvantage is that federal regulations restrict how many withdrawals you can make from a money market checking account.

In Andrew's case, he decides he needs a checking account where he can deposit money from his part-time job with the Recreation Department and withdraw money for expenses. He realizes that he needs to save money for college and beyond. True, he already has the U.S. Savings Bonds that his aunt has been giving him on his birthdays; they're in his desk drawer at home. However, Andrew does some research and decides that saving money in a money market account would be a better idea.

Money Market Account, noun

An account you set up at the bank, like a checking account, but that earns interest.

He and his mother visit the local credit union so Andrew can set up two accounts: a checking and money market account. Andrew asks the personal banker to set up the checking account so that the Recreation Department can automatically deposit his paycheck each month, and so that $100 is automatically transferred to his money market account at the same time. That way the $100 will not be available for him to spend when he's tempted by all those ads on television. Instead, it will be sitting in the money market account, earning good interest. When he graduates from high school, he hopes to have some money set aside for college expenses.

HOW DO YOU SET GOALS?

Andrew has a goal of going to college and saving up some money to help him reach his goal of financing college. What are your goals? Goals are an important part of your life, whether or not they involve money. A **goal** is something you work toward, a result you want to achieve. Goals help you focus your attention and plan for the future. They also provide something against which you can measure your achievements and see how you are doing.

There are three types of goals, depending on your time frame: short-term, medium-term, and long-term. It's always a good idea to start with the long-term goals because they may end up defining the medium-term and short-term goals required to achieve them.

- **Long-term.** These are goals you hope to achieve in at least five years down the road, or in the distant future. These goals might include graduating from college, getting married, buying a house, or eventually retiring.

- **Medium-term.** These are goals you hope to achieve within one to five years. These goals might include getting a part-time job, graduating from high school and going to college, or buying a car. Medium-term goals are often the stepping stones to accomplishing long-term goals.

- **Short-term.** These are goals that you hope to achieve in the near future—the next day, week, month, or year. For example, you may have a goal of finishing a history project by the end of the week, fixing your car's broken windshield, or trying out for the school musical.

Many of your goals will have financial components because they take money to achieve. Let's return to Andrew and look at some of the goals he wrote down in Exhibit 9-3.

EXHIBIT

9-3   Andrew's goals

My short-term goals

1. Pass Spanish test on Thursday.

2. Clean out car this weekend.

3. Get present for Hannah's birthday on Friday.

My medium term-goals

1. Graduate from high school.

2. Get my windshield fixed.

3. Go to college.

My long term goals

1. Graduate from college.

2. Buy a new car.

3. Travel to Australia.

Short-term goals 1 to 3 all have financial components. Andrew puts his change in a jar so he can pay for a Spanish tutor, the trip to the car wash, and a gift certificate for Hannah's birthday.

Medium-term goals 2 and 3 have financial components. To achieve them, Andrew sets up an automatic transfer from his checking account to his saving account. Every two weeks when he gets paid, the bank transfers $50 into his savings account.

Long-term goals 1 to 3 all have financial components. Andrew will have to get a part-time job and financial assistance to pay for college, as well as save money for a car and a trip to Australia.

now you try it

1. Write down three to five short-term life goals and include any financial goals that might need to accompany them.

   _____

   _____

   _____

   _____

   _____

2. Write down three to five medium-term goals and include any financial goals that might need to accompany them.

   _____

   _____

   _____

   _____

   _____

3. Write down three to five long-term goals and include any financial goals that might need to accompany them.

   _____

   _____

   _____

   _____

   _____

HOW DO YOU RESEARCH COLLEGE COSTS?

I f one of your goals is to attend college or some type of training school after high school, it's never too early to start exploring colleges and their costs.

Since a college education can be expensive, it's important to do the necessary research to find the right college at the right cost. It's also important to involve your family in the research so they can have some say in the decision, since they will probably be helping you with finances.

What Kind of School Do You Want to Attend?

Your research typically starts by identifying the type of school you might like to attend. This involves asking yourself a number of questions to help narrow the number of schools you will have to research. These questions appear in Exhibit 9-4.

By answering these questions honestly, you define the criteria for your college search.

EXHIBIT

9-4   Questions to ask yourself about schools

THINK ABOUT WHAT YOU WANT IN A SCHOOL ...

1. Do you prefer a large school or a small school? A school nearby or a school far away?

2. If you want to go away to school, do you have an idea of the region where you would like to live (coast vs. inland, mountains vs. flat lands)? Do you have a preference about the climate of the region where you will be living (four seasons vs. mild all year)?

3. Would you prefer a co-ed college or a men-only or women-only college?

4. Do you have an idea of what you would like to study, or are you interested in a general, liberal arts education?

5. Do you want to get a credential for a specific vocation or get a degree?

6. Do you want to go to a four-year college (private or public), a community college, or a vocational school?

In a survey, 86 percent of college graduates said that college was a good investment for them.[3]

What Is on Your List of Choices?

Next, you can move on to finding colleges that fit your criteria. This typically occurs by talking with your school counselor, visiting the library, and checking out college websites. It also involves sending away for college catalogues.

EXHIBIT

9-5   Andrew's college research

COLLEGES	YEARS FOR DEGREE	TUITION COST	ROOM AND BOARD COST	TYPES OF FINANCIAL ASSISTANCE
University of California at Berkeley	4	$11,300/yr.	$13,000/yr.	Parent loans, work study, savings, state education grants
California State University at Monterey Bay	4	$5,131/yr.	$10,353/yr.	Parent loans, work study, scholarships, savings, state education grants
San Diego Mesa College	2	$624/yr.	$7,800/yr.	Parent loans, work study, savings, state education grants
University of Hawaii at Manoa	4	$23,932/yr.	$9,410/yr.	Parent loans, work study, savings, scholarships
University of Oregon at Eugene	4	$5,544/yr.	$10,333/yr.	Parent loans, work study, savings, scholarships

- Organize your findings in a chart that you can share with your family.
- List your choices from least expensive to most expensive.
- Include the school name, years necessary to get a degree or certificate, tuition cost, room and board, and whether or not financial aid is offered. **NOTE:** We will talk about financial aid later in this chapter.

Andrew finished his research and came up with the chart of information shown in Exhibit 9-5.

What Are the Pros and Cons?

Once you have your information ready, sit down with your parents and share what you have learned. Together you can discuss the pros and cons of each school. Your parents may have some insights that you don't have. They may even have done some research on their own and you

EXHIBIT

9-6   Pros and cons list

COLLEGE	PROS	CONS
UC Berkeley	Prestigious school, good biology program, within commuting distance for visiting friends and family	Expensive, housing is hard to find
CSU at Monterey Bay	Good biology program, scholarships are available, within commuting distance for visiting friends and family	Expensive
San Diego Mesa College	Could live at home, save money, see friends and family	Biology program is not very prestigious
University of Hawaii	Excellent biology program with a work-at-sea program	Could come home only in the summer, expensive with out-of-state tuition, housing is hard to find
University of Oregon	Excellent biology program with a work-at-sea program, could come home for holidays and summer break	Expensive with out-of-state tuition, housing is hard to find

can compare notes. Most importantly, you can use the time to discuss finances with your parents and find out what they can and cannot afford, so you know whether you will have to investigate financial aid.

Exhibit 9-6 identifies the pros and cons list that Andrew and his family drew up after examining Andrew's information and discussing each school.

After talking with his parents, Andrew sees he could save money by first attending community college for two years and then transferring to California State University at Monterey Bay. When he examines room and board estimates, he sees that living at home is the least expensive choice.

His parents know that if he goes to community college for two years and lives at home, he will save money. But they also know that they are planning to sell their house and move to a smaller condo. So they agree to help Andrew pay for living on campus for four years at California State University.

FINANCIAL FIGURES

LEARNING FROM THE EXPERIENCE OF OTHERS

Anya Kamenetz, *Fast Company Magazine staff writer, Brooklyn, N.Y.*

"Think outside the box." It's 21st century advice that fits for more than fast food. Fast Company Magazine staff writer Anya Kamenetz urges young adults to take creative approaches to investing for their financial futures, from non-traditional college options to how they take on the stock market.

Kamenetz, author of *Generation Debt* and *DIY U: Edupunks, Edupreneurs and the Coming Transformation of Higher Education*, says the typical college graduate faces $24,000 in loan repayments. "A good rule of thumb is not to borrow more than you expect to earn in your first year after graduation," Kamenetz says.

She stresses that students need to be proactive and think in non-traditional ways. "What I hear all the time is anxiety of how college costs connect to the real world opportunities," Kamenetz says. "With the Internet and technologies, there's so much more options for students to create their own relevant learning experiences, whether internships or online networks, blogging networks, sites like Twitter, to connect to the real world. That's a key strategy for success, because you're never going to learn everything in the classroom."

In the Yahoo! Finance online article "Don't Wait to Invest in Your Future," Kamenetz stresses the importance of contributing to employer-sponsored retirement accounts, knowing the ins and outs of IRAs, and getting into the stock market early. Life-cycle funds, index funds, and international funds are good options for young investors.

Kamenetz recommends a handful of online tools and blogs for managing and learning about finances, including mint.com, *The Simple Dollar* and *I Will Teach You To Be Rich*. She also has some smart credit card advice. "You don't need more than one credit card when you are starting out," Kamenetz says. "Reserve it for emergencies. Start with just one category or purchases, like plane tickets home or monthly gas bills. It's easy to charge it and pay it off each month. That goes toward building the kind of credit record that will serve you well in the future."

WHAT IS FINANCIAL AID?

Once you and your family come up with a school you can all agree on, it's important to identify how much money you can contribute to school expenses, how much your parents can contribute, and how much money will have to come from other sources, such as scholarships, grants, or loans.

According to a survey conducted in 2007 by the student-loan provider Sallie Mae, a college education is worth the cost, although only 42 percent believed college was affordable.[4]

Scholarships

A **scholarship** is a form of financial assistance provided by individuals, organizations, schools, and state or federal government. There are four different kinds of scholarships.

- **Need-based.** These are provided to students whose family income is less than a certain amount so their parents cannot afford to send them to college without financial assistance. For example, the Sallie Mae Fund provides scholarships to low-income, minority students around the United States who might otherwise be unable to attend college.

- **Merit-based.** These are provided to students whose grades and academic achievements are exceptional. For example, a private college might provide a scholarship for students who have maintained a 4.0 grade-point average throughout high school and have consistently worked on volunteer projects in the community to benefit those in need.

- **Field of study.** These are provided to students pursuing specific degrees in certain disciplines. For example, a pediatrician who graduated from a particular college might in turn provide a scholarship to a student who is considering a medical degree at that school and also wants to work with children.

- **General.** These are scholarships that don't seem to fall into the other three categories. For example, a business owner who came from an uneducated family and worked hard to create a successful business may provide a scholarship to a student who is the first person in his or her family to attend college.

EXHIBIT

9-7   Different types of financial aid

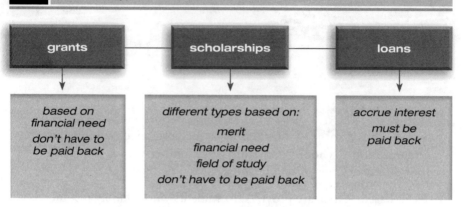

NOTE: For more details about different types of scholarships, grants, and loans,
please see **Appendix B, College Finances**

Grants

A **grant** is a form of financial aid that does not need to be repaid.
Grants are need-based awards to students who might not otherwise
be able to go to college. There are two typical kinds of grants.

- **Foundation grants.** These are offered by private or public foundations for students who meet very specific guidelines, usually associated with the type of work the foundation does. These grants are typically very restrictive about what students can or cannot use the money for.

- **Government education grants.** These are offered by the federal government to help students pay for college or training. They are typically based on financial need only. The most common type of federal grant is the Pell Grant, awarded to undergraduate students in financial need.

Grant, noun

A needs-based financial aid reward that does not need to be repaid.

Loans

A **loan** is a form of financial aid that must be repaid. **Federal loans** are
offered by the government and **private loans** are offered by individuals
and organizations. Federal loans typically have lower interest rates than
private loans, longer repayment periods, and easier credit requirements.

Don't think you qualify for any scholarships? Think again. You can get a scholarship for being a male over 6'2" or a female over 5'10", being left-handed, being of the name Van Valkenburg, or for being a vegetarian, among many other bizarre qualifications.

Both federal and private loans may be subsidized or unsubsidized.

- **Subsidized** means the loan does not accrue interest while you are still in school. You usually do not have to start making payments until six months after you graduate. These types of loans often have a limit on how much you can borrow. The benefit of subsidized loans is that you have less money to pay off when you graduate.

- **Unsubsidized** means that interest starts accruing from the time you take out the loan. There is generally no limit on how much you can borrow, and you do not have to start making payments until you graduate. However, if you take out a very large loan and interest has been accruing from the day you got the loan when you started college, you will be paying off a very large amount of money.

quickcheck ✔

What's the difference between a loan and a grant?

What are the different types of scholarships available to students?

What's financial aid?

HOW DO YOU FIND AND APPLY FOR FINANCIAL AID?

Think about Andrew and his family. Even though his parents agreed to help him pay for living on campus at California State University at Monterey Bay, they aren't sure they can cover all of his tuition. Andrew does have money set aside from his part-time job, as well as the savings bonds from his aunt. But it's still not enough. However, because Andrew has good grades, he is probably eligible for several merit scholarships. All he needs to do is find out what's available.

Many students aren't as lucky as Andrew and must foot the bill for college all by themselves. Fortunately, paying for college completely

FiNaNCiaL FouL-UPS

LEARNING FROM THE MISTAKES OF OTHERS

D.J. wasn't excited about going to college until after he graduated from high school. Even though he wouldn't go back to high school if someone paid him, he wished he had something to do with his time besides working a crummy, minimum-wage job. And not only that, most of his friends were going to the state college in his hometown and he felt like he was missing out.

He decided to apply, and a few weeks later, he was opening his acceptance letter. D.J. couldn't wait to register for classes, see his friends again, and get an education that could release him from behind the concession counter at the movie theater.

But as the registration process progressed and D.J. started realizing the cost of a college education, he regretted not preparing for the possibility of going to college. His grades were average, which limited any merit-based scholarships; his parents made too much money to get a large sum from federal grants, even though his parents weren't contributing to his college expenses; and D.J. hadn't set any money aside to pay for college out-of-pocket.

He went to the financial aid office and they suggested he take out the maximum amount he was offered for loans. He saw it as his only option. He waited for the paperwork in the mail. The school was offering him $5,000 in subsidized and unsubsidized loans, but he didn't really know what either of them meant. However, the school was offering him money and he had no other choices. He checked both boxes, accepting all the loans offered, and sent the paperwork back to the school. Within moments D.J. was $5,000 in debt without any idea about what he signed up for, how he was going to finance the following three-plus years of college, or how he was going to pay it all back.

on your own teaches you to be 100 percent responsible and show a prospective employer that you can make your goals a reality.

That's what this section is all about—finding the financial aid you need and applying for it.

Fill out the FAFSA

If you decide to apply for a federal grant or loan, the U.S. Department of Education requires that you and your family fill out the Free Application for Federal Student Aid (FAFSA) to determine the expected family contribution. This form looks at your family's income, assets, and other

214

EXHIBIT

9-8   The FAFSA application is the basis of awarding all need-based grants or loans from the federal government

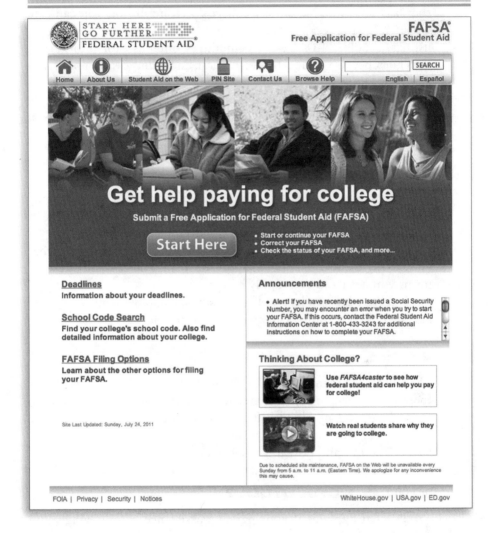

family information, and determines how much money in federal grants and loans you can receive.[6]

The **FAFSA** is an online application. Your guidance counselor or teacher can help you and your parents fill it out. Once you get a federal grant or loan, your family must continue to fill out the FAFSA every year that you are in college to keep track of all your financial details.

FAFSA, noun

An acronym that stands for Free Application for Federal Student Aid. You are required to fill out the FAFSA if you decide to apply for federal grants or loans to determine your family contribution.

Apply for a Scholarship

Every college or university has a scholarship program. Most scholarship lists are available on any college's website. If not, you can call, e-mail, or go to the college financial aid office to ask about scholarship listings. Scholarship selection committees often ask for information that goes beyond financial information, including essays about you and your family.

There are more than a million different scholarships available for students around the world and there's one out there that's just right for you.

Apply for a Grant

The federal government has a wide array of grants that you can apply for. A good place to start looking for them is on the U.S. Department of Education website: **www.ed.gov/fund/grants-apply.html**

There you can find out what type of grants are available, what you are eligible for, and how to apply for them. You can find out what forms you need and even apply online.

NOTE: Many college websites also list available grants and have financial aid offices that can answer your questions.

Apply for a Loan

The federal government also has a variety of low-interest direct loans for students. You and your parents can explore loan information on the Federal Student Aid website: **www.direct.ed.gov/**.

The site will explain the different types of loans, interest rates, payback terms, and how to get started applying for them.

WHAT IS WORK STUDY?

What happens if your parents' assistance, your savings, and financial assistance from a scholarship, grant, or loan still cannot cover all your college costs? There is always work study. **Work study** is a financial aid program that allows undergraduate and graduate students to work on campus or with approved off-campus employers to earn money to pay college expenses. Work-study programs are usually funded by the federal or state government, often with matching funds from the college.[7]

How to Apply

To apply for work study, you must fill out your FAFSA and request work study. To determine eligibility, most schools look at cost of attendance and then subtract your expected assistance (family contribution plus free assistance, like grants and scholarships). The remaining amount is the amount you are eligible for through work study.

Type of Work and Pay

Work study is not a grant because you have to work to earn it, and it is not a loan because you don't have to pay it back. Being awarded work study means you are eligible for part-time jobs with flexible hours that are usually related to your field of study or provide community service of some type. These jobs are typically listed at the college career center. For example, you might end up shelving books at the library, dishing out food at the cafeteria, running the cash register at the bookstore, or working in a lab.

Work Study, noun

A financial aid program that allows students to work on or off campus to earn money for their college expenses.

Your work-study earnings will vary, depending on the type of job you get and the region of the country where you live. The nice thing about work-study earnings is this: You can use the money for any type of expenses you want (not just tuition or housing) and your earnings are not used to determine your financial need when filing the FAFSA.

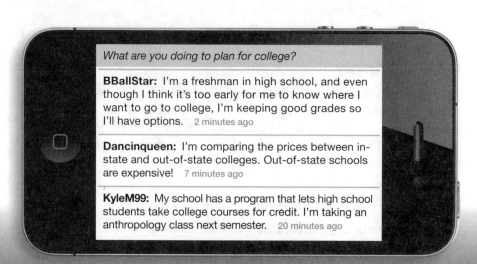

What are you doing to plan for college?

BBallStar: I'm a freshman in high school, and even though I think it's too early for me to know where I want to go to college, I'm keeping good grades so I'll have options.   2 minutes ago

Dancinqueen: I'm comparing the prices between in-state and out-of-state colleges. Out-of-state schools are expensive!   7 minutes ago

KyleM99: My school has a program that lets high school students take college courses for credit. I'm taking an anthropology class next semester.   20 minutes ago

LET'S REVIEW

Learning to use checking and savings accounts, as well as coming up with money for college, takes some pre-planning. So does researching colleges and finding financial aid. Being able to research and evaluate your choices, whether they are types of bank accounts or colleges, is critical to your success.

What Did You Learn?

1. Finding a bank or credit union and opening an account is easy if you understand what you need from the financial institution.
2. Goals help you prepare for the future, focus your efforts, and gauge your progress.
3. Researching colleges and weighing the pros and cons can help you choose the best option for you.
4. Financial aid is available from private and government sources in the forms of scholarships, grants, and loans.
5. Unlike scholarships and grants, loans must be paid back, and they often have different amounts of interest depending on whether they are subsidized or unsubsidized.
6. Work study is a form of financial aid where you earn money that you don't have to pay back. While the earnings are taxed, they are not considered part of your income when applying for aid.

New Terms

- Checking Account
- Short-term Saving
- Money Market Checking Account
- Medium-term Goals
- Scholarship
- Loan (Subsidized and Unsubsidized)
- Work Study

- Savings Account
- Long-term Saving
- Short-term Goals
- Long-term Goals
- Grant
- FAFSA

END-OF-CHAPTER ACTIVITIES

Here's your chance to put pen to paper, as well as discuss what you've learned with others. Doing activities and talking about them are great ways to make sure you really do understand the concepts you've read about.

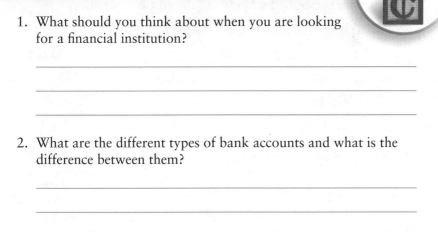

Remember the Basics

1. What should you think about when you are looking for a financial institution?

_____

_____

_____

2. What are the different types of bank accounts and what is the difference between them?

_____

_____

_____

_____

_____

_____

3. How do you open a checking or savings account?

_____

_____

_____

4. What are the different types of goals you can set based on time frame?

_____

_____

_____

5. What factors should you look at when choosing a college or university?

_____

_____

_____

_____

6. What are some good ways to cut the cost of college?

_____

_____

_____

_____

7. What is the difference between scholarships, grants, and loans?

_____

_____

_____

8. What makes a loan different from both scholarships and grants?

_____

_____

9. How can you find out about financial assistance?

_____

_____

_____

10. What is work study and why should you apply?

_____

_____

Put Math into Practice

1. **Scenario:** Suppose you decide to go to a community college for your first two years before attending Harvard. How much can you save by going to community college for two years and then Harvard for two, instead of going to Harvard for all four years?

   - Harvard costs: $55,000 per year
   - Community college costs: $624 per year

   Answer:
   Four years at Harvard: $55,000 x 4 = $220,000
   Two years at community college: $624 x 2 = $1,248
   Two years at Harvard: $55,000 x 2 = $110,000
   Total with two years at community college and two at Harvard: $1,248 + $110,000 = $111,248
   Money saved: $220,000 - $111,248 = $108,752

2. Andrew's aunt has given him a $50 savings bond on every one of his birthdays. Each individual savings bond earns 1 percent a year. Andrew just turned 18 years old this June and received another savings bond. He plans to go to college in the fall.

   - Figure out how much money Andrew will have when he starts attending college (don't count the interest on the savings bond he received on his recent birthday).

   _____

Answer:

Face value of the bonds:

$50 x 18 = $900

Interest (using a compound interest calculator):

$9.81 = interest earned over 18 years on the savings bond he got for his 1st birthday

$9.22 = interest earned over 17 years on the savings bond he got for his 2nd birthday

$8.63 = interest earned over 16 years on the savings bond he got for his 3rd birthday

$0.50 = interest earned over 1 year on the savings bond he got for his 17th birthday

Total interest = $9.81 + $9.22 + $8.63 ... + $0.50 = $90.55

Total value of the investment = $900 + $90.55 = $990.55 for college

3. Choosing the right bank is important, especially when interest rates often differ between banks. Imagine that you want to open a savings account and one bank offers 1 percent annual interest, while the other offers 2.5 percent.

   - If you were to invest $5,000 in each bank, how much interest would you earn from each bank in one year? Which one would you rather bank with?

   Answer:

   Interest at 1% = $5,000 x .01 = $50

   Interest at 2.5% = $5,000 x .025 = $125

   Better interest: You earn $75 more in interest by investing with the bank that offers a savings account that earns 2.5 percent interest.

4. The four-year college you want to attend is out of state and costs $40,000 per semester. Your state college costs only $5,000 per semester because the state is actually paying for part of your tuition.

   - Figure out how much you will save by going to your state college versus going to the out-of-state college.

Answer:

Out-of-state college = $40,000 per semester x 2 semesters
per year x 4 years = $320,000

In-state college = $5,000 per semester x 2 semesters per year
x 4 years = $40,000

Money saved = $320,000 - $40,000 = $280,000

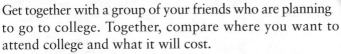

Work With a Team

Get together with a group of your friends who are planning
to go to college. Together, compare where you want to
attend college and what it will cost.

1. Do any of you want to go to the same college? If so, which one?

_____

2. Look into how much it costs to rent a house or an apartment if
   you and your friends were to become roommates.

APARTMENT COMPLEX	RENT	DISTANCE FROM CAMPUS

HOUSE ADDRESS	RENT	DISTANCE FROM CAMPUS

For more activities, assessments, and examples, visit www.lifebound.com.

Higher Education Can Mean a Higher Salary

Median annual income of persons with income 25 years old and over, by gender and highest level of education, 2009

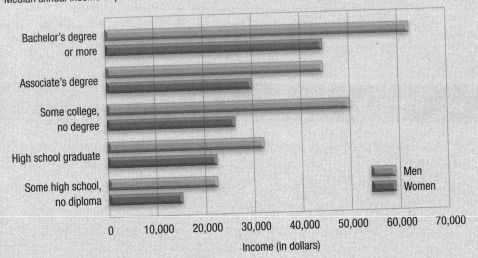

Income (in dollars)

What does it mean when people say college is an "investment"?

Do you plan on making an investment in your education? Why or why not?

Financial Planning for College, Career, and Life

"If nothing ever changed, there'd be no butterflies."

ANONYMOUS

Questions you will answer. . . .

1. How do you find and live with a roommate?
2. How can you manage a budget and chores with a roommate?
3. Where do you want to be 10 years from now?
4. How does a bad financial record affect how companies perceive you?
5. What are some common financial struggles and how do you get through them?
6. How much money should you have in an emergency fund?

Test your financial skills with the Dollars & Sense chapter assessment at www.lifebound.com.

COLLEGE
CAREER

7. How do you plan a financial future with your life partner?

8. What are the pros and cons of buying a house?

9. What are the pros and cons of buying or leasing a car?

10. What is a health savings account?

11. What is retirement and when should you start planning for it?

Meet Daniel

During his economics class, Daniel learns that if he starts investing $805 a year in a savings account that earns 12 percent interest he could be a millionaire by the age of 60! Daniel thinks becoming a millionaire sounds like a great idea, but where is he going to get the $805 a year that he needs to start growing his fortune?

Daniel thinks $805 is a large sum of money to invest all at once, but when he divides the amount by 12 months, he realizes he only needs to set aside $67 a month. That's still a lot of money to Daniel. But when he divides that amount by 30 days, he realizes he only needs to set aside $2.23 a day. That's about the cost of his afternoon snack from the vending machine.

Daniel decides to buy his snacks in bulk from the grocery store and bring his own food to school. He knows there's no time like the present, so before he finds a bank that offers a savings account with a high interest rate, he starts inserting his $2.23 in a box instead of the vending machine. By the end of the school week he has saved an easy $15 that will start paving the way toward his financial security.

LIVE AND LEARN

 ike Daniel, you can start planning today for college, career, and the rest of your life. In this chapter, we will give you some ideas and some resources to help you plan for your financial future.

COLLEGE: HOW DO YOU FIND AND LIVE WITH A ROOMMATE?

You've done your research and chosen which college to go to and how you are going to pay for it. Now, whom are you going to live with? Many colleges require freshmen to live on campus. So, unless you are going to live with your parents, you will probably have to share your dorm room with someone else during your first year of college.

Most people have roommates at different times in their lives, during and after college. Why? Because splitting the cost of living with at least one more person lessens the financial stress of paying for rent, groceries, electricity, and everything else that comes with being independent. However, just because you find someone who wants to be your roommate doesn't necessarily mean he or she accepts the responsibility of cleaning, paying expenses, being respectful of your space, or staying until the end of the lease. This is why knowing how to choose a roommate is so important.

Having bad roommates can cost you money directly if they decide not to pay their portion of the bills. They can cost you money indirectly if their habits keep you from sleeping or cause you stress that prevents you from doing your best at work and school.

Compatibility is important with roommates and dormmates—especially when it comes to cleanliness, study habits, party habits, and sleeping habits. It's also important that the person you live with be reliable, trustworthy, considerate, friendly, and have good communication skills.[1] Consider some of the not-so-great alternatives: 1) living with someone who lies, someone you can never count on or trust; 2) living with someone who couldn't care less about how his or her words and actions affect you; or 3) living with someone who barely talks at all or only yells to communicate. You certainly don't want to live like that. So how do you find a compatible dormmate or roommate? Here are some tips for you.

Be Honest

When answering questions about what you are looking for in a dormmate or roommate, it is essential that you be honest. Otherwise, you may end up with someone whom you cannot get along with.

Dormmates. When you get accepted to a college, you will typically receive a housing questionnaire from the college. Be honest when you fill it out. If you are more of a night owl than a morning person, or prefer a messy house rather than a tidy one, put that on the questionnaire. The more your college knows about you, the better the chances of you getting paired with someone you can live with.

Roommates. If your college doesn't require you to stay in the dorms or you choose to move into your own place when your college allows it, you will have to find roommates on your own. You might ask your friends, put an ad in the college paper or on a college bulletin board, put an ad on Craigslist, or spread the word on Facebook. You might find it more comfortable to move in with people you know, but living with someone is a lot different than hanging out with them on the weekends. A lot of people prefer living with strangers because it's easier to set ground rules and make a clean break. Ask your prospective roommates about their lifestyles and be honest about yours in return.

Invite People You Already Know

If possible, it's always safest to choose a dormmate or roommate whom you already know or have at least met a few times.

Dormmates. If you have a friend from high school who is going to the same school, try to room with him or her. Most colleges will let you request your dormmate. If you don't have a friend from high school who is looking for a dormmate, make a new friend during one of the orientation sessions. If you get along with that person and have lots in common, ask if he or she would like to room with you.

Roommates. If you're living off campus, you might decide to get a roommate to save money. Invite someone you already know or someone who is referred through mutual friends. As you learned earlier, even if you know the person, it's important to set ground rules and be honest about each of your preferred lifestyles.

Ask Questions

Whether you plan to share a dorm room or share an apartment, it is essential to ask your potential dormmate or roommate a lot of questions so you can assess whether the two of you will get along.

Dormmates. The college will send you a notification of who your dormmate is before you go to college and provide you with the individual's contact information so you can connect before move-in day. Come up with a list of questions you would like to ask your future dormmate and strike up a conversation with them via e-mail or phone. You might ask questions such as:

- How much studying do you typically do, and do you like to study in the dorm room?
- Do you do much partying?
- Are you neat or messy by nature?
- Are you extroverted or introverted?
- Do you need quiet when you study?
- What kind of music do you listen to?
- What time to you like to get up and go to bed?

Your future dormmate's answers will be a good indication of whether the two of you will be compatible.

Roommates. If you're living in off-campus housing, asking questions before signing a lease is extremely important. Any of the questions you might ask a dormmate are useful, but here are some additional questions you might ask for off-campus living:

- Do you plan on staying for the whole year?
- Have you ever lived on your own before?
- Do you have a boyfriend or girlfriend who plans on being over all the time?
- Do you plan on throwing parties?

Unlike campus living, off-campus living doesn't come with a safety net. Your landlord collects a check; he or she is not your mediator, support system, or friend. If the idea of being held responsible for caring for a property terrifies you, you might want to reconsider dorm life.

Bond

It's important to get to know your dormmate or roommate. It makes living together a lot easier.

Dormmates. Try to get to know your dormmate the first day. Take him or her out to lunch or dinner, introduce the person to your parents and meet your dormmate's, shop for books, or tour the campus together.

Roommates. Getting to know your roommate can lessen friction when awkward situations occur. These situations might include someone having a girlfriend or boyfriend the other person doesn't like, or being unable to pay part of the expenses because one of you has a job loss or a cutback in hours. If your schedules keep you from getting to know each other, schedule a time so you can go to lunch and get caught up on what's going on in each other's lives.

Work Out a Budget and Chores

One of the most common complaints about roommates is the division of money and chores. When you live with another person in a dorm, house, apartment, or condo, you have to work out a budget and chore schedule with your roommate to keep your sanity.

Make your responsibilities known, such as cleaning schedules and bill payment, during the first day or week you move in together. It's easy for these everyday problems to get out of control. Avoid the passive-aggressive behavior, the finger pointing, and the passionate fights by instilling the following practices right when you move in.

Budget. In the dorms, the budget is not that critical because your housing and food has mostly been paid for. However, if you live off-campus, a budget is crucial. No one wants to get stuck paying all of the rent or utilities because the other person runs out of money.

A good way to handle the budget is to list all shared expenses, such as rent, utilities, phone (if you have a land line), groceries, and household goods. Estimate the amounts and divide them up. Then get a calendar and write down when the bills are due. For example, you might need to pay the energy, water, and Internet bill by the first of every month. The expense list and bill-paying calendar should prevent any sudden surprises later in the month and ensure that bills are paid on time.

30–40 percent of college students drop out before earning a degree, and many won't return to finish. A student's ability to adjust and transition successfully to college both socially and academically plays a large role in whether or not students will become part of the statistic.[2]

Chores. It's no fun to live with people who won't clean up after themselves or want to live in a pigsty. Also, if you are female, beware of male roommates who think that just because they are "guys" they don't have to clean up after themselves and expect you do everything.

Once people are out of high school, living on their own, they are responsible for cleaning up after themselves, no matter what their gender or age. If you happen to be someone who never cleans up after yourself, beware. You will have to change your ways when you move in with other people. Part of being independent involves taking care of the place where you live and not expecting other people to do it for you.

The best way to avoid issues around chores is to do the following:

1. **List everything that needs to be done and how often.** For example, your chore list might include cleaning the bathroom, kitchen, and floors once a week, and taking the trash out every other day.

2. **Split the responsibility.** Decide which chores you and your roommate will be in charge of on a weekly, biweekly, or monthly basis. You may find that one person hates doing one type of chore but doesn't mind another. Try to assign people chores they are willing to do so they will do them regularly. If no one likes a particular chore, share it.

3. **Make a calendar.** After you've divided up your chores and decided how often they need to be performed, record

them on a blank calendar. Put the calendar on the refrigerator or another high-traffic area where it will be difficult to ignore.

4. **Open the door to communication.** It's very possible that with a busy work and school schedule, your roommate might legitimately forget or feel like they don't have enough time to do the chores. Politely remind the person that he or she missed their chores that week. Don't suffer in silence or blow up in anger.

5. **Reassess.** Once you get into the schedule, you might find that what you sketched out was easier said than done. For example, maybe you offered to clean the entire house every other week and your roommate would do the same on the opposite week. However, you find that cleaning the entire house in one day takes more time than you have to commit, so you reassess and split the weekly chores between you and your roommate throughout the week.

If chores, budgets, personality, or behavior become a problem, and you feel you cannot live with your dormmate or roommate, what should you do? On campus, if you and your dormmate don't mesh well together, you can go to the housing department at your school and ask for a different roommate. Your college wants you to do well, and will usually try to match you with someone you can live with.

If you're living off campus, you'll have to consider the consequences to your choices and which ones you can live with. When you sign a year lease, you're agreeing to pay rent for 12 months. If you duck out earlier in three months, you end up owing the landlord for nine months of rent. Or, your landlord may charge you a hefty fee for breaking the lease. The fee would be less than nine months of rent, but it would still be quite a penalty.

And the penalties don't stop there. Just as it looks bad on a résumé to quit a job every few months or get fired here and there, it looks bad on your record to break a lease, get evicted, or leave your rental a mess. An employer isn't going to hire an unreliable employee and a landlord isn't going to risk renting property to an irresponsible tenant.

Hopefully you can now see how your choices in college, like choosing roommates, can affect the future. What are some other choices that impact your future—especially your financial future?

In the first nine chapters you developed an understanding of you and your family's relationship with money, the importance of healthy financial behavior, how to manage your money for today and the future, and more. Throughout the rest of this chapter, you will apply those financial literacy skills to plan for the rest of your life.

now you try it

Consider you're about to move in with your new roommate. What is a non-confrontational way you can start the conversation you need to have about laying ground rules for your home?

_____

_____

_____

Imagine you've lived with your roommate for the last three months and they haven't been pulling their weight when it comes to cleaning chores. You think it's unfair, so you decide to talk to your roommate about following through on the schedule you both agreed upon. What do you say?

_____

_____

_____

After college, most people expect to start their career. In the next section you will learn how you can start setting goals today so you can end up where you want to be in your professional life.

CAREER: WHERE DO YOU WANT TO BE 10 YEARS FROM NOW?

Have you ever been asked, "What do you want to be when you grow up?" Whether you have a single career goal like Andrew in Chapter 9 or you have several life goals that could be met by various careers, assessing your dreams and goals is important. As you grow, your dreams and goals will grow with you. You'll probably notice the career dreams you had in elementary or junior high school have evolved or dissipated. Continually reassess your dreams as you grow older to stay true to your always-changing self.

When you graduate from college, you will most likely search for a career that is in your field and pays you a large enough salary to pay back your college loans and support you. Whether you graduate from college, opt for another life path, or don't make it to graduation day, you'll have plenty of other expenses to start planning for, like

People who pursue higher levels of training and education will earn more money out of school and throughout their careers, according the U.S. Bureau of Labor Statistics.[4]

marriage, family, traveling, taking art lessons, becoming an Olympic athlete, or anything else your heart desires.

Statistically, your grandparents' and parents' generations had 10 jobs in their lifetime.[3] With the explosion of telecommuting and technology jobs that change at the speed of innovation, that number will probably be higher for your lifetime.

Do you have multiple aspirations for the future? That's great! Trying new things can expose you to opportunities you never imagined and get rid of ones that no longer fit. If you're interested in nursing, try volunteering at a hospital or nursing home. You might find you have a knack for listening and solving family problems, and instead aspire to go to school to become a social worker. Expose yourself to as many options as possible. Can any of your dreams work as stepping stones to achieve another dream?

To help you think about your career possibilities, take a look at Exhibit 10-1. It lists data from the Bureau of Labor Statistics showing the top 20 fastest-growing careers from 2008 to 2018. Notice the percent of growth and the amount of training or degrees required. Maybe you would be interested in some of them.

EXHIBIT

10-1 30 fastest-growing careers (2008 – 2018)[5]

OCCUPATION	NUMBER OF JOBS (in thousands)		PERCENT CHANGE	REQUIRED DEGREE OR TRAINING
	2008	2018		
Biomedical engineer	16	28	72.0	Bachelor's degree
Network systems and data communications analysts	292	448	53.4	Bachelor's degree
Home health aides	922	1,383	50.0	Short-term on-the-job training
Personal and home care aides	817	1,193	46.0	Short-term on-the-job training
Financial examiners	27	38	41.2	Bachelor's degree
Medical scientists	109	154	40.4	Doctoral degree
Physician assistants	75	104	39.0	Master's degree

EXHIBIT

10-1 30 fastest-growing careers (2008 – 2018)[5] continued

OCCUPATION	NUMBER OF JOBS (in thousands)		PERCENT CHANGE	REQUIRED DEGREE OR TRAINING
	2008	2018		
Skin care specialists	39	54	37.9	Postsecondary vocational award
Biochemists and biophysicists	23	32	37.4	Doctoral degree
Athletic trainers	16	22	37.0	Bachelor's degree
Physical therapist aides	46	63	36.3	Short-term on-the-job training
Dental hygienist	174	237	36.1	Associate degree
Veterinary technicians	80	108	35.8	Associate degree
Dental assistants	295	401	35.8	Moderate-term on-the-job training
Computer software engineers	515	690	34.0	Bachelor's degree
Medical assistant	484	648	33.9	Moderate-term on-the-job training
Physical therapist assistants	64	85	33.3	Associate degree
Veterinarians	60	79	33.0	First professional degree
Self-enrichment education teachers	254	335	32.1	Work experience in a related profession
Compliance officers	260	341	31.1	Long-term on-the-job training
Occupational therapist aides	8	10	30.7	Short-term on-the-job training
Environmental engineers	54	71	30.6	Bachelor's degree
Pharmacy technicians	326	426	30.6	Moderate-term on-the-job training
Computer software engineers	395	515	30.4	Bachelor's degree
Survey researchers	23	31	30.4	Bachelor's degree
Physical therapists	186	242	30.3	Master's degree
Personal finance advisors	208	271	30.1	Bachelor's degree
Environmental engineering technicians	21	28	30.1	Associate degree
Occupational therapist assistants	27	35	29.8	Associate degree
Fitness trainers and aerobics instructors	261	338	29.4	Postsecondary vocational award

now you try it

WHAT DO YOU WANT TO BE?

What is one occupation you're interested in
pursuing in the future? Is it listed in Exhibit 10-1?

_____

Pick 2-3 professions from Exhibit 10-1 that sound interesting. Using the
Occupational Outlook Handbook at www.bls.gov, research what kinds of
tasks the professions entail and if the work environments sound like a
good fit for you.

_____

_____

_____

Dreams and Goals

In Chapter 9, it was helpful for Andrew to write down his goals so he
didn't let them slip away. Writing down your hopes and dreams makes
them more real and helps you remember just how important they are to
you. When you identify a goal, it means you're attempting to move from
where you are right now to somewhere you want to be in the future. The
act of moving toward that goal will add up to new experiences, unexpected roadblocks, and new people who can easily throw you for a loop.

To help manage these important goals and stay on track, try doing
the following:

1. **Set short-term, medium-term, and long-term goals.** First, make a
   list of three to five short-term goals, those you want to accomplish
   in the next year. Next, make a list of three to five medium-term
   goals, those you want to accomplish in the next two to five years.
   Finally, make a list of three to five of your long-term goals, those
   you want to accomplish in the next six to 10 years. The time
   frames on these goals are just a loose guideline. You can break
   short-term plans into days, weeks or months, and you can length-
   en long-term goals to encompass the rest of your life.

2. **Use a calculator to determine the cost of a long-term goal.** After
   you've made a list of your long-term goals, choose one you would

like to finance. For example, remember Daniel at the beginning of the chapter and his goal to be a millionaire by the time he is 60? He calculates that he needs to put away $805 per year in an account that has 12 percent interest.

3. **Apply systematic decision making to a long-term goal.** Daniel calculates that $805 per year is $2.23 per day. Then he looks at what kinds of savings accounts pay 12 percent interest, but cannot find one. Instead, he chooses a Roth IRA, with an interest rate of 9 percent, which he decides is close enough. But, now, he has to recalculate his numbers based on his new decision.

4. In **recalculating his numbers,** he discovers he would have to put away $2,136 a year. This means he would have to save $178 a month or $5.93 daily to reach his financial goal at 9 percent interest rate. With that recalculation alone, Daniel is looking at saving $111 more a month or $3.70 more a day.

5. **Analyze how inflation and taxes affect financial decisions:** Daniel won't be affected by taxes because any money he puts into his IRA is tax free, as long as he keeps it there until retirement. But IRAs are a fixed-rate investment, which means that if inflation goes up, the interest rate on the IRA won't go up to match it, which would make Daniel's IRA worth less.

How Bad Finances Affect Your Adult Life

If retirement still seems too far away to think about, there are many other things, like finding a rental apartment, buying a house, or financing school that will be a reality before you know it. Even if you aren't setting money aside every month for a large, faraway investment like retirement, you can still be smart about paying your bills and paying them on time. A poor bill-paying record can threaten your eventual career or home.

- **Career.** As we saw in Chapter 6, Kevin didn't get the job he really wanted because his credit score was not good. For many companies, how you treat your personal finances affects their opinion of how you will treat their company's funds and resources, whether or not your job involves working with money. Having your personal finances in order tells an employer you are a responsible adult, which can make it easier for you to get hired or get a promotion.

- **Expenses.** Every bank, credit union, utility company, insurance company, and rental agency runs a credit check before letting you open an account or rent an apartment. If you have your personal finances in order, you will not have to pay hefty deposits or be turned down for insurance coverage.

Common Financial Struggles

Even people with top-notch financial skills encounter financial struggles at some point in their lives. Depending on your life situation or the state of your finances, all the planning, saving, and investing might not be enough to protect you from two common financial difficulties: job loss and sudden debt.

- **Job loss.** This is a common occurrence during a recession. Large companies often downsize or consolidate to save money. This causes them to close their branches and lay off large portions of their staff. For small businesses, a recession may cause their customers to: 1) look for cheaper prices and bulk deals that only large companies can offer or 2) stop spending. Both behaviors can cause small businesses to close their doors and lay off their employees.

- **Sudden debt.** This happens when you least expect it, like in the event you must suddenly pay for an unexpected purchase, a medical emergency, or a repair. If you don't have any savings and live paycheck-to-paycheck, an emergency can send you whirling into debt. Whether your car needs a new radiator, or you break your leg and have to pay a large deductible on a health insurance policy, you may not have the funding to cover it. Either situation means you will probably need to use a credit card or arrange a payment plan.

quickcheck

What is one way you can bond with a roommate?

What are two common financial struggles?

What are three of the fastest growing careers?

REAL-WORLD MATH

Suppose your rent is $650 a month. Your utilities add up to $100 a month and you spend $400 a month on food, with an extra 10 percent to cover the unexpected. How much should you put aside for emergencies or job loss for a three-month fund? How about for a six-month fund?

Expenses

$650 + $100 + $400 = $1,150

.10 x $1,150 = $115

$1,150 + $115 = $1,265 per month

Emergency Fund

3 x $1,265 = $3,795 emergency fund for 3 months

6 x $1,265 = $7,590 emergency fund for 6 months

How much would you need to put aside every month if you wanted to have half of your emergency fund put away in two years?

2 years x 12 months per year = 24 months

.5 x $3,795 = $1,897.50 (half of your 3-month emergency fund)

$1,897.50 ÷ 24 = $79.06 per month for half of a 3-month emergency fund

.5 x $7,590 = $3,795 (half of your 6-month emergency fund)

$3,975 ÷ 24 = $165.63 per month for half of a 6-month emergency fund

Your salary, employment status, and health can change at a moment's notice. One of the best ways to overcome unanticipated expenses associated with a job loss, change in salary, or illness, is to have a savings plan, as we discussed in Chapter 7. Your emergency savings account should have enough in it to cover three to six months of necessary expenses such as rent, utilities, and food.[6]

In the third section of this chapter we will discuss the miscellaneous financial decisions you will face throughout your life. These financial

FINANCIAL FIGURES

LEARNING FROM THE EXPERIENCE OF OTHERS

Mark Kantrowitz, *financial aid and college planning author, Cranberry Township, Pa.*

"Bad things happen to everybody, but they shouldn't be a reason to derail you from your path." Take Mark Kantrowitz's words to heart—he survived cancer and a lightning strike to his home and still became an esteemed financial aid and college planning author.

Planning your career and life often starts with the decision to attend college or go another route. "College is a credential. It's not just teaching you skills and knowledge that help you in the job market or in life, it's also a kind of stamp of excellence. Alternate routes usually don't involve this kind of certification of your abilities," Kantrowitz admits.

For those who choose college, Kantrowitz's FinAid website (finaid.org) is the online holy grail of financial aid insight, serving up sections on scholarships, loans, savings, and military aid, plus key tips for financial aid applications. His companion website is FastWeb (fastweb.com), a free scholarship matching service that Kantrowitz runs. Some of Kantrowitz's pointers: Answer the optional questions on scholarship questionnaires; smaller scholarships can add up, so apply for them; and apply early, well before your senior year.

FinAid and FastWeb are invaluable tools for making your education a financial reality. "The real point is, before you incur that debt, pay attention to what that debt is going to mean and how you will repay that debt," Kantrowitz stresses. That includes doing a ton of career research. Kantrowitz notes that tech, science, and health fields tend to pay higher salaries.

In his many writings, Kantrowitz also weighs in on topics such as taking a year off after high school. "Taking a gap year can help with your maturity level," he says. "The problem with a gap year is you might get out of the habit of studying. It can make it more difficult to get back into the mode of academic work. There are tradeoffs."

scenarios will probably make themselves known while you're in college, during your career, and into retirement. That's life!

LIFE: HOW DO YOU JUGGLE FINANCES, RELATIONSHIPS, AND RETIREMENTS?

inances are complicated enough when you just have to worry about your own, but most of us will be in relationships where we have the option to merge finances, in the case of a long relationship or marriage, or lend family or friends money, in the case of an emergency. Arguments about money are one of the most common problems in modern marriages and relationships. Financial disagreements are often based in some of the issues we discussed in Chapter 2.

Discussing Money with Your Partner

Everyone has a unique relationship with money. Discussing finances is just as important to the health of your romantic relationships as is discussing children, politics, and religion. Yet, according to many financial advisors, money is one of the last things couples discuss with one another. When you are in a serious relationship, consider the following financial talking points to make sure you are both on the same page.

1. **Talk about your financial goals and values.** What are your spending priorities? What do you want to accomplish together in 10 years? Are you frugal or frivolous? Agreeing on what you want together will give both of you an idea of how the other person thinks about money.[7]

2. **Try to stay objective.** As we discussed before, money can be an emotional topic. Your relationship with money is often tied up with issues of security, trust, and self-esteem. It's important to untangle the emotional issues from the financial issues.

3. **Use "I" statements.** This keeps the other person from thinking you are blaming him or her. If you feel like you are being attacked, stop, take a breath, and remember that the other person loves you and you love him or her. You want that person to be happy and you want to be happy together.[8]

4. **Talk about your goals.** Present any financial goals you have made over time. Once you have presented your goals, such as buying a house within five years, make sure your partner shares that goal. If your partner doesn't, find out why not. But keep the discussion objective and avoid being judgmental or accusatory.[9]

5. **Be honest.** When people are first dating, they often try to present their best faces to one another. As their relationships become more serious and complex, they don't want to do anything to jeopardize the other person's love, and they may go along with things that they do not really want to do. If you are in this situation, you may be tempted to give in to the other person's financial wishes even when you don't agree. But to create a realistic household budget and list of financial goals, you have to be honest about what you really want and how much it will cost.[10]

6. **Financial goals are a team effort.** As a couple, you are building a financial foundation together. You will have different approaches and priorities; one of you may be good at organizing financial paperwork and keeping track of where the money is going, and one may not. Or both of you may be good at finances, or neither of you may be. The most important thing is to make decisions together. If only one person makes the financial decisions, that person might feel that he or she has power over the other, and resentment can build up over financial decisions and priorities.[11]

In an article on finances and marriage, Utah State University's Jeffrey Dew writes, "Research that I have done indicates that conflict over money matters predicts divorce better than other types of disagreement."[14]

7. **Have weekly financial meetings.** Keeping each other informed on what you are spending and what you are earning makes a financial plan work. If the person who handles day-to-day finances doesn't know you spend an extra $10 on gas that week, then he or she can't accurately calculate the family budget. At your meeting, you can review the budget and any problem areas, like a rise in the price of gas or a month full of birthdays, as well as any bonuses or tips you may be getting.[12]

8. **Share your credit reports.** People in the U.S. are getting married later and later in life, which means they have more debt when

they get married. That's why it's so important to share your credit report with your "soon-to-be." Once you understand each other's credit score and outstanding debt, you will have a clearer picture of your financial goals, priorities, and past so you can start building an honest future together.[13]

If you argue with your spouse about finances once a week, your marriage is 30 percent more likely to end in divorce than if you argue with your spouse about finances less frequently.[15]

Understanding the Cost of Divorce

People don't want to think about getting divorced before they're even married, but with 50 percent of marriages ending in divorce, it's a reality that cannot be ignored.[16] Divorce is unappealing for many reasons, but one costly reason is that it is expensive. According to marital status.com, a website geared toward divorce and remarriage, divorce is a $28 billion-a-year industry with an average cost of about $20,000.[17]

Approximately 10 people per 1,000 people got married in 2008, while 5 people per 1,000 people got divorced.[18] These numbers account only for people who were married; there are many unmarried people in relationships who "break up" outside of the statistics.

The more emotional and complicated a divorce is, the more expensive it is. Any assets or liabilities you accumulate as a couple must be evaluated, and depending on the state you are getting divorced in, split between the two of you.

Planning for Big Purchases

Beyond marriage and divorce, there are other expenses and issues to be aware of. Large purchases require planning, whether it's setting aside money in your teens to finance a comfy retirement, or doing research a month in advance to purchase a car. In the following section we will discuss what you need to know before making a big purchase and questions you should ask yourself along the way.[19]

1. **Figure out what you really need.** Take the time to think about why you need the purchase. This helps you identify features and details that are important to you about the purchase. Make a list of what you need and what you want.

2. **Set a budget.** Know how much you can afford to spend before you go shopping. It's easy to be tempted by great values and overspend.

3. **Do your homework.** Become an expert on the item you want to buy. There are many resources to help you make an informed decision, including online product and price comparison tools, online forums, consumer guides, or even your friends and family.

4. **Take your time.** Don't feel pressured to sign on the dotted line. Ask the retailer or seller questions about anything you don't understand before you buy. If you're feeling pressured, walk away. In fact, a good rule of thumb is to wait 24 hours before making a large financial decision.

5. **Remember hidden costs.** With many items, the purchase price is just part of the cost of ownership. Add in the expense of insurance, maintenance, or fuel when comparing your options.

6. **Check your credit report.** Review your credit report before making any large purchase and take steps to correct any errors. Knowing your credit score before you start shopping may cause you to rethink financing a large purchase.

Buying a Car

One of the first big purchases you might make in the near future is a car. There are so many choices that shopping for a car can be overwhelming. That's why it's important to isolate the things that you really need from a car, for example: transporting you three miles to work and back, and going grocery shopping. With a clear list of requirements, you can skip the expensive frills and choose something more practical and affordable for your lifestyle. Here are four practical suggestions:[20]

1. **Figure out what you really need from a car.** Do you need reliable transportation for work and school? Do you need good gas mileage because you are commuting more than five miles to work or school? Do you need a compact car or a sedan? Sit down and make a list of what you will be using your car for and work out what you can afford to pay for a down payment, monthly payments, gas, insurance, and maintenance.

2. **Ask questions.** Do some research in your local newspaper, on the Internet,

or in Kelley Blue Book to get an idea of how much the car you are thinking of buying is worth. Also research the "lemon laws" in your state. These are important if you unknowingly buy a car with a major mechanical problem.

3. **Get the car checked out.** Once you've looked at some cars and decided to test drive one, take it to a mechanic to have it checked out. The cost is usually minimal, and well worth it if the mechanic catches a problem that could cost you hundreds or thousands of dollars. If you are not able to take the car to a mechanic, bring along someone who knows about cars to check for common problems on the spot.

4. **Know the difference between "under warranty" and "as is."** If you are buying a used car from a dealer or dealership, there will be a window sticker with the vital statistics of the car. On that sticker are two boxes, one is "under warranty" and the other is "as is." Notice which box is checked.

   - The "under warranty" box tells you there is a guarantee stating that the car is reliable and free from known defects and that the seller will, without charge, repair or replace defective parts within a given time limit and under certain conditions.

   - The "as is" box tells you that the car has not been examined to see if it is reliable or free of defect, and if any defects are found after purchase, the buyer has no legal recourse to recover money from the seller.

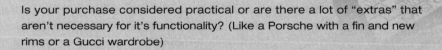

now you try it

Do you have a dream car or dream purchase, like a big-screen TV, house, new wardrobe, etc.?

_____

Is your purchase considered practical or are there a lot of "extras" that aren't necessary for it's functionality? (Like a Porsche with a fin and new rims or a Gucci wardrobe)

_____

Not only do you have options about what kind of car you want to buy, but also you have options about how to finance the car. You can buy or lease a car. Use Exhibits 10-2a and 10-2b to compare and contrast the pros and cons of buying and leasing a car.[21]

EXHIBIT

10-2a	Pros and cons of buying a car

PROS	CONS
1. You will eventually own it someday and be free of car payments.	1. Monthly payments are higher when buying a car than when leasing a car.
2. The car is yours to sell at any time and can be used as an asset for loans.	2. Dealers require a down payment.
3. You aren't tied down to a fixed ownership period.	3. Depreciation can eat away at your equity. Cars lose value much more quickly than houses. By the time you finish paying off your car, you could have paid much more than it is worth.
4. Insurance limits are lower for buying a car than leasing a car.	
5. You can put as much mileage on the car as you want without worrying about paying penalties.	

10-2b	Pros and cons of leasing a car

PROS	CONS
1. There are lower out-of-pocket costs to maintain the car. Leasing has fewer upfront costs.	1. You always have a car payment.
2. The monthly payments are lower.	2. You have restrictions on how many miles you can put on the car.
3. You get a new car every couple of years.	3. Insurance is higher on a leased car.
4. You are not penalized for loss of value on the car.	

Buying a Home

Whether you're single, married, or in a long-term relationship, you're going to need a place to live. Renting works fine for a while, but eventually many people decide they're ready to own their own homes. It might sound like a happy dream to own your own home, but it comes with lots of paperwork, large bills, and big commitments. Here are some tips for getting ready for the big purchase.[22]

Depreciation, noun

How much of an asset's value has been used up. Putting mileage on a car will use up its value.

1. **Make sure you have good credit.** As we discussed in previous chapters, your credit score and rating are very important. A mortgage is probably the largest loan you will ever apply for, so having good credit will make it possible and affordable. The lower your credit score, the less apt you are to get a loan, and if you do get the loan, it will be at a higher rate of interest.

2. **Have a down payment.** The rule of thumb for the down payment on a home is 20 percent. For example, if you want to buy a house that is selling for $250,000, you should have a down payment of $50,000. If you qualify for a loan with your good credit, you will usually be offered low-interest mortgages that require a down payment as small as 3 percent of the purchase price. But the more you have for a down payment, the smaller your monthly payment will be and the less interest you will pay back.

> **Equity,** noun
>
> *The difference between what the asset is worth versus how much you still owe on the asset.*

If you cannot afford to make the down payment out of pocket, there are a variety of public and private lenders who can provide loans, usually at a higher rate of interest.

3. **Get help.** There are several professionals who can help you understand what's involved in buying a home: a title company representative, a personal banker, a professional mortgage agent, a financial planner, or a home inspector. They can help you understand the ins and outs of the mortgage process, as well as tell you whether or not the house you are interested in is worth buying. With their help, you may be able to avoid using a Realtor, who usually charges you 3 percent or more of the home's price as a commission.

> **Mortgage,** noun
>
> *An agreement where you borrow money from a lender to buy property, especially a house. In exchange for the loan, the lender may take possession of the property if you fail to repay the money with interest.*

4. **Get pre-approved.** Getting pre-approved for a mortgage from your financial institution will save you the time and effort of looking at houses that you find out later you cannot afford. It also puts you in a better position to make serious offers on homes you like.

> **Down Payment,** noun
>
> *The part of the purchase price paid in cash up front, reducing the amount of the loan or mortgage.*

EXHIBIT

10-3   Pros and cons of owning a home[23]

PROS	CONS
1. **You own it.** You can paint, decorate, renovate, without having to get permission from the landlord, because you are the landlord. You have a level of privacy that you don't get as a renter.	1. **High cost of buying a home.** Property taxes, homeowner's insurance, utilities, and upkeep added to your mortgage can be much more than you would pay for rent.
2. **It is an asset.** Owning a house and paying a mortgage builds your credit and gives you a tangible asset to borrow against in the case of job loss or emergency expenses.	2. **Harder to move.** If you get transferred for your job, or find a better job in another location, you have to figure out what to do with your house. Do you sell it? Do you rent it out? It takes time to sell a home or to find a renter.
3. **Tax incentives.** You get deductions on your taxes for owning a home.	3. **High cost of home ownership.** Since you are the landlord, you pay the property taxes, the repair bills when hail puts holes in your roof, landscaping, snow removal, and many other costs you might not see on the surface.

Still not convinced buying a home is for you? **Exhibit 10-3** helps you examine the pros and cons of owning a home.

Handling Health Emergencies

Health insurance is a very important expense to add into your budget. In Chapter 2, we stated that the Federal Trade Commission defined insurance as a "necessary expense." Today, health insurance can be expensive, especially if you are self-employed or have lost a job. More and more people are uninsured, and even if you do have health insurance, it won't cover every cost.

What Insurance May Not Cover

How much insurance companies actually pay for accidents, cancer treatment, or surgery depends on what kind of insurance you have, but there are some limits. Just because you have insurance, does not mean the insurance company will pay. After all, they are for-profit companies and want to pay out as few claims as possible.

Here are some facts for you to consider:

- **Cost of illness.** Most insurance companies have a cap on how much they will pay for a long-term illness.

- **Emergency room cost.** If you have an accident that requires emergency treatment and you end up in an emergency room outside your insurance network, you may not be covered.

- **Surgical coverage.** You may be surprised at what your insurance company considers non-covered surgery. There can be a big gray area between covered "reconstructive" surgery and uncovered "cosmetic" surgery. Even when surgery is covered, your deductible may be $500 or more, and you may still be responsible for up to 25 percent or more of surgical costs, depending on the specifics of your plan.

Health Savings Accounts (HSAs)

Some people opt to purchase **high-deductible health insurance plans** because the plans are less expensive than conventional plans and have lower monthly payments. However, when a medical emergency arises, people with such plans must pay a large, out-of-pocket deductible before the insurance kicks in. To help people with those types of plans, the federal government created **health savings accounts** (HSAs) in 2003.

An HSA lets you put aside tax-free money for a health emergency if you are already covered by a high-deductible insurance plan. Any contribution you make to the HSA is tax-deductible. Your employer may also make tax-deductible contributions.[24] The money accumulates in the account year after year and serves as both a tax-free emergency health fund and a savings fund.

If you do not have insurance, you can still open up a traditional savings account where you set aside money that will be accessible for unexpected expenses, especially health-related ones. The savings account will earn interest, but the money in it will not be tax-deductible like the contents of an HSA.

How to Save for Your Emergency Health Fund

Whether you open an HSA or a traditional savings account as your emergency health fund, consider the following tips for building up the fund.

- Put any money you get from a tax refund or earned income credit into your emergency fund.

- Ask your bank or credit union to automatically transfer funds into your emergency fund.

- Explain the importance of an emergency fund to your family and get everyone involved in cutting back on unnecessary spending.[25]

FINaNCiaL FOUL-UPS

LEARNING FROM THE MISTAKES OF OTHERS

Jenna just returned from her five-year college reunion. It was great to see her friends again. Her former roommate, Krista, seemed so happy. Krista, like Jenna, is entrenched in a teaching career. But Krista has already paid off her college loans, drives a new car, and takes two vacations a year.

Jenna is an elementary school teacher, making $35,000 a year before taxes. After four years of college and a teacher certification class, she has to pay back $60,000 in student loans. That's more than twice as much as Krista, who applied for scholarships early in high school and used an online scholarship matching service to land some very lucrative awards.

Unlike Krista, Jenna waited until spring of her senior year in high school to target scholarships. A competitive ice skater, Jenna had the opportunity to apply for a scholarship through her skating club, but she did not apply, because the payout was "only" $5,000. Jenna did apply for another scholarship, offered by a local Rotary Club, but she did not complete the optional essay, and was passed over.

Jenna assumed her education would be funded primarily by federal grants and her parents' contributions. But federal cutbacks directly affected her grant money, and when the economy soured, her father was laid off from his job for six months. Her parents were able to chip in just enough money to cover Jenna's housing, food, and transportation expenses.

It wasn't until two years after graduating from college that Jenna read the advice that you should borrow only as much as you expect to make in your first year out of college. Now, she's revisiting her choice of college in the first place. Maybe, she wonders, she would have been better off attending her community college for two years, then transferring to the private college. She cannot change her past decisions, but hopefully she will make better decisions in the future.

How to Avoid Health Problems in Later Life

One way to avoid unexpected health-related expenses is to take care of your health. As some people are fond of saying: "My health is my insurance." You can prevent several health issues later in life by maintaining good health habits earlier in life. Diabetes, stroke, heart disease, osteoarthritis, and several other diseases become more common with age. But you can prevent or manage them with a healthy diet, reduced stress, and sufficient rest and exercise. The best health insurance is keeping your body healthy from the inside out!

Practicing Charitable Giving

Once you get your career under control and begin to build your own wealth, you will be in a position to financially help others. Your ability to do so demonstrates your financial and personal maturity.

Sharing your wealth with others by donating your money, skills, belongings, or time is a way to give back to your community. It is also a way to become less self-centered and more aware of the needs of others. The more you volunteer and give, the more you see how serving others can have a direct impact on yourself and the world around you. Your charitable efforts can help individuals, families, and organizations

Just as you budget money to put into savings or into retirement, you can also budget money for charitable giving. At first the amount may not be much, but it still adds up. For example, suppose you donate $10 a month to your local animal shelter. That adds up to $120 a year, which helps pay for food, shots, and neutering. Or maybe you choose to donate pet food or blankets to the shelter. Many animals will be thankful. Or perhaps you decide to volunteer a few hours a week. When it comes to charitable giving, your money, donations, or volunteer hours will make a difference.

Saving for Retirement

At some point in your life, you are going to want to stop working, and the sooner you start planning for it, the sooner you'll have the funds to retire. A generation ago, retirement often meant never working and simply relaxing: puttering in the garden, playing golf, or traveling. However, a generation ago, people often had pensions provided by their employers that provided some funding for their retirement, along with their Social Security.

6 out of 10 non-retirees believe Social Security won't pay them benefits when they retire.[26]

But those days are over. As you learned in prior chapters, in today's world, you are unlikely to have a funded pension you can live off when you retire, unless you work for a government agency (city, county, state, or federal), or a school. And even if you work for such an organization, unless you stay with that organization for your entire career, it's doubtful you will receive a pension.

R E A L - W O R L D   M A T H

Imagine that your mortgage payment is $1,150 a month, your utilities are $200 a month, your car payment is $550 a month, and you spend $400 a month on food, making your monthly expenses about $2,300. You imagine you might need an extra 10 percent cushion for retirement, which means you should have at least $607,000 put aside when you retire.

That may seem like a lot of money. But if you break it down, like Daniel did, you will find that if you start investing $110 a month when you are 18 at a 9 percent interest rate, you will have $618,968.17 put aside by the time you are 65. Of course, that's just an estimate.

This means that you will have to save your own money for retirement. It also means that you may end up working part time late in life to pay the bills. And it means that as an active senior, you may decide to volunteer and help others, something you may not have had much time for when you were working full time. So, it's likely that you may still be "working" in some way or another when you retire.

In chapters 7 and 8, you learned about 401K plans (for those who are not self-employed), savings accounts, and investments. These are the methods you can use to plan for retirement, so the earlier you start planning, the better. Many people put off planning for retirement until they are middle-aged, but as we saw with Daniel's example, if you begin planning for retirement when you are 18, you will be much better off than your friends who decide to wait. Plus, the money you put aside for retirement can be used for emergencies, buying a house, or sending your children to college.

To make sure you put aside enough money for retirement, you can use the same formula we mentioned earlier for your emergency fund, but use it to calculate for years rather than months.[27]

There are several ways to plan for your retirement. You can find more ideas for retirement plan strategies in the online exercises for Chapter 10 under Time to Explore.

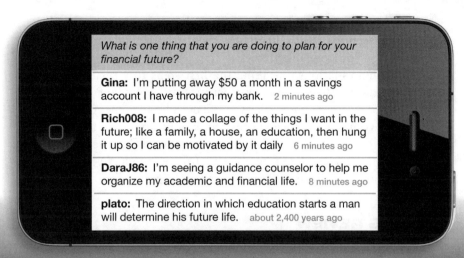

What is one thing that you are doing to plan for your financial future?

Gina: I'm putting away $50 a month in a savings account I have through my bank.   2 minutes ago

Rich008: I made a collage of the things I want in the future; like a family, a house, an education, then hung it up so I can be motivated by it daily   6 minutes ago

DaraJ86: I'm seeing a guidance counselor to help me organize my academic and financial life.   8 minutes ago

plato: The direction in which education starts a man will determine his future life.   about 2,400 years ago

THE SOCIAL MEDIA FEED

SUMMARY

I f you have worked through this book in a class or on your own, you now have financial know-how for daily life in high school, college, career, and future personal affairs, including relationships and family goals.

If the information you learned here was somewhat new to you, you are like the majority of high schools students. If you are lucky enough to have financial role models who took you under their wings, you are in the fortunate minority. If you are like most of us, you are striking out on your own without the help of family members who can teach you how to be dollars and sense smart.

Either way, completing this book is the first step to financial independence. You might not believe it, but there are many adults in the world who aren't as financially literate as you are after reading this book. You've done a good job with your follow-through and your goal to be smart about money through your entire life.

You are now empowered by the financial tools you mastered in this book and online. Use the online study guide to show yourself and your teacher what you know. Once you work through those exercises, you are ready for your financial final exam, which you can take online and give to your teacher or your parents.

Being smart about money is more than how much money you may or may not have in the bank. Being smart about money means being smart about your personal relationships, mental and physical health, security, family, happiness, as well as learning how money can work for you now and always.

Congratulations on taking the first steps to a secure and happy life. May you live a long, prosperous, and abundant life, and be a financial role model for others in the decades to come. Once you take care of your own financial needs, think of how you can use your hard-earned savings and investments to help others in need. With your help, they will be able to get on a positive, productive path so that they, too, can contribute to the world in larger ways.

LET'S REVIEW

Building a relationship with money is a lifelong process. As your dreams and goals change, your financial strengths and weaknesses change as well. As you move through life, it is important to plan for emergencies, job loss, sudden debt, and retirement.

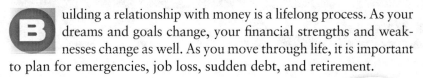

What Did You Learn?

- Roommates are common, both in and out of college. Being honest, respectful, and responsible will help to make your roommate experience a positive one.
- In 10 years, your life will be very different from what it is now. You may have a full-time job, a career, a college degree, a home, a husband, wife, or partner, and possibly children. Those life passages will affect your relationship with money.
- Financial struggles happen to everyone. Unemployment and unexpected expenses are two common struggles. However, if you plan for your financial future, these struggles become more bearable.
- There are pros and cons to buying a house vs. renting one, just as there are pros and cons to buying a car vs. leasing one.
- Talking to your future partner about money now can save your relationship in the future.
- Saving for possible health costs can save time and money in the future.
- Taking care of your health throughout your life will lower your healthcare costs as you grow older.
- It's never too early to plan for retirement.

New Terms

- Dormmate
- Long-term vs. Short-term Goals
- Down Payment
- Equity

- Roommate
- Mortgage
- Depreciation
- Retirement

END-OF-CHAPTER ACTIVITIES

Here's your chance to put your pen to paper, as well as discuss what you've learned with others. Doing activities and talking about them are great ways to make sure you really do understand the concepts you've read about.

Remember the Basics

1. What should you do to find a compatible roommate?

2. Where do you want to be 10 years from now?

3. What does your ability to handle money tell your employer?

4. How can you get through common financial struggles?

_____

_____

_____

_____

5. How do you negotiate with your future partner to come up with common financial goals?

_____

_____

_____

6. Where should you put your savings?

_____

_____

_____

7. What are the pros and cons of buying a house?

_____

_____

_____

_____

8. What are the pros and cons of buying a car vs. leasing a car?

_____

_____

_____

9. What is a health savings account?

_____

_____

_____

10. How can you have good health as you get older?

11. What is retirement and when should you start planning for it?

Work With a Team

1. Think about having a roommate in college.
   - What things do you want in a roommate?

   - What things do you think you would like to know about your roommate?

   - What habits would you not put up with?

   - What habits do you have that might bother a roommate? Which ones are you willing to change?

2. Take your list of roommate requirements to your friends, parents, and grandparents.

   ■ Ask them what they think you should know about the person you will be living with.

   ■ Think about their suggestions. Then adjust your list accordingly.

3. Talk to any of your friends who have purchased a car.

   ■ What was their experience?

   _____

   _____

   ■ What advice do they have for you?

   _____

   _____

4. Talk to your parents or friends in relationships about their financial goals as a couple.

   ■ Did they choose someone who had similar goals?

   _____

   _____

   ■ Did they have to negotiate their goals?

   _____

   _____

Practice Your Math

1. Based on a long-term goal you want to achieve, calculate how much money you would have to save or invest each month or each week to reach it.

   ■ What is your goal?

   _____

   ■ What is the cost of the goal?

   _____

- When do you want to achieve it?

  _____

- How much money would you have to save each month? Each week?

  _____

2. Consider your own retirement and calculate how much money you would have to save to prepare for it.

   - How long do you want to work?

     _____

   - When would you like to retire?

     _____

   - How much money would you like to retire with?

     _____

   - How much money will you have to save each year to retire when you want to? How much will you have to save each month?

     _____

3. Talk to people who own their homes (your parents, a friend, a teacher, a co-worker).

   - Ask them how much the home is worth.
   - Go to www.mortgagecalculator.org and calculate how much your payment would be if you were buying a similar home today.

For more activities, assessments, and examples, visit www.lifebound.com.

Good fortune is what happens when opportunity meets with planning.

—THOMAS EDISON

The best thing about the future is that it comes one day at a time.

—ABRAHAM LINCOLN

Using a quote book, an online quote database, this book, or words of wisdom from friends, family, or the famous, pick a few motivational quotes about the future and record them in the blank spots to personalize your quote board.

Do, or do not. There is no try.

—YODA

Failing to plan is planning to fail.

—ALAN LAKEIN

It pays to plan ahead. It wasn't raining when Noah built the ark

—ANONYMOUS

Accessing Financial Resources

There is such a wide range of resources to help answer all your financial questions: books, databases, websites, tools, and advisors. Take the initiative and find out what these resources have to offer.

Books

Here are some excellent books you can purchase or get from the library.

- Lawrence, Judy. *The Budget Kit*. Riverside, NJ: Kaplan Publishing, 2011.
- Leeds, Regina. *One Year to an Organized Financial Life*. New York, NY: Da Capo Press, 2010.
- Opydke, Jeff D. *Piggy Banking: Preparing Your Financial Life for Kids and Your Kids For a Financial Life*. New York, NY: Harper Business, 2010.
- Orman, Suze. *The Money Book for the Young, Fabulous, and Broke*. New York, NY: The Berkley Publishing Group, 2007.

Online Tools

Looking for free financial resources? Go online and check out these sites or do an Internet search for your specific financial needs.

Credit Reports

Credit reports are a great way to keep track of your credit history and watch your credit score increase or decline. An ideal score is 720. It takes some time to establish this kind of score but it's very possible. Here are some websites you can visit to discover your detailed credit score.

- www.freecreditreport.com
- www.equifax.com
- www.creditreport.com

Financial Applications

An app is a software program (application) for smartphones or tablets. You can find an app for just about anything these days, even ones that manage your finances. Here is an introduction to a few apps that can turn your phone or tablet into a money-managing machine:

CHECKING ACCOUNT

- *Wells Fargo, Bank of America*, and *Chase* are just a few banks that offer apps for their customers to track their spending, check their balance, transfer money, and much more.

INVESTMENTS

- *Bloomberg*: Get trusted financial information to your phone just like hundreds of thousands of business professionals around the world are doing right now. Get news, stock quotes, market trend analysis, and more at **www.bloomberg.com/mobile**.

PERSONAL MONEY MANAGEMENT

- *Mint*: "Mint brings all your financial accounts together online, automatically categorizes your transactions, lets you set budgets & helps you achieve your savings goals." For more information, go to **www.mint. com**.

TIP CALCULATOR

- *Checkplease*: Calculate a tip and even split it between everyone in your party. Look for *Checkplease* at your online app store.

Financial Calculators

There are many helpful online calculators available to you. Do an online search for the following calculators to get help crunching important numbers.

- **Compound Interest Calculator.** This calculator is an online tool that can help you determine interest if you're borrowing or lending money.
- **Saving for College Calculator.** There are many sites out there ready to calculate how long and how much you need to save to finance your college education.
- **Spending Calculator.** These calculators can help you get a budget started by comparing how much you make to how much you spend.
- **Additional Financial Calculators.** Do you have more numbers that need crunching? Go to **www.financial-calculators.com** for the rest of your calculation needs.

Budgeting Worksheets

There are many websites that provide free, printable budgeting worksheets to help simplify and organize your finances. A budget worksheet lets you compare how much money you are spending with how much money you are making. Different people have different financial situations and may require different budgeting worksheets to fit their specific needs.

Check out websites like **www.budget worksheets.org** or **www.kiplinger.com/ tools/budget** to find the budgeting worksheet that's right for you. For information on how to fill out a budget worksheet, refer to **Chapter 3, Budgeting and Goal Setting for Success.**

Podcasts

Podcasts are audio or video media files that you can subscribe to using any computer that can play media files. Listening to a podcast is much like listening to a radio segment, but on your own schedule.

The following are some podcasts you can subscribe to for financial tips. Do an Internet search for each name to find out how to subscribe to them on your computer:

- *Kiplinger's Personal Finance* podcasts are audio versions of Kiplinger magazine's top stories. Subscribe and listen to a new podcast every Tuesday.
- *The Dave Ramsey Show: Take Control of Your Money* podcast teaches you practical money skills for everyday money management with every listen.
- *Money Girl's Quick and Dirty Tips for a Richer Life* podcast offers tips on personal finance, real estate, and investing in easy-to-understand language in about 10 minutes.

Do an Internet search for podcasts on your specific financial needs and subscribe today!

Advice

Many websites give students advice on how to pay for college, campus life, and career development programs and ideas. Here are a few advice websites you can visit:

- www.students.gov
- www.FAFSA.ed.gov
- www.princetonreview.com/ FinancialAidAdvice.aspx

Community

Besides books and the Internet, there are plenty of real people who can help you understand finances. Don't be afraid to talk to people in your community for financial advice.

- **School counselors** specialize in giving advice to students. They can help you with relationships, college applications, finances, and anything else you can think to talk about.
- **A parent or guardian** might be able to give you honest financial advice. Whether the person practices good or bad money behavior, they probably have some words of wisdom on finances. Also, asking if you can be an observer or participant in the family finances can teach you valuable financial skills, like paying bills, balancing a checkbook, and making a budget.
- **A close friend** might know something you don't. For teens, friends are often easier to talk to than parents.
- **Financial counselors** are scattered throughout the area where you live. They can give you their professional insight into your bright and successful future.
- **A boss or general manager** has some experience in the business world and might be able to give you some advice as well. This individual can offer personal opinions on how he or she makes a living and juggles his or her time accordingly. This person might even have stories of how he or she became successful in the business environment.

Getting Assistance with College Finances

Not everyone can afford college without financial assistance from parents, scholarships, grants, or work study. This appendix provides more detailed information about financial aid programs and the history behind them.

Financial Aid

Financial aid was established by the U.S Department of Education to help young people pay for higher education. The paperwork involved in filing for FAFSA determines your **expected family contribution (EFC)**. Depending on you and your family's income, the government can help decide how much financial assistance you are eligible for.[1]

To learn more about FAFSA and fill out an application, visit this website:

- www.fafsa.ed.gov

Scholarships[2]

There are many different scholarships offered to students every year. Scholarships are awarded to those who meet specific qualifications, including good grades, involvement in extracurricular activities, and diverse cultural influences.

There are some scholarships specifically geared toward students with financial struggles. These are known as **need-based scholarships**. There are others provided to students who have accomplished tremendous academic achievements throughout high school. These are known as **merit-based scholarships**. Another type of scholarship is **ethnicity-based**, which looks at a student's race, religion, or nationality as a qualification. Lastly, you may qualify for **general scholarships**, which are all other scholarships that don't fall in any of the three scholarship types already mentioned.

When you fill out your FAFSA application, you will be alerted to all the federal grants and loans you qualify for and only a few, if any, scholarships. The odds are you'll be better at finding a scholarship you qualify for yourself, since there's a scholarship for nearly everything and you know the most about you. Visit the following websites for more information on scholarships the government and sponsors have to offer:

- www.receivescholarships.org
- www.scholarships.com
- www.fastweb.com
- www.brokescholar.com

Grants[3]

A grant is money that is given to you to finance your education that, unlike loans, doesn't need to be paid back. There are many grants that have varying qualifications you must meet to be considered eligible for the reward, such as amount of income and GPA.

The **Federal Pell Grant** is the most popular grant issued by the U.S. government to undergraduate students. This grant is a need-based grant for undergraduate students with financial needs.

The Academic Competitiveness Grant (ACG) is a merit- and need-based grant for college freshmen and sophomores or those enrolled in a qualifying certificate program. Students must both qualify for and receive a Federal Pell Grant to be eligible for the ACG.

As with scholarships, there are grants specifically geared toward juniors and seniors in college who have their minds set on a specific technical major. Students involved in computer science, technology, mathematics, and engineering may qualify for the **SMART Grant**: the National Science and Mathematics Access to Retain Talent Grant.

There is even a grant for students who are interested in becoming educators. The Teacher Education Assistance for College and Higher Education, or TEACH Grant, may be available for those who want to become an elementary or secondary teacher.

There are many grant websites with more information on specific grants you may qualify for. Use the following websites to start your search for the grants that are right for you:

- www.usagovernmentgrants.org
- www.grants.gov
- www.blackexcel.org
- www.grantsalert.com
- www.smart-grant.com

Loans

One of the most popular loans for students is known as the **Federal Stafford Loan**. This is an option for many young students getting ready for higher education because no credit is required for approval. The Federal Stafford Loan is attractive to borrowers for two main reasons: 1) the low interest rates and 2) the loan does not require you to start paying back the tuition until six months after you graduate.[4]

Some students have parents or guardians who are financially able and willing to help their student apply for more loans that can go toward paying for tuition, housing, books, and anything else. The Federal Parents **PLUS Loan** allows for parents and guardians to take out money for their student's college education at a low fixed rate with easy repayment options.[5]

Unlike the Stafford Loan, which is funded by the government, the **Federal Perkins Loan** is funded through the school. Not every school has this loan available, so check with your prospective college or university. Like other loans, you must pay back what you borrowed in installments after graduation.

For private loans, check with your nearest banks and credit unions. They have many options for students who are in need of financing options for college. It is a good idea to do research in your surrounding area to make sure you get the lowest interest rate and best option for you. Don't be afraid to ask questions.

9 Ways to Get Out of Serious Financial Trouble

Follow these nine simple steps to financial freedom. . . .

1. Acknowledge the problem.

Admitting that you are in debt is the first step to getting out of it. Many people get into debt by spending money they don't have. Once you acknowledge the problem, you can start taking the appropriate steps to getting help.

2. Realize how much debt you have.

Once you admit you are in debt, it's important to assess how much debt you are in. Gather all of your bills and make a chart of how much you owe: log each creditor (credit card company, cell phone company, store, etc.) and the balance you owe them. This step helps you get organized so you know exactly what needs to be paid off.

3. Stop spending.

Review your list of monthly purchases, like cable, cell phone, Internet, food, restaurants, clothes, etc. Decide which are needs (required) and which are wants (optional). Choose at least one item from your want pile that you can cut back on or cut out completely, allowing you to refocus the funds on your needs.

4. Make a budget.

Write a budget so you can see where your money is going and how much you are spending each month. How much money would you save if you ate out only once a week instead of five days a week? Could you live without paying for transportation until you pay off a big bill? Share your new commitment with the people who are closest to you so they can help keep you on track. For more information on making a budget, see **Chapter 3, Budgeting and Goal Setting for Success.**

5. Increase your income.

If you cut back on unnecessary expenses and are still unable to pay for your essentials, it's probably time to increase your income. You can do this by seeing if you qualify for a raise, working more hours, or finding a second job. You might feel stretched thin for a while if you're required to work more hours, but the more money you make, the faster you will be out of debt and back to your old work schedule.

6. Talk to a financial counselor.

If you feel overwhelmed by debt, have questions about finances, or cannot seem to stick to a budget, talk to a financial counselor. He or she can help you stay within your goals and give expert advice on overcoming your financial struggles.

To find a counselor, consider contacting the **National Foundation for Credit Counseling.** The organization has offices in all 50 states of the U.S. and offers free and low-cost counseling from trained, certified counselors. For more information, visit **www.nfcc.org**.

7. Prioritize your bills.

Paying your bills on time is vital to maintaining a good credit score. Determine which bills must be paid now and pay them. If you cannot make a full payment, make a partial payment. A partial payment on time is better than a full payment late. Look at the credit cards with the largest balances and the most interest. Stop using them and focus on paying them off. Call the credit card companies and see if you can negotiate a lower interest rate. By paying on time and paying down large balances, you will eventually raise your credit score and pay off some of those bills that have been taunting you for so long.

8. Commit to your plan.

Write down your financial goals and stick the list on a high-traffic area, like the refrigerator or bathroom mirror. This becomes a daily reminder to help you stay motivated and on task throughout your day.

9. Have some fun.

It is OK to celebrate your success. Budget some money for the occasional celebration. Be proud of your accomplishments.

Examining Careers in Finance

Do you think you have a knack for finances? If you are interested in a financial career, there are many choices out there for you. Below is a sample of popular financial careers and resources where you can find more information.

Debt or credit counselor. This is an individual who assists people with issues around credit, debt, mortgages, and bankruptcy. Counselors work with individuals or companies. Counselors usually must be trained and certified, and sometimes need a degree in social work.[6]

Stock broker. Most stock brokers will need a bachelor's degree in business, finance, accounting, or economics. A stock broker advises investors, who can be individuals or retail investors, on what their best investment options are considering their needs and state of their finances.[7]

Real estate agent. To consider this career, you must have at least a high school diploma and become a licensed real estate agent from the state you hope to work in. Real estate agents help people buy and sell homes, but they also must have knowledge of neighborhoods, how much real estate is worth, and the laws involved in buying and selling a home.[8]

Insurance agent. Insurance agents must be licensed in the states where they sell. Employment opportunities are more plentiful for insurance agents who also have college experience with sales, interpersonal skills, and expertise in insurance and finances. Insurance agents offer car, life, health, and disability policies, as well as mutual funds, annuities, and financial planning services.[9]

Accountant. There are four kinds of accountants: Public accountants, management accountants, internal auditors, and government accountants and auditors. Most accountants are required to have a college degree in accounting and may require further tests and certifications.[10] People who enjoy numbers, are detail oriented, and well-organized are ideal for accounting positions.[11]

Bank teller. A bank teller is required to have a high school diploma and on-the-job training. Bank tellers process financial transactions, like cashing checks and making deposits, loan payments, and withdrawals.

For more information about financial careers, visit any of the following websites:

- The Bureau of Labor Statistics: **www.bls.gov**
- Careers in Finance: **www.careers-in-finance.com**
- eFinancial Careers: **www.efinancial careers.com**

Managing Risk

Risk management refers to ways to deal with common risks that exist in everyday life, such as car accidents, home damage, injuries, or illness. The most common way to do this is by purchasing insurance. In fact, several chapters in this book mentioned life and health insurance.

This appendix briefly describes the most common types of insurance: car, home, health, life, disability, and long-term care. It also outlines wills, which help manage your assets after you die.

Insurance

Insurance policies are meant to protect people and things, such as you, your family, your car, and your home. Most insurance policies work the same way. You pay a certain amount each month, called a **premium**. In exchange, if something happens to what you have insured, the insurance company is supposed to pay for some of the damage. Of course, you must submit a claim explaining what happened and then pay a particular deductible before the insurance company will pick up the bill.

How much the insurance company will pay under what circumstances, depends on the policy you have. In general, the higher the premium, the lower the deductible, and the greater the coverage. However, insurance companies can deny your claim for any number of reasons, and the claim process is often long and tedious.

With that in mind, here are the typical types of insurance, with a brief description of each one.

Auto Insurance

Anyone who owns a car needs insurance, no matter how old or young they are. This type of insurance protects you and your car. The type of coverage you have is up to you, but each state in the U.S. requires a certain minimum coverage. In general, insurance for younger people is higher because they typically pose the highest risk in terms of accidents.

Here are some of the most common types of coverage:[12]

- **Liability.** Covers other people whose property you might damage with your car.
- **Bodily Injury.** Covers other people whom you might injure with your car. It helps pay for their medical bills and loss of income.
- **Collision.** Covers damage to your car if you hit another car or are hit by a car.
- **Uninsured Motorist.** Covers you, your family, and passengers in the car if anyone in your car is injured by another driver who is at fault and has **no insurance.**
- **Underinsured Motorist Bodily Injury.** Very similar to the previous type of insurance, except that it covers you, your family, and passengers in the car if anyone in your car is injured or killed by another driver

who is at fault and has **insufficient insurance** to cover your costs.

- **Underinsured Motorist Property Damage.** Covers damage to your property by another driver who is at fault and has insufficient insurance to cover your costs.

The amount and type of coverage is up to you. Auto insurance rates vary by age and by geographic location. That's why it's wise to talk to your insurance agent about required minimum coverage and then decide if you need more. You don't want to end up paying a large premium each month for insurance you don't need, especially if you could use that money to meet other basic needs.

Home Insurance

Anyone who owns a home needs some form of home insurance. This type of insurance protects your home from a wide range of damage, protects the personal property inside your home, and protects other people who may get injured in your home.

There are several levels of coverage that differ according to the circumstances they protect you against. Here are some of the most common levels of coverage.[13]

- **HO-1 (Basic).** Insures your home against the most common natural disasters: aircraft, wind/hail, explosion, riots/civil unrest, fire/lightning, vehicles, volcano eruptions, vandalism, smoke, and self-damage (the building falls on itself).
- **HO-2 (Broad Coverage).** Protects your home against everything in HO-1, plus more specific disasters, such as snow, falling objects (for example, trees), water damage (for example, the washing machine over-

flows), and electrical damage (for example, a power surge).

- **HO-3 (Special).** Protects your home against everything in HO-1 and HO-2 EXCEPT for those things that the insurance company explicitly excludes. This is the most common type of insurance policy, so it is important that you identify and understand what is excluded.
- **HO-4 (Renter's).** If you do not own a home, but rent a home, condo, or apartment, this policy protects your household contents and personal belongings against the disasters covered in an HO-2 policy.

Each level of coverage deals with both property and liability. **Property** refers to the house itself, as well as personal property within it. **Liability** refers to people who might be injured on your property, including people you have invited (friends, workers, contractors) and even trespassers. Like auto insurance, the amount of property and liability coverage you need depends on the value of your home and what's inside it, as well as where you live, how many people outside of the family come in and out of your home (and might get injured), and whether natural disasters are a likely occurrence.

Health Insurance

You already learned a lot about health insurance in earlier chapters. To recap, a health insurance policy is supposed to help pay for medical bills in case you get sick—this might include hospital stays, visits to the doctor, and prescriptions. However, coverage and price varies greatly. The younger and healthier you are, the less likely you are to need health insurance.

Some health insurance policies cover preventative care, such as annual exams, eye exams, and dental exams. Others cover doctor visits, hospital stays, and physical therapy. Some may cover prescriptions and others may cover alternative treatments such as acupuncture, massage therapy, and chiropracty. In general, the broader the coverage, the more expensive the policy. In addition, some health insurance companies will not insure you if you have specific pre-existing conditions, will only pay up to a certain amount, or deny your claim under certain conditions.

In many cases, the insurance company will pay 80 percent of whatever is covered in the policy, but only if you use a doctor in the insurance health network; otherwise, the company pays less. But in either case, you must first pay a certain amount of money out of your own pocket ("deductible") before the insurance company will pay anything. In general, policies with large deductibles have smaller monthly premiums, and policies with small deductibles have larger monthly premiums.

Disability Insurance

A disability insurance policy helps you in case you are unable to work due to an accident or illness and cannot earn any money. This type of insurance is important for anyone who is responsible for making monthly payments, such as home mortgage, auto insurance, utilities, or groceries and works at a job where injury is a real possibility.

Disability insurance is designed to replace 45 to 60 percent of your gross income on a tax-free basis. Its cost varies, but it is usually wise NOT to pick the cheapest policy. Why? Because if you are injured, it's more difficult to get paid.[14]

Long-term Care Insurance

Long-term care insurance is for people who are concerned that if they live a long time, they may end up needing care when they get older, or may need to live in a retirement home or assisted-living facility. Many people with extended families and friend networks and no health problems do not need this type of insurance.

Did you know that the average life span of a male living in the U.S. is 75 years, and that of a female is 84 years?[15] With people living longer, they are more likely to suffer from age-related health issues, such as Alzheimer's, stroke, Parkinson's, or frailty due to age. People suffering from these ailments will often require in-home care services or need to live in an assisted-living facility for many years, which is quite expensive and usually not covered by health insurance or Medicare. That is why long-term care insurance was developed—to pay for care you may need when you are elderly.

The cost of a long-term care insurance policy is based on the type and amount of services you choose, the daily benefit (in dollars) you want to receive, and how old you are when you buy the policy. If you are in poor health or already receiving long-term care services, you may not qualify for long-term care insurance, or you may only be able to buy a more limited amount of coverage, or buy coverage at a higher rate.

Most long-term care insurance policies limit the number of years they will pay out or limit the maximum amount of money they will pay out. However, once you start receiving payments, most policies no longer require you to pay any premiums.[16]

Wills

You've learned about insurance from autos through long-term care, which covers the time period from when you are a young driver to when you are an elderly citizen. So now it makes sense to talk about wills. Like insurance, a will is a form of protection—it actually protects you, the things you love, and the people you love.

A **will** is a legal document that states how you want to distribute your property when you die and how you want your children cared for if they are under the age of 18 when you die. There are several varieties of wills which are briefly described below:

- **Testamentary Will.** This is a traditional will that a lawyer prepares and you sign in the presence of witnesses.
- **Holographic Will.** This is a handwritten will that you write and sign without any witnesses. To be legal, there needs to be proof that you wrote it and were mentally competent at the time, and the will must contain your specific wishes about how your property is to be distributed.
- **Oral Will.** This is a spoken will, stated in front of witnesses. It rarely stands up in court.
- **Living Will.** This has nothing to do with property; it has to do with whether or not you want any life support in case you are incapacitated—and if you do, what type. Some people choose not to be hooked up to machines or feeding tubes; others want every medical device possible to keep them alive. To ensure that your wishes will be carried out, make sure your living will is in writing and signed by you and your witnesses.

Making a will is important because it's the one way that you will have control over what happens to what you own after you die—your home, your belongings, and your investments. It also allows you to specify how your children or pets are to be cared for after your death. And it gives you a chance to pass on your assets to charities or organizations so you can make a difference, even when you are no longer here.

Mapping National Standards for Personal Financial Literacy

This book was written with you in mind, and with certain standards in mind: the National Standards for Personal Financial Literacy. These standards were created by the Jump$tart Coalition for Personal Financial Literacy. This coalition is a national group of over 150 organizations dedicated to improving financial literacy in students of all ages, from those just entering kindergarten to those graduating from high school.

These standards identify the personal finance knowledge and skills that students of different ages should posses. The idea is that by meeting the standards, when you graduate from high school, you will be able to take responsibility for your own personal economic well-being, which should make you feel more confident and capable as you move through your life.

This book was specifically designed to focus on the personal financial standards for high school students. If you have carefully read all the chapters in this book and completed all activities, you should now be financially literate enough to do the following:[17]

- Find, evaluate, and apply financial information
- Set financial goals and plan to achieve them
- Develop income-earning potential and the ability to save
- Use financial services effectively
- Meet financial obligations
- Build and protect wealth

Exhibits F-1 through F-6 list the personal finance standards for high school students[18] and identify the chapters containing the information that help you meet each standard.

EXHIBIT

F-1 Financial responsibility and decision making

Overall competency: Organize personal finances and use a budget to manage cash flow.

	STANDARD	TOPIC DISCUSSED IN
1	Take responsibility for personal financial decisions.	Chapter 1
2	Find and evaluate financial information from a variety of sources.	Chapter 1
3	Summarize major consumer protection laws.	Chapter 2 and online study materials.
4	Make financial decisions by systematically considering alternatives and consequences.	Chapters 1, 2, 9, 10
5	Develop communication strategies for discussing financial issues.	Chapters 6, 10
6	Control personal information.	Chapter 6

EXHIBIT

F-2 Income and careers

Overall competency: Use a career plan to develop personal income potential.

	STANDARD	TOPIC DISCUSSED IN
1	Use a career plan to develop personal income potential.	Chapter 10
2	Identify sources of personal income.	Chapters 4, 8
3	Describe factors affecting take-home pay.	Chapters 4, 11

EXHIBIT

F-3	Planning and money management

Overall competency: Organize personal finances and use a budget to manage cash flow.

	STANDARD	TOPIC DISCUSSED IN
1	Develop a plan for spending and saving.	Chapters 3, 7, 4
2	Develop a system for keeping and using financial records.	Chapter 4
3	Describe how to use different payment methods.	Chapters 4, 5
4	Apply consumer skills to purchase decisions.	Chapters 3, 7
5	Consider charitable giving.	Chapters 7, 10
6	Develop a personal financial plan.	Chapter 4
7	Examine the importance of a will.	Appendix F

EXHIBIT

F-4	Credit and debt

Overall competency: Maintain creditworthiness, borrow at favorable terms, and manage debt.

	STANDARD	TOPIC DISCUSSED IN
1	Identify the costs and benefits of various types of credit.	Chapters 5, 6, 10
2	Explain the purpose of a credit record and identify borrowers' credit report rights.	Chapters 5, 6
3	Describe ways to avoid or correct credit problems.	Chapters 5, 6, 7
4	Summarize major consumer credit laws.	Chapter 5

EXHIBIT

F-5	Risk management and insurance

Overall competency: Use appropriate and cost-effective risk management strategies.

	STANDARD	TOPIC DISCUSSED IN
1	Identify common types of risks and basic risk management methods.	Appendix F
2	Explain the purpose and importance of property and liability insurance.	Appendix F
3	Explain the purpose and importance of health, disability, and life insurance protection.	Chapters 8, 10

EXHIBIT

F-6	Saving and investing

Overall competency: Implement a diversified investment strategy that is compatible with personal goals.

	STANDARD	TOPIC DISCUSSED IN
1	Discuss how saving contributes to financial well-being.	Chapters 7, 9
2	Explain how investing builds wealth and helps meet financial goals.	Chapters 7, 8
3	Evaluate investment alternatives.	Chapter 8
4	Describe how to buy and sell investments.	Chapter 8
5	Explain how taxes affect the rate of return on investments.	Chapter 8
6	Investigate how agencies that regulate financial markets protect investors.	Chapter 8

Endnotes

CHAPTER 1

1. Source: http://www.chevrolet.com/pages/mds/pricing/affordability.do

2. "Debt Facts." Manage All Debt. Accessed on 14 March 2011 from http://www.managealldebt.com/debtfacts.html

3. Woolsey, Ben and Schulz, Matt. "Credit card statistics, industry facts, debt statistics." CreditCards.com. Accessed on 13 March 2011 from http://www.creditcards.com/credit-card-news/credit-card-industry-facts-personal-debt-statistics-1276.php

4. "50% of Americans One Paycheck Away from Needing Government Assistance." Infowars.com. Accessed on 13 March 2011 from http://www.infowars.com/50-of-americans-one-paycheck-away-from-needing-government-assistance/

5. Knox, Richard. "The Teenage Brain: It's Just Not Grown Up Yet." NPR. March 1, 2010. Accessed on 13 March 2011 from http://www.npr.org/templates/story/story.php?storyId=124119468

6. Yurgelun-Todd, Deborah. "Inside the Teenage Brain." Frontline. © 2002. Accessed 13 March 2011 from http://www.pbs.org/wgbh/pages/frontline/shows/teenbrain/interviews/todd.html

7. "HTC EVO Shift™ 4 is HTO EVO™ 4G's Little Sibling." Announcements. Accessed on 13 March 2011 from http://community.sprint.com/baw/community/sprintblogs/buzz-by-sprint/announcements/blog/2011/01/05/htc-evo-shift-4g-is-htc-evo-4g-s-little-sibling?decorator=print

8. O'Dell, Jolie. "How Big Is the Web & How Fast Is It Growing?" Mashable.com. Accessed on 8 August 2011 from http://mashable.com/2011/06/19/how-many-websites/#17197How-Fast-Is-the-Web-Growing

9. "New Study Shows Time Spent Online Important for Teen Development." Macfound.org. Accessed on 8 August 2011 from http://www.macfound.org/site/c.lkLXJ8MQKrH/b.4773437/k.3CE6/New_Study_Shows_Time_Spent_Online_Important_for_Teen_Development.htm

CHAPTER 2

1. Kim, Helen. "Border Patrol—How Saying 'No' Increases Your Net & Self Worth." *More Loving, More Life* website. Accessed on 24 June 2011 from http://geofflaughton.com/newsletters/feb-2-2011/

2. Miller, Arlene C. "How Not to Raise Future Gamblers of America: Perspectives on Helping Children Build Healthy Relationships to Money." Accessed on 24 June 2011 from www.888betsoff.org/links/06_presentations/B3a.pdf

3. Ratz, Chaim. "The Untold Story of a Consumer Nation." *Kabbalah Today*. April–May 2008, #14: pp. 1-2. Print

4. "Five Ways to Promote Ad Savvy." PBS.org website. Accessed on 27 June 2011 from http://www.pbs.org/parents/childrenandmedia/ads-teens.html

5. Rubin, Gretchen. The Happiness Project. New York, New York: Harper, 2009

6. "Money Studies and Statistics." Accessed on 27 June 2011 from http://www. character-education.info/Money/money-studies-and-statistics2.htm "Advertising to Children." Advertising Educational Foundation. Accessed on 8 August 2011 from http://www.aef.com/on_campus/classroom/speaker_pres/data/3005

7. Story, Louise. "Anywhere the Eye Can See, It's Likely to See an Ad." The New York Times. Accessed on 8 August 2011 from http://www.nytimes.com/ 2007/01/15/business/media/15everywhere.html

8. "Advertising to Children." Advertising Educational Foundation. Accessed on 8 August 2011 from http://www.aef.com/on_campus/classroom/speaker_pres/ data/3005

CHAPTER 3

1. "College freshmen face a major dilemma," by Gayle B. Ronan. Accessed on 27 June 2011 from http://www.msnbc.msn.com/id/10154383/ns/business-personal_finance/t/college-freshmen-face-major-dilemma/

2. "Tips on Budgeting." E Home Fellowship Help with Life. Accessed on 25 June 2011 from http://www.way2hope.org/tips_on_budgeting.htm

3. Vohwinkle, Jeremy. "School Year Budget Worksheet for College Students." About.com. Accessed on 25 June 2011 from http://financialplan.about.com/ library/blyrcolbud.htm

4. "Frugal Recipes and Frugal Cooking." Frugal-Living-Tips.com. Accessed on 25 June 2011 from http://www.frugal-living-tips.com/frugal-recipes.html

5. Ibid

6. Ibid

CHAPTER 4

1 "Electronic Fact Sheet: Social Security and Medicare taxes." Social Security. Online website. SSA Publication No. 05-10003 (January 2011). Accessed on 30 June 2011 from http://www.ssa.gov/pubs/10003.html

2. Ibid

3. "2011 vs. 2010 Federal Income Tax Brackets, Rates and Taxable Income Thresholds." Saving to Invest website. Accessed on 28 June 2011 from http://www.saving toinvest.com/2010/04/2010-and-2011-tax-brackets-new.html

4. Cole, Gina. "Fed set to limit debit-card swipe fees." The Leader (PtLeader. com). Accessed on 29 June, 2011 from http://www.ptleader.com/main.asp? SectionID=36&SubSectionID=55&ArticleID=29523

5. Browne, Clayton. "Financial Privacy—U.S. Financial, Data & Internet Privacy Rights." Corporate Social Responsibility@suite101.com website. Feb. 28, 2011. Accessed on 29 June 2011 from Corporate Social

6. "How to recognize phishing e-mails." Microsoft Online Safety. Accessed on 29 June 2011 from http://www.microsoft.com/protect/fraud/phishing/ symptoms.aspx

7. "Defend: Recover from Identify Theft." Fighting Back Against Identity Theft. *Federal Trade Commission* website. Accessed on 30 June 2011 from http://www.ftc.gov/bcp/edu/microsites/idtheft/consumers/defend.html

CHAPTER 5

1. "5 Rules for responsible credit card use." *Money Cone* website. July 24, 2010. Accessed 3 July 2011 from http://www.moneycone.com/5-rules-for-responsible-credit-card-use/

2. Consumer Federation of America and Fair Isaac Corporation. "Your Credit Scores." *Consumer Federation of America website.* © 2005. Accessed on 7 June 2011 from http://www.consumerfed.org/elements/www.consumerfed.org/file/finance/yourcreditscore.pdf)

3. "What is AnnualCreditReport.com?" *Federal Trade Commission* website. Accessed on 2 July 2011 from http://www.ftc.gov/bcp/edu/microsites/free reports/index.shtml

CHAPTER 6

1. "5 Rules for responsible credit card use." *Money Cone* website. July 24, 2010. Accessed 3 July 2011 from http://www.moneycone.com/5-rules-for-responsible-credit-card-use/

2. "APR Matters on Payday Loans." CRL Issue Brief (June 2009). *Center for Responsible Lending* website. Accessed on 7 July 2011 from http://www.responsiblelending.org/payday-lending/research-analysis/apr-matters-on-payday-loans.html

3. "APR Matters on Payday Loans." CRL Issue Brief (June 2009). *Center for Responsible Lending* website. Accessed on 7 July 2011 from http://www.responsiblelending.org/payday-lending/research-analysis/apr-matters-on-payday-loans.html

4. King, Uriah and Parrish, Leslie. "Springing the Debt Trap." *Center for Responsible Lending* website. Accessed on 7 July 2011 from http://www.responsiblelending.org/payday-lending/research-analysis/springing-the-debt-trap.html

5. "Chapter 13 Bankruptcy Information." *BankruptcyHome.com* website. Accessed 8 July 2011 from http://www.bankruptcyhome.com/chapter13.htm

6. "Chapter 7 Bankruptcy Basics." *Lawyers.com* website. Accessed on 8 July 2011 from http://bankruptcy.lawyers.com/Bankruptcy-Basics/Chapter-7-Bankruptcy-Basics.html?page=2

7. "Consumer Bankruptcy: How long does a bankruptcy stay on your credit report?" *Free Advice.com* website. Accessed on 8 July 2011 from http://bankruptcy-law.freeadvice.com/consumer_bankruptcy/credit_report.htm

CHAPTER 7

1. "Seventeen Spending Teen Survey." Accessed on 27 June 2011. http://www.money-management-works.com/teen-spending.html

2. "Navigating the Best Bargains in Dollar Stores." *Today Money*. 15 August 2009. Accessed 6 June 2011 from http://today.msnbc.msn.com/id/32275269/ns/today-money/t/navigating-best-bargains-dollar-stores/

3. Petrecca, Laura. "Secondhand stores reap benefits of recession." *USA Today website.* Dec. 9, 2008. Accessed on 6 June 2011 from http://www.usatoday.com/money/industries/retail/2008-12-08-secondhand-recession-stores_N.htm

4. Williams, Kim. "Rise of the thrift store shopper provides steady growth in retail industry." *Retail Customer Experience website.* April 15, 2011. Accessed on 6 June 2011 from http://www.retailcustomerexperience.com/article/180664/Rise-of-the-thrift-store-shopper-provides-steady-growth-in-resale-industry

5. "Donate," *Goodwill Industries International website.* Accessed on 6 June 2011 from http://www.goodwill.org/get-involved/donate/

6. "Comparison of Personal Savings in the National Income and Product Accounts with Personal Savings in the Flow of Funds Accounts." Bureau of Economic Analysis U.S. Department of Commerce. March 25, 2011. Accessed on 6 June 2011 from http://www.bea.gov/national/nipaweb/Nipa-Frb.asp

CHAPTER 8

1. "Financial Concepts: The Risk-Return Tradeoff." *Investopedia* tutorials. Accessed on 13 June 2011 from http://www.investopedia.com/university/concepts/concepts1.asp

2. "50 Fun Facts About the Stock Market." Accessed on 29 June 2011 from http://www.bargaineering.com/articles/50-fun-facts-about-the-stock-market.html

3. http://www.wholesaleinsurance.net/consumer-reports/term-life-facts.asp

4. "Mutual Funds." *Securities and Exchange Commission* website. Accessed on 10 June 2011 from http://www.sec.gov/answers/mfprospectustips.htm

5. "Mission." *BetterInvesting Community* website. Accessed on 13 June 2011 from http://www.betterinvesting.org/public/default.htm

CHAPTER 9

1. "Too Many Hours on the Job May Put Teens at Risk." Accessed on 30 June 2011 from http://consumer.healthday.com/Article.asp?AID=649480

2. "Avoiding ATM Fees: Easier than You Might Think." By CBSNews. Accessed on 30 June 2011 from http://www.cbsnews.com/stories/2010/08/11/early-show/living/money/main6762952.shtml

3. "Is College Worth It?" Time magazine. Accessed on 30 June 2011 from http://www.time.com/time/interactive/0,31813,2072670,00.html

4. "Financial Aid." Financial Aid Facts website. Accessed on 18 June 2011 from http://finaidfacts.org/

5. "32 Weird Scholarships Almost Anyone Can Get." College and Finance. Accessed on 2 August 2011. http://www.collegeandfinance.com/32-weird-scholarships-almost-anyone-can-get/

6. "Understanding College Financial Aid." *Student Financial Aid Services Inc.* website. Accessed on 18 June 2011 from http://www.fafsa.com/understanding-fafsa/

7. "What is Work Study?" Western Washington University website: Employment Center. Accessed on 19 June 2011 from http://www.finaid.wwu.edu/studentjobs/students/resources/ws_faq.php#WhatIs

CHAPTER 10

1. Cunningham, Annie. "How to Choose a College Roommate." *CampusLife@ Suite 101* website. Accessed on 14 July 2011 from http://www.suite101.com/content/how-to-choose-a-college-roommate-a69878

2. "Social adjustment of college freshmen: the importance of gender and living environment," By Wendy K. Enochs and Catherine B. Roland. Accessed on 20 July 2011 from http://findarticles.com/p/articles/mi_m0FCR/is_1_40/ai_n 26844259/?tag=content;col1

3. "Number of Jobs Held, Labor Market Activity, and Earnings Growth Among the Youngest Baby Boomers: Results from a Longitudinal Survey." Bureau of Labor Statistics U.S. Department of Labor News Release. September 10, 2010. Accessed on 14 July 2011 from http://www.bls.gov/news.release/pdf/nlsoy.pdf

4. "Career Choices," Accessed on 20 July 2011 from http://www.educational dividends.com/students/career_choices.asp

5. "The 30 fastest-growing occupations, 2008-18." Bureau of Labor Statistics Economic News Release, December 11, 2009. Accessed on 14 July 2011 from http://www.bls.gov/news.release/ecopro.t07.htm

6. "The Emergency Fund." *It's Your Money* website. Accessed on 14 July 2011 from http://www.mdmproofing.com/iym/emergency_fund.html

7. Babauta, Leo. "Six Key Steps to Healthy Finances in Your Relationship." *Zen Habits* website. Accessed on 14 July 2011 from http://zenhabits.net/six-steps-to-healthy-finances-in-your-relationship/

8. Chu, Kathy. "Many marriages today are 'til debt do us part." *USA Today* website. Accessed on 14 July from http://www.usatoday.com/money/perfi/basics/2006-04-27-couples-cash-series_x.htm

9. Babauta, Leo. "Six Key Steps to Healthy Finances in Your Relationship." *Zen Habits* website. Accessed on 14 July 2011 from http://zenhabits.net/six-steps-to-healthy-finances-in-your-relationship

10. Ramsey, Dave. "The Truth About Money and Relationships." *DaveRamsey .com* website. Accessed on 14 July 2011 from http://www.daveramsey.com/article/the-truth-about-money-and-relationships/lifeandmoney_relationships andmoney/

11. Babauta, Leo. "Six Key Steps to Healthy Finances in Your Relationship." *Zen Habits* website. Accessed on 14 July 2011 from http://zenhabits.net/six-steps-to-healthy-finances-in-your-relationship/

12. Ibid

13. Chu, Kathy. "Many marriages today are 'til debt do us part." *USA Today* website. Accessed on 14 July 2011 from http://www.usatoday.com/money/perfi/basics/2006-04-27-couples-cash-series_x.htm

14. Dew, Jeffrey. "Bank On It: Thrifty Couples are the Happiest." *The State of Our Unions* website. Accessed on 14 July 2011 from http://www.stateofourunions. org/2009/bank_on_it.php

15. Rufus, Anneli. "15 Ways to Predict Divorce." Website. Accessed on 14 July 2011 from http://www.thedailybeast.com/articles/2010/05/19/15-ways-to-predict-divorce.html

16. "Divorce Rate." *Divorcerate.org* website. Accessed on 14 July 2011 from http://www.divorcerate.org

17. McDonald, Kevin. "The cost of divorce." *Bankrate.org Archives* website. Accessed on July 2011 from http://www.bankrate.com/brm/news/advice/ 19990903a.asp

18. "Marriage and Divorce Rates by Country: 1980 to 2008." U.S. Bureau of Labor Statistics. updated and revised from "Families in Work in Transition in 12 Countries, 1998-2001," *Monthly Labor Review*, Sept. 2003, with national sources, many of which may be unpublished. Accessed on 14 July 2011 from http://www.census.gov/compendia/statab/2011/tables/11s1335.pdf

19. "Making the Big Purchase a Little Less Daunting." *Fifth Third Bank* website. Accessed on 14 July 2011 from https://www.53.com/wps/portal/pv?New_WCM_ Context=/wps/wcm/connect/FifthThirdSite/Personal/Planning%20Center/ Budgeting%20for%20the%20Future/Big%20Purchases/

20. Hearn, Al. "Welcome to First Car Guide." *Website*. Accessed on 14 July 2011 from http://www.firstcarguide.com/your-first-car-new-or-used.html

21. Pareto, Cathy. "New Wheels: Lease or Buy?" *Investopedia website*. Accessed on 14 July 2011 from http://www.investopedia.com/articles/pf/05/042105. asp#axzz1QzzmjLXQ

22. "Money 101, Lesson 8: Buying a Home—Top Things to Know." *Money.com website*. Accessed on 14 July 2011 from http://money.cnn.com/magazines/ moneymag/money101/lesson8/index.htm

23. "Preparing for Home Ownership." *First Time Home Buyer Center.net* website. Accessed on 14 July 2011 from http://www.first-time-home-buyer-center. net/advantages_disadvantages.htm

24. Iliades, Chris. "Why You Need a Health Emergency Fund." *Website*. Accessed on 14 July 2011 from http://www.everydayhealth.com/healthy-living/ why-you-need-a-health-emergency-fund.aspx

25. Ibid

26. "Poll: Faith in Social Security system tanking," By Susan Page. Accessed on 20 July 2011 from http://www.usatoday.com/news/washington/2010-07-20- 1Asocialsecurity20_ST_N.htm

27. Updegrave, Walter. "How much do I need to save?." *CNN Money* website. Accessed on 14 July 2011 from http://money.cnn.com/2009/10/29/pf/expert/ retirement_save.moneymag/index.htm

APPENDICES

1. "About Federal Student Aid." Accessed on 26 July 2011 from http://federal-studentaid.ed.gov/-about/index.html

2. "Four Basic Groups of Scholarships." Accessed on 26 July 2011 from http://www.colleges.com/-financialaid/scholarships.html

3. "Government College Grants." Accessed on 24 July 2011 from http://www.studentgrants.org/government/

4. "Stafford Loan Information." Accessed on 26 July 2011 from http://www.staffordloan.com/stafford-loan-info/

5. "Parent PLUS Loans." Accessed on 26 July 2011 from http://www.parent-plusloan.com/

6. "Occupational Employment and Wages, May 2010: Credit Counselors." Accessed on 24 July 2011 from http://www.bls.gov/oes/current/oes 132071.htm

7. "Securities, Commodities, and Financial Services Sales Agents." Accessed on 24 July 2011 from http://www.bls.gov/oco/ocos122.htm

8. "Real Estate Agent." Accessed on 24 July 2011 from http://www.bls.gov/k12/money05.htm

9. "Insurance Sales Agents." Accessed on 26 July 2011 from http://www.bls.gov/oco/ocos118.htm

10. "Accountants and Auditors." 26 July 2011 from http://www.bls.gov/oco/ocos001.htm

11. "Accounting." 26 July 2011. http://matsu.alaska.edu/office/student-services/degree-programs/accounting/

12. "Types of auto insurance coverage explained." *Car Insurance website.* January 23, 2011. Accessed on 21 July 2011 from http://www.carinsurance.com/Articles/content27.aspx

13. "Home Owners/Renters Insurance Center." *FreeAdvice.com* website. Accessed on 21 July 2011 from http://insurance.freeadvice.com/information/home/article/15

    "Types of Home Insurance." *Insurance Finder* website. Accessed on 21 July 2011 from http://www.insurancefinder.com/homeinsurance/homeinsurance plans.html

14. Crawford, Steve. "Personal Disability Insurance." *About Disability Insurance* website. Accessed on 21 July 2011 from http://www.about-disability-insurance.com/

15. "Long Term Care Insurance." *Long Term Care Insurance National Advisory Center* website. Accessed on 21 July 2011 from http://www.longtermcare insurance.org/

16. "What is Long-Term Care Insurance?" *National Clearinghouse for Long-Term Care Information* website. Accessed on 21 July 2011 from http://www.longtermcare.gov/LTC/Main_Site/Paying_LTC/Private_Programs/LTC_Insurance/index.aspx

17. Jump$tart Coalition for Personal Financial Literacy. "National Standards in K-12 Personal Finance Education"

18. Jump$tart Coalition for Personal Financial Literacy. "National Standards in K-12 Personal Finance Education"

other success books by carol carter

The books at right are available through LifeBound. Visit www.lifebound.com.

The books below are available through Prentice Hall Publishers. Visit www.prenhall.com (search by keywords "keys to").

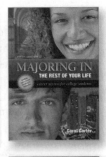

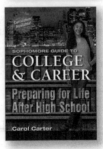

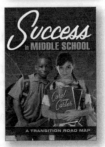